PRENTICE HALL

HISTORY OF MUSIC SERIES

H. WILEY HITCHCOCK, editor

FOLK AND TRADITIONAL
MUSIC OF THE
WESTERN CONTINENTS

third edition

FOLK AND TRADITIONAL MUSIC OF THE WESTERN CONTINENTS

BRUNO NETTL

University of Illinois

with chapters on Latin America by
Gerard Béhague (University of Texas)

Revised and edited by
Valerie Woodring Goertzen (Wesleyan University)

PRENTICE HALL, ENGLEWOOD CLIFFS, NEW JERSEY   07632

Library of Congress Cataloging-in-Publication Data

Nettl, Bruno
    Folk and traditional music of the Western continents / Bruno
  Nettl. -- 3rd ed. / revised by Valerie Woodring Goertzen.
      p.   cm. -- (Prentice-Hall history of music series)
    Includes index.
    ISBN 0-13-323247-6
    1. Folk music--History and criticism.   I. Title. II. Series.
  ML3545.N285 1990
  781.62'009182'1--dc20   89-34653
                                                          CIP
                                                           MN

Editorial/production supervision and interior design: Jan Stephan
Manufacturing buyer: Ray Keating

On the cover: *Mbira* player from the Njombe district, Tanzania. Illustration by
Roger Aasback, based on a photograph from the field collection of Ola Kai Ledang.

© 1990, 1973, 1965 by Prentice-Hall, Inc.
A Paramount Communications Company
Englewood Cliffs, New Jersey 07632

Printed in the United States of America

20   19   18   17   16   15   14   13   12   11   10   9   8   7   6   5   4   3   2

ISBN   0-13-323247-6

Prentice-Hall International (UK) Limited, *London*
Prentice-Hall of Australia Pty. Limited, *Sydney*
Prentice-Hall Canada Inc., *Toronto*
Prentice-Hall Hispanoamericana, S.A., *Mexico*
Prentice-Hall of India Private Limited, *New Delhi*
Prentice-Hall of Japan, Inc., *Tokyo*
Simon & Schuster Asia Pte. Ltd., *Singapore*
Editora Prentice-Hall do Brasil, Ltda., *Rio de Janeiro*

FOR GLORIA

FOREWORD

Students and others interested in the history of music have always needed books of moderate length that are nevertheless comprehensive, authoritative, and engagingly written. The Prentice Hall History of Music Series was planned to fill these needs. It seems to have succeeded: revised and enlarged second editions of books in the series have been necessary, and now a new cycle of further revisions exists, as well as a completely new book on music in the Middle Ages.

Six books in the series present a panoramic view of the history of music in Western civilization, divided among the major historical periods— Medieval, Renaissance, Baroque, Classic, Romantic, and Twentieth-Century. The musical culture of the United States, viewed historically as an independent development within the larger Western tradition, is treated in another book; and one other deals with music in Latin America. In yet another pair of books, the rich folk and traditional musics of both hemispheres are considered. Taken together, these ten volumes are a distinctive and, we hope, distinguished contribution to the history of the music of the world's peoples. Each volume, moreover, may of course be read singly as a substantial account of the music of its period or area.

The authors of the books in the Prentice Hall History of Music Series are scholars of international repute—musicologists, critics, and teachers of exceptional stature in their respective fields of specialization. Their goal in contributing to the series has been to present works of solid up-to-date scholarship that are eminently readable, with significant insights into music as a part of the general intellectual and cultural life of man.

H. WILEY HITCHCOCK, *Editor*

PREFACE

Dividing the world into two halves for the purpose of investigating and discussing its traditional and folk or its so-called ethnic music is perhaps a dangerous proposition. But if such a division must be made, it seems logical to group together Europe, sub-Saharan Africa, and the Americas. During the last several centuries, these areas have come greatly under the influence of Western civilization and its music—and they have influenced Western high culture also—while the rest of the world appears to have been more under the aegis of the Oriental high cultures. Moreover, in an American publication it seems appropriate to treat together those areas of the world which, broadly speaking, are responsible for the musical culture of the Americas today: Europe, sub-Saharan Africa, and aboriginal America. Finally, the areas covered here can be thought to have produced about half of the world's music and musical styles, if such concepts can be quantified at all. On the other hand, there is not much unity but there is a tremendous variety of musical styles, values, functions, and instruments in the part of the world that is the subject of this volume.

Our approach is essentially geographic. After two chapters dealing with the general characteristics of traditional music and its cultural context, and with some of the methods used to study folk music, we devote four chapters to Europe, one to sub-Saharan Africa, and three to the Americas. It has been impossible, of course, to survey comprehensively the music of each area, nation, and tribe, and we must content ourselves with examples of the kinds of musical styles that are found, and with sampling the types of songs that are sung, the various uses to which music is put, and the plethora of instruments past and present. The musical examples are intended to illustrate points made in the text rather than to serve as a representative anthology of musical forms, but most of the things discussed are musically illustrated, and a few of the most important and unusual instruments are depicted.

Valerie Goertzen prepared this third edition and I would like to thank her for her devoted work in making the necessary revisions. I would also like to express my thanks to the various publishers, collectors, and authors who have given permission to quote musical and textual material; individual credit is given with each quotation. I am indebted to William P. Malm for advice and criticism and for arranging to have the exquisite line drawings of instruments by the prominent Japanese artist Masakazu Kuwata. I am also grateful to H. Wiley Hitchcock for advice and guidance and to my wife for technical assistance.

B. N.

Note to the Third Edition

In the sixteen years that have passed since the second edition of this book appeared, knowledge of the folk and traditional musics of Europe, Africa, and the Americas has increased greatly. A one-volume survey can just present a sample of these traditions and only suggest the scope and complexity of issues relating to the study of them. For this edition, Gerard Béhague has expanded his chapter on Latin American music. I have revised and added material to other chapters, and have rewritten the bibliographical and discographical notes entirely, incorporating significant contributions made to the field in recent years. Besides guiding readers who wish to explore particular topics further, the updated reference material will indicate the directions of current and recent scholarship.

V. W. G.

CONTENTS

ONE

FOLK AND TRIBAL MUSICS IN THEIR
CULTURAL SETTING

INTRODUCTION

We are concerned here with a body of music called ethnic, folk, or traditional, as it is found in Europe, a large part of Africa, and the Americas. This music consists essentially of two groups of styles and repertories: (1) folk music, which is found in those cultures and areas in which there is also a longtime development of urban, professional, cultivated musical tradition, something that is often called art or classical music, and (2) tribal music, the music of nonliterate cultures, that is, those peoples without a tradition of literate, sophisticated musical culture living alongside the musical folk culture. The latter kind of music is sometimes referred to as "primitive," but the description is to be used with caution. The world's tribal musical cultures are not in essence different from the cultivated ones, except that they have less in the way of music theory and of professionalization of

1

musicians, and they have no musical notation. Quantitatively, their musics are simpler than the art musics of the world. (But even this statement is only generally true; for example, the rhythmic structures of African music are often much more complex than those of nineteenth-century European classical music.) Nevertheless, the musical creations of tribal cultures are genuine works of art and can be analyzed, judged, and appreciated in the context of their own cultural background.

Although we really have no way of telling just what happened in the musical history of all the world's cultures, we may assume that an earlier stage of the musical development of all cultures, including the modern ones, was something like the musical culture of contemporary tribal and folk societies, in the sense that it involved mainly people who were not professional musicians, and that it consisted of music that all of the people could understand and in which many or most could participate. Then, among some peoples, there must have taken place the development of a separate musical life for an educationally sophisticated and economically or politically powerful segment of the population, while the rest of the people held on to the older musical tradition. In Western civilization, we tend to be dominated by this more sophisticated musical culture, which includes our concert music and also the vast body of popular music. We are less aware of the folk traditions that, before the invention of recording and radio, were dominant, especially in the rural parts of Europe and the Americas, and that still live in relatively isolated pockets of society. But we are learning more about our folk music, about the great impact it has had on urban musical culture, and also about the ways in which the musical folk culture has changed under the influence of the urban mass media, but still remains somewhat intact.

We are concerned, then, with two kinds of music, the folk and the so-called primitive, which—when they are first heard by the novice—may seem to have very little in common. European and American folk music is, after all, part of our own cultural tradition as members of Western culture. The traditional musics of the American Indians and Africans are generally quite outside our experience. Moreover, each nation, each tribe, has its own music, and one kind of folk music may sound quite unlike another; Indian and African musics are quite dissimilar; indeed, they are as different as two kinds of music can be. Our only justification for including such a diverse group of musics in a single volume is the fact that in each culture in the Western half of the world this is the music that belongs, in some sense, to a large number of people.

Contemporary musicians trained in the Western art music tradition tend to concentrate on the degree to which a piece of music is unique and on the complexity of its structure and texture. They may not care particularly whether it is understood by many listeners, by a few professionals, or even by the composer. In tribal and folk musics, the values are usually turned around. Uniqueness may not be important and in fact the innovator may be discriminated against, but a new musical creation must be acceptable to others in order to live. This distinction is important, even if the case for it has sometimes been overstated.

Early students of folk music believed that in a tribal or folk community all individuals knew all of the songs in the repertory and could perform them more or less equally well. It is true that in order for a song or other music to be viable in such a culture, it must be understood and accepted by a large segment of the population. But we know that in African societies there have for a long time been musicians recognized as such, we know that American Indian shamans or medicine men knew more songs than other members of their tribes, and we are aware that in European folk cultures individuals who knew many songs and could sing well were singled out for recognition. Moreover, in all of these cultures, there was a tendency for certain songs or pieces to be reserved for specific groups, such as men, women, children, members of religious cults, political subdivisions, and so on. Thus it is impossible to conclude that there is a difference *in essence* between the musical cultures of primitive tribes and those of the modern Western world. The simplest tribal group and the most intellectual group of avant-garde musicians (which throughout the world has perhaps only a few thousand adherents) might be thought of as occupying places at different ends of one continuum; most of the world's musics fall at various points between them. And a great deal of the world's music is at borderlines between such conventional categories as tribal, primitive, folk, popular, and classical.

If there are specific features common to all of the musics discussed in this volume, they are (1) ready acceptability to large segments of the society in which they exist, and (2) the fact that they live in and are preserved by oral tradition.

ORAL TRADITION

To say that a culture has oral tradition means simply that its music (like its stories, proverbs, riddles, methods of arts and crafts, and, indeed, all its folklore) is passed on by word of mouth. Music is learned by hearing; instrument making and playing are learned by watching. In a literate musical culture, music is usually written down, and a piece need never be performed at all during its composer's lifetime; it can be discovered centuries later by a scholar and resurrected. But in a folk or a nonliterate culture, or even in a sophisticated culture without musical notation, a song must be sung, remembered, and taught by one generation to the next. If this does not happen, it dies and is lost forever. Surely, then, a piece of folk music must in some way be representative of the musical taste and the aesthetic judgment of all those who know it and use it, rather than being simply the product of an individual, perhaps isolated, creator.

As we have just indicated, a folk song must be accepted or it will be forgotten and die. There is another alternative: it may be changed to fit the needs and desires of the people who perform and hear it. And because there is not, in the case of most folk or tribal music, a written standard version which people can consult, changes made over the years tend to become integral to the song.

Of course this kind of change occurs for several reasons and at various levels. Imagine, for instance, that a Kentucky mountaineer makes up a song—both melody and words. He may compose the melody by putting together snatches of other songs he knows, or simply by humming aimlessly until he hits upon something that strikes his fancy, or by systematically changing a melody he already knows. (We know very little about the way in which composing is done in folk and nonliterate cultures or, for that matter, in any culture.) This man then teaches his song to his three children. Son number one is a musical fellow who has a large collection of recordings and occasionally goes to the city (where he hears a variety of musics), and over the years he whittles away at the song, changing notes here and there, adding ornaments, and evening out the meter, until he has made very substantial changes, which he no doubt considers improvements. Son number two likes to sing, but has a poor musical memory. He forgets how the song begins but remembers the second half of the tune. In his rendition, the song, which originally had, say, four different musical phrases (ABCD), consists only of a repetition of the last two and now has the form CDCD. (This is what evidently happened in the case of an old English and American song, "The Pretty Mohea," which is often sung to a tune with the form of AABA. The last two lines, repeated, seem to have become the tune of a popular hillbilly song, "On Top of Old Smoky.") The mountaineer's daughter moves to Mexico, and although she likes to sing her father's song, she becomes so saturated with Mexican popular and folk music that her version of the song begins to sound like a Mexican folk song with the kind of rhythmic and ornamental structure characteristic of that country's tradition. You can imagine what might happen at a family reunion: The three children sing their three versions, and although a person who knew the old man and his song the way it was first sung would surely realize that he had heard three versions of the same song, a newcomer to the group might hardly guess that the children's songs actually were descendants of one original. Add a few generations, and one song has become a large number of variants. The original form is forgotten and can no longer be reconstructed from the later versions.

HOW DOES TRADITIONAL MUSIC ORIGINATE?

We have looked at the way in which folk music comes to us. Most of it is quite old, but it has changed. To be sure, new songs are made up in most cultures at all times. In some cultures, many new songs are composed every year or every generation; in others, only a few new ones may appear in a century. But a great deal of the material, in all cases, is old, and thus we frequently hear about the great antiquity of folk and primitive music. But we must keep in mind the fact that this music, no matter how far back its roots, has probably undergone a great deal of change—because people wanted to improve it, because they forgot parts of it, or perhaps because they felt it necessary to make it sound like other music that they were hearing. Folk and primitive musics, then, have for us the fascinating quality of being both old and contemporary, of being representative of a people's ancient traditions as well as indicators of current tastes. And they are simultaneously the product of individual composers and of the creativity of masses of people. This historical development—far more than the artistic merit of the individual composition, which may be considerable in the opinion of some, but which may also seem insignificant in comparison to Bach fugues and Brahms symphonies—is the main justification for a detailed consideration of traditional music on the part of modern urban students and musicians.

We have implied that folk music is composed by individuals, but that subsequent to the original act of composition many persons may make changes, thus in effect recreating the piece. This process, called *communal recreation*, is one of the things that distinguishes folk music from other kinds. But the way in which folk music is created has not always been recognized. Among the earlier definitions of folk music, that which stresses the anonymity of the creator is one of the most persistent. According to this definition, a song whose composer is unknown is a folk song. Of course there is a fallacy here; should our ignorance of the identity of a composer make such a difference in our classification of musics? Still, there is some truth in this view, for the composers of European folk music and in most nonliterate cultures are indeed not known to scholars. Moreover, they are not usually known to the members of their own culture; in most of the cultures with which we are concerned here it makes little difference just who makes up a song. There are exceptions, of course; in some Plains Indian tribes people remember very specifically who "made" a particular song, or who "dreamed" it (some tribes believe that songs come to people in dreams).

It was believed by some nineteenth-century scholars that folk songs were made up by people improvising in groups. Actually this is rare, if indeed it occurs at all. Controlled improvisation under the leadership of a music master does seem to occur here and there—in the gamelan orchestras of Java and Bali, for instance, and among the Chopi of Southeast Africa. We have reports of American black slaves in the nineteenth century making up songs by calling to each other and gradually arriving at a song-like formula. But this kind of communal creation is rare. Nevertheless, those who formulated the theory that folk songs are the product of the communal mind were not unwise, for they must have realized the importance of the contributions of generations of singers, players, and listeners in determining the forms of the songs they heard. Of course, folk songs are normally composed by individuals, and in the case of Western European folk music these may be professional composers, popular songwriters, members of the clergy, or even the great masters of music. There are many instances of tunes from the classics—Schubert's "Linden Tree" and Papageno's aria from Mozart's *Magic Flute* come to mind—which have found their way into the folk tradition.

When speaking of the importance of change due to communal recreation in folk and tribal music, let us not fail to realize that the amount of change that a song undergoes is also determined by the culture's view of change. Some of the world's cultures regard change as a positive value—the United States today is certainly a good example—whereas others regard an adherence to tradition as immensely important; the culture of India is one of many possible examples. On the whole, folk and tribal cultures have tended to avoid rapid change, at least until confronted with modern technology. But there is variation even within a group of related and similarly complex societies. For example, the Pueblo Indians of the southwestern United States resisted change much more than did the Indians of the North American Plains, and this difference in attitude has affected many aspects of their history, including the recent history of their music. Thus, although we must assume that we never find complete stability and that some change always results from oral tradition and communal recreation, some cultures experience rapid and dramatic change, while slow and often barely perceptible change occurs in others.

FOLK MUSIC AS NATIONAL EXPRESSION

The idea that folk music is closely associated with a people, a nation, or a culture has long been widely accepted. In some languages, the words for "folk music" and "national music" are the same. This popular notion is quite opposed to that which deems music a universal language. Neither is really correct or objective. Of course, it is possible to identify music as music, whether it is in a style known to us or not. Music is a universal phenomenon, but each culture has its own, and learning to understand another culture's music is in many ways like learning a foreign language. No culture can claim a body of music as its own without admitting that it shares many characteristics and probably many compositions with neighboring cultures. But we must also assume that some of the essential and distinctive qualities of a culture somehow find their way into its music. Balancing the idea of traditional music as a national or regional phenomenon against the concept of folk music as a supranational kind of music is one of the fascinations of this field.

At the root of the concept of uniting nation and musical style is the idea that a nation's folk music somehow is bound to reflect the inner characteristics of that nation's culture, the essential aspects of its emotional life—its very self. This feeling has at times given rise, among the general population as well as among folk song scholars, to a politically nationalistic view of folk music. Folk music has at times been made the tool of aggressive and racist policies. This was to an extent the case in Nazi Germany, where the high quality of German music was extolled and the "poorer stuff" of Slavic folk song was denigrated, and in the Soviet Union during the 1950s, when traditional folk tunes of all peoples, including the non-Slavic minorities in Soviet Asia, were fitted with words praising Lenin and Stalin, collective farms, and the dictatorship of the proletariat. Although we may question the authenticity of music treated or arranged in this way, and although we may wonder whether it is really representative of or accepted by a nation's culture, it behooves us to study this use of folk music in order to understand its importance in the political and cultural processes.

There is some validity to the notion that the folk music of a nation or a tribe has a special relationship to its culture. We have mentioned the need for general acceptance of a song if it is to be remembered. There are other points. For example, it seems likely that the general characteristics of a language—its stress patterns, its patterns of intonation, and of course the structure of its poetry—are reflected in the music of its people. Moreover, if we plotted the characteristics of the folk music of each people—the characteristics of its scales, its melodic movement, its rhythm, and so on—and if we fed this information, nation by nation, into a computer and examined the results statistically, we would probably find that no two peoples have identical styles of music. And although various musical characteristics may be present in the music of many peoples, each people has its own particular proportion and combination of musical traits, and these interact in a unique way.

Studies of this sort have been carried out by a group of scholars headed by Alan Lomax.[1] Using many characteristics of music, they plotted

[1] Alan Lomax, *Folk Song Style and Culture* (Washington, DC: American Association for the Advancement of Science, 1968). See also his *Cantometrics: An Approach to the Anthropology of Music* (Berkeley: University of California Extension Media Center, 1976).

the typical stylistic profile of many musical cultures, finding correlations between certain kinds of music and certain culture types, but also finding each unique. According to Lomax, the favorite song style of a culture reflects its style of social relationships. Thus he believes that the difference between Middle Eastern music (which is prevailingly soloistic and has long, drawn-out, ornamented melodies) and sub-Saharan African music (which is often performed by ensembles or choruses, requires close cooperation by the musicians, and frequently involves interaction of independent melodic lines or rhythmic patterns) is due to differences between these cultures in their attitudes toward cooperation, sex, and the stratification of social classes. This theory has generated a fair amount of controversy,[2] but it does make us aware of the fact that each culture has its distinctive music, and that this distinctiveness is probably in some way related to the basic values and attitudes of the culture.

Despite the distinctiveness of each people's music, the musical relationships between neighboring peoples may be very close. It has been shown many times that melodies and songs travel from people to people. A tune may appear as a ballad in Germany and (in slightly different form) as a Christmas carol in Poland, as a dance song in Slovakia, and so on. It is possible, of course, that the same tune was made up separately in each of these countries, but this is not the most plausible explanation. The more complex an idea or a cultural artifact is, the smaller the possibility that it was invented more than once by different people. And a song, even a very simple one, is, after all, a complicated creation. More likely a melody found in several countries was simply taught by people on one side of the border to friends on the other side, or taught in many communities by a wandering minstrel. The tune could be easily learned, but the words were strange, could not be readily translated, and thus were replaced by a poem in the language of the second country. But because the tune did not fit perfectly into the repertory of the second country, and it did not have the characteristics of that country's preferred musical style, it was gradually changed to make it conform. If the styles of the two countries involved were very different, the song would probably not take root at all in the second country. It so happens that the various folk music styles of Europe are rather similar, and probably for this reason there are many tunes that have spread from people to people until they covered the entire continent. In contrast, when the Spaniards and British settled North America, they did not absorb into their repertories many (or perhaps any) tunes of the American Indians, probably because, among other reasons, they were too strange for absorption into their style.

[2] See, for example, Edward O. Henry, "The Variety of Music in a North Indian Village: Reassessing Cantometrics," *Ethnomusicology*, XX (1976), 49–66.

We see that songs can be passed from culture to culture. The same is true, to an extent, of musical characteristics or, as we frequently call them, stylistic traits. A type of scale, a kind of rhythm, a way of singing can be passed from one people to another without a simultaneous passing of songs. If one country has a particular kind of technique—for example, *antiphony*, the alternation between two groups, each singing a phrase at a time—that technique can be taken up by the people in a second country, who may then impose it on their own songs. There is some evidence that this actually happened in North America. Antiphonal technique is highly developed in some African cultures, and when Africans came to America as slaves, some began living with certain Southeastern Indians, both as slaves and as refugees from slavery. The Indians, who already practiced some singing in which a leader and a chorus alternated, seem to have started using the specifically African variant of this technique in their own songs. It is obvious that in spite of the national or tribal identity of a folk music style, there is much sharing of songs and of ways of performing music among the peoples of the world.

Discussion of the uniqueness of each people's musical style brings us to a consideration of authenticity. This concept is rooted in the idea that each culture has a primordial musical style of its own, and that songs and traits learned at a later date in its history are not properly part of its music. An authentic song is thought to be one truly belonging to the people who sing it, one that really reflects their spirit and personality. To be sure, each culture has its unique musical style, but within this there may be subsumed a number of varieties, some of them resulting from the introduction of new techniques of composition and of new inventions, such as instruments, or from contacts with other cultures. All of the kinds of music that reside within a culture are worthy of study and are important for an understanding of that culture. We are entitled and, indeed, obligated to find out and interpret the differences in age among certain songs, the difference in complexity among various strata of the repertory of a culture, and the attitudes that members of a culture take toward various kinds of music that they perform. But that is quite different from deciding that a particular kind of music is the authentic music of that culture, and that other kinds of music, particularly those that have come about under the pressure of outside influences, are somehow inferior, debased, or contaminated, and not worthy of attention. It is probably safe to say that the majority of the musics in use in the world today are in some way hybridized, as a result of contact among widely divergent cultures. Surely this is true of most of the popular musics in use; Western popular music has elements of African musical styles, Middle Eastern popular music is a mixture of traditional and Western. The same is true of older and less modernized tribal or folk musics. Thus one must be careful not to make a too narrow identification of one kind of music with a given culture or nation. A people's favorite style and the limits of its musical development will be determined to some extent by the culture type, economic development, and the range of long-term outside influences that apply; but within these limits there is ample room for variety and change.

HISTORICAL PERSPECTIVE

A characteristic of folk and tribal music that is frequently stressed is its great age, although often it is not certain whether the age of individual songs or of musical styles is meant. But to assume that each people is, for all time, tied to one kind of music is to assume that no change has ever occurred in its tradition. This view we cannot accept, for we can observe change in the world's folk music traditions going on constantly. And although change has certainly been accelerated in recent times by the rapid Westernization of many non-Western cultures and by the growth of mass media, we must assume that change also occurred in the more distant past. After all, migrations of peoples have always taken place, cultural diffusion and acculturation have occurred at all times, and there is no reason to believe that peoples who learned from each other to use the wheel, to construct instruments, and to smelt iron refrained from exchanging songs.

It is rarely possible to reconstruct the music history of a culture with oral tradition alone, but we can find out something about the growth, change, and geographic movements of musical styles, instruments, and even specific songs from their geographic distribution throughout the world, from archeological investigation of instruments, and from observation of the types of change that have occurred recently. But the fact that a culture has, today, a limited repertory does not mean that it may not, in an earlier time, have possessed musical styles that were later forgotten or that merged with new materials learned from outside influences.

About the history of folk and tribal musics, then, we can make only the most general sorts of statement. We must assume that there has been a history, that change, rapid or slow, took place. In general, but probably not always, simple musical styles were followed by more complex ones. Several kinds of change were involved: changes in the repertory, brought about by the introduction of new compositions; changes in the uses of music and of attitudes toward music; and changes in individual compositions, for example, the addition of new musical phrases, or of ornamentation, or of harmony to an extant song, or perhaps the changing of a song from one mode to another, as from major to minor. And finally, we must assume that in general those cultures which were exposed most to outside influences also had a more rapidly changing music history than did the more isolated ones, and that societies whose culture changes rapidly also exhibit more rapid musical change than do those with greater cultural stability.

MUSIC IN CULTURE

The forgoing paragraphs may give the impression that we reject the concept of authenticity outright. To be sure, there seems to be little to justify some of its implications. We are approaching the study of folk music with the assumption that we are studying the musical expression of many people. And we cannot neglect any aspect of this expression simply because it is not ancient, because it was brought from the outside, or because it does not seem to reflect the personality of the culture. On the other hand, we are not concerned here with music that is disseminated primarily by the mass media, although this music today has an enormous role in the world, and although some of it is closely related in style to the orally transmitted musics that are our subject. Similarly, we shall not deal with arrangements of folk songs, as performed by professional urban musicians, nor shall we deal with rock, jazz, and country music, except to mention their ultimate derivation, in part, from folk styles. This exclusion may seem arbitrary, because there is an unbroken historical line connecting rural folk music and urban popular music, but the entire field of world music is historically interrelated and arbitrary lines must be drawn for practical reasons. Thus the concept of authenticity has its practical uses: We are discussing, in this volume, that part of the music of the world's Western continents which was and is entirely or largely maintained in oral tradition.

But we are also interested in the music of particular groups of people. Those classified as nonliterate or tribal cultures can be defined with no great difficulty. Until recent times, for instance, there was no doubt that all American Indians were in this category. In the nineteenth century, there were individual Indians who learned to read, and some became learned; later, some became anthropologists who studied their own cultures. But the Indian languages were not written down except under the stimulus of white missionary scholars, and in each Indian tribe, more or less all the people shared one kind of music.

In the folk cultures of Europe and America it is more difficult to separate folk music from cultivated or fine art music, or from popular music. Distinctions are gradual and unclear. The musical life of cities and courts, directed by trained professional musicians with the use of written music, is certainly different from that of the villages in which music is passed on by oral tradition and in which most of the people participate actively without much specialization. But a considerable amount of folk music also exists in urban areas, and influence from the cities has always trickled down to the villages and at times inundated them. Everyone has a bit of folk heritage; on the other hand, the folk songs of most areas in Europe and America have for centuries felt the influence of urban musical traditions. Popular music, essentially an urban development with a written tradition, but belonging to a large part of the populace, seems to occupy a sort of middle ground.

Much has been said about the differences between folk and art musics as far as their uses or functions in the culture are concerned. We frequently hear the statement that folk and primitive musics are functional, whereas art music is not, or less so. This would imply that folk and primitive music usually accompany other activities in life, and that art music exists as "art for art's sake." There is some truth in this distinction, but the overall picture is a very complex one.

If we scrutinize the role of music in Western civilization, we find that it is not at all solely a giver of pleasure and a device for aesthetic edification. On the contrary, music is frequently designed to accompany activities of all sorts. We need to mention only church music, dance music, marching music, and the background music of drama, film, and television. On the other hand, the ideal kind of music, the music generally considered as best and greatest by those most concerned with music, is the music designed primarily for hearing in recital or concert. Thus we would be right in stressing the role of music in Western civilization as one not involving other activities, but only because this is the idealized role of music, not because most music necessarily conforms to this image. And, to be sure, we are more apt to respond to music on the basis of its aesthetic qualities than its suitability for a particular use.

The converse picture is, on the whole, found in folk and tribal cultures. We are frequently told that all folk music accompanies other activities, that it never fills a role of entertainment, that it does not provide simple enjoyment. Of course this is not the case; there are many examples, in European folklore and in African and American Indian cultures, of music's being used as entertainment. Individual singers may entertain groups or themselves with music. In some African cultures, music is performed by professional or semiprofessional musicians to entertain. But generally speaking—and here there are great differences among the world's cultures—the traditional music is directed toward another purpose or goal. Songs are typically referred to as "good" or "powerful," indicating that it is not the aesthetic quality of the song but the manner in which it fulfills its task (persuading the spirits, accompanying a dance, or giving an account of history) that is essential. Is it possible to indicate for any culture the main function of its music? No doubt, in any culture, music has many uses. But seen in the overall perspective of a culture, and compared with other activities, music may in each society have one special role. In some tribal cultures, music has essentially an enculturative function, that is, it serves to introduce members of the tribe to various aspects of their own culture. Elsewhere, its main function may be specifically religious in the strict sense, that is, it may be used as a language in which the supernatural or divine is addressed. Elsewhere again, music is the tribal stamp of approval for an activity; the activity must be accompanied by the appropriate music in order for it to be carried out correctly. Or music may be an important force for tribal unity and cohesion. In modern Western culture, all of these functions are present, but the fact that our most valued musical creations are intended for concerts and for entertainment (in the broad sense of that word) indicates that in our lives music has a different role from that which it has in most tribal and folk societies.

THE GENESIS OF FOLK MUSIC

The way in which Western folk music (or, for that matter, the folk music of Asian civilizations) came about is a fascinating one. The question whether "the folk creates" or whether it only utilizes material created by a higher social stratum has frequently been asked. We have already stated that all music is composed by individuals. But the source of the materials used in folk music is still a bone of contention. Tribal cultures, of course, must have acquired their songs and the musical components of these songs from their own creativity or possibly from occasional outside contacts, although it is sometimes argued that even the most remote peoples have had contact with the high cultures of the world, and that they have derived their musical accomplishments by absorbing the music of the high culture, diluted though it may be by passing through tribes and nations. Thus it has been argued that the Indians of South America, some of whose music is exceedingly simple, must in primordial times have derived their style from that of China, and there are remote similarities to substantiate this theory. This, however, is quite different from the everyday contact that has existed between folk and art music in some European countries. In Europe, it has sometimes been thought, both the songs and the style of the folk music of a given nation have derived from that nation's art music. This idea, based on a theory known by the German term *gesunkenes Kulturgut* (debased culture), assumes that the folk communities are inherently incapable of creating music or literature or art, and that instead they assimilate what trickles down to them from the sophisticated urban societies. A time lag is assumed as well, so that the style found in German art music in one century, for instance, is likely to turn up in its folk music centuries later.

No doubt there has been a great deal of influence from the cities on folk culture. We know of folk songs that originated in the city, and we know of sophisticated dances that decades later became folk dances. But we cannot accept the notion that all folk music is simply debased city culture. The evidence of folk song influencing the learned composer—from Schubert and Liszt to Bartók and Enescu—is too great. Rather, let us accept a theory of mutual give-and-take to describe the relationship between folk and art music.

Let us now summarize, on the basis of the considerations given in this chapter, the criteria we shall use for determining the materials to be discussed in the rest of this volume. Defining tribal music is not too difficult, but defining folk music is not an easy task. Several criteria can be used, but each, applied alone, is unsatisfactory. The main one is the transmission by oral tradition. Folk music, in its native setting, is not written down. As a result, its compositions develop variants, and the original form of a folk song is rarely known. Folk music may originate anywhere, but it is most frequently created by untrained, nonprofessional musicians, and performed by singers and players with little or no theoretical background. Folk song is frequently old, and the style of folk music may be archaic. But folk and nonliterate cultures do have a music history; they allow their music to change, their compositions to be altered, and their repertory to be turned over. Folk music is frequently associated with other activities in life, but it also serves as entertainment. And most important, because folk music is the musical expression of a whole people or tribe, or a significant portion of a culture, it must be performed and accepted in order to remain alive.

BIBLIOGRAPHICAL AND DISCOGRAPHICAL NOTES

Introductions to the general nature of traditional music and its functions in society and as an aspect of human behavior include some of the articles in the Funk and Wagnalls *Standard Dictionary of Folklore, Mythology and Legend,* ed. Maria Leach (New York, 1949–50), notably "Song" (by George Herzog), "Dance" (by Gertrude P. Kurath), and "Oral Tradition" (by Charles Seeger). Articles on individual nations in *The New Grove Dictionary of Music and Musicians,* 20 vols., ed. Stanley Sadie (London: Macmillan Press, 1980), contain sections devoted to folk music written by authorities in their fields. In addition to providing informative overviews of folk music traditions, these articles include bibliographies, and often survey folk music scholarship and major collections. Further information about instruments is to be found in *The New Grove Dictionary of Musical Instruments,* 3 vols., ed. Stanley Sadie (London: Macmillan Press, 1984); for discussion of topics relating to folk and traditional music in the United States, see pertinent articles in *The New*

Grove Dictionary of American Music, 4 vols., ed. H. Wiley Hitchcock and Stanley Sadie (London: Macmillan Press, 1986). The survey of non-Western music in the first volume of *The New Oxford History of Music* (London: Oxford University Press, 1957), although dated in its approach, contains some useful material. *Worlds of Music: An Introduction to the Music of the World's Peoples*, ed. Jeff Todd Titon (New York: Schirmer, 1984) is a collaborative effort by specialists; two cassetes of recorded examples are available separately. Alan P. Merriam, *The Anthropology of Music* (Evanston, IL: Northwestern University Press, 1964), provides much material on the role of music in various nonliterate cultures.

Several scholarly periodicals specialize in non-Western and folk music; among them, we should note *Ethnomusicology* (Journal of the Society for Ethno-musicology); *Journal and Yearbook of the International Folk Music Council* (*J-IFMC* and *Y-IFMC*, since 1981 the *Yearbook for Traditional Music*); *Asian Music*; *Jahrbuch für musikalische Volks- und Völkerkunde*; *Selected Reports* of the UCLA Institute of Ethnomusicology; *African Music*; *World of Music*; *Yearbook for Inter-American Musical Research*; and *Latin American Music Review/Revista de música latinoamericana*. Bruno Nettl, *Reference Materials in Ethnomusicology* (Detroit: Information Coordinators, 1961), is a bibliograph-ical guide to the whole field. Each issue of *Ethnomusicology* includes a list of current publications in the field, grouped according to geographical region and covering printed sources, recordings, and films.

Many of the issues raised in this chapter are discussed more fully in Bruno Nettl, *The Study of Ethnomusicology: Twenty-nine Issues and Concepts* (Ur-bana: University of Illinois Press, 1983). Roger P. Elbourne, "The Question of Definition," *Y-IFMC*, VII (1975), 9–29, is an effort to define the concepts of folk, folk music, and folk life. Other studies relevant to points made in this chapter include Alan Lomax, "Folk Song Style," *American Anthropologist*, LXI (1959), 927–54; Maud Karpeles, "Some Reflections on Authenticity in Folk Music," *J-IFMC*, III (1951), 10–16; and K. P. Wachsmann, "The Trans-plantation of Folk Music from One Social Environment to Another," *J-IFMC*, VI (1954), 41–45. Lomax's *Folk Song Style and Culture* (Washington, DC: American Association for the Advancement of Science, 1968) and *Cantometrics: An Approach to the Anthropology of Music* (Berkeley: University of California Extension Media Center, 1976), the latter with seven training cassettes, detail his system of cantometrics. A study of the relationship between geographic distribution and tune history is Chris Goertzen, "American Fiddle Tunes and the Historic-Geographic Method," *Ethnomusicology*, XXIX (1985), 448–73. Musical change as the result of contact among cultures is the subject of Bruno Nettl, "Some Aspects of the History of World Music in the Twentieth Century: Questions, Problems, and Concepts," *Ethnomusicology*, XXII (1978), 123–36; *The Western Impact on World Music: Change, Adaptation, and Sur-vival*, ed. Bruno Nettl (New York: Schirmer, 1985); and Margaret J. Kartomi, "The Processes and Results of Musical Culture Contact: A Discussion of Termi-nology and Concepts," *Ethnomusicology*, XXV (1981), 227–50. *World of Music*, Vol. XXVIII, no. 1 (1986), is devoted to studies of musical change. Philip V.

Bohlman, *The Study of Folk Music in the Modern World* (Bloomington: Indiana University Press, 1988), advocates a broad view of folk music and folk music scholarship.

The following recordings present samples of the music of many of the world's cultures: *Music of the World's Peoples*, ed. Henry Cowell (four albums), Folkways FE 4504–4507; *Primitive Music of the World*, ed. Henry Cowell, Folkways FE 4581 (a smaller selection overlapping with the former); *Columbia World Library of Folk and Primitive Music*, compiled by Alan Lomax (over twenty records, partly reissues of older recordings, partly new material collected by Lomax and others); *The Demonstration Collection of E. M. von Hornbostel and the Berlin Phonogrammarchiv*, Folkways FE 4175 (reissue of an early collection that attempted to show the great variety of the world's musical styles); *Man's Early Musical Instruments*, Folkways P 525; *An Anthology of the World's Music*, Anthology records; the UNESCO Collection, comprising sets of African and Asian music; *World Collection of Recorded Folk Music*, established by Constantin Brailoiu (six volumes containing reissues of recordings of African, Asian, Eskimo, and European music made 1913–53), Disques VDE-Gallo 30 425–30; *Collection anthologie de la musique populaire*, produced under the auspices of the International Folk Music Council on the OCORA(ORTF) label; and *Documenti originali del folklore musicale europeo*, issued by Vedette of Milan on its Albatros label (Vedette Records, Via Lumiere, 2 (Cinelandia), 20093 Cologno Monzese, Milano, Italy).

TWO

STUDYING THE STYLE
OF FOLK MUSIC

Music of any sort, but folk and tribal music especially, should be examined in two ways: (1) for itself, that is, its style and structure, and (2) in its cultural context, its function, and its relationship to other aspects of life. Ideally, of course, a blending of the two approaches should be achieved. The second approach has been briefly covered in Chapter 1. We have tried to show how folk music and the music of nonliterate cultures, despite their diversity, differ as a group from other kinds of music in their origin, transmission, and cultural role. We turn now to the question of musical style. In order to talk about music we need to develop a vocabulary, and talking about or describing folk music and the music of non-Western cultures requires special adaptations of the technical vocabulary normally used for describing the music of Western civilization. Also, in order to distinguish the various styles of folk music throughout the world from each other, we should have some idea of what is common to all or most of them. Here, then, we wish to talk about the music itself, not about the use that is made of it, nor about the words of the song, nor about the instrument used to play it.

We are interested in finding out how a piece of music is put together, what makes it tick. We also want to know what aspects of music characterize a repertory of a community or a country or a tribe, and we want to know what it is that distinguishes the musical sound of one culture from that of another. Answering these questions, that is, describing musical styles, is something that ultimately requires great sophistication. But a written description can tell only part of the story. In order to become familiar with a given folk music tradition, one must listen a great deal to pieces from that tradition (on recordings, if not in live performances). Even a person with no background at all can, by listening and repeated listening, learn a great deal about how a piece of music is put together.

It is important to realize that a music is something like a language. It must be understood to be appreciated. The listener must know that certain kinds of sounds are signals, for example, of points of tension, of relaxation, of beginnings or endings of musical thoughts. A music, or musical repertory, is a system with an internal logic, structure, and typical modes of expression. And this is true whether the music is written by professional trained composers, as in Western classical music; whether it is composed by highly trained professionals who do not use musical notations, such as the composers of Indian classical music; whether it is by the formally untrained composer of folk and tribal cultures who may not be able to explain what he or she is doing; or whether it is an improviser of Middle Eastern music who composes during the course of the performance. In no music is material made up simply at random. The absence of an articulated music theory does not imply the absence of rules which composers must follow; on the contrary, composers in a folk or tribal culture are likely to be surrounded with musical limitations, to which they feel it necessary to adhere. (This is partially related to the need of having one's compositions accepted by performer and listener in order for the music to remain alive.)

Because in folk and tribal cultures so-called rules of composition are not stated by music theorists and composers, we must derive them from the music itself, and the statements in the following chapters regarding the characteristics of various musics may be regarded as partial or introductory statements of the rules and logic of their musical systems. These brief statements are of necessity superficial, for if we delve with sufficient depth into any musical repertory, we discover that it is a system of communication with a complicated grammar, syntax, and vocabulary of musical materials and devices.

SOUND AND SINGING STYLE

The first thing that strikes listeners when they hear an unfamiliar musical style is the overall sound, which has many components but among whose chief traits are tone color and texture. Musical cultures differ in their sound ideals. The way in which the human voice is used, particularly, is characteristic of a culture and tends to be maintained throughout the variety of forms, scales, rhythmic patterns, and genres in its repertory. The way in which American Indians sing is quite different from that of Africans; Spanish folk singers sound different from English ones. One needs to hear only two seconds of Arabic singing to identify it as Middle Eastern. The characteristics of singing in a culture may reflect characteristics of speech and language, but there are sufficient exceptions to make us suspicious of any simple explanation that automatically relates these two methods of communicating.

Describing the characteristics of a singing style in words is difficult. We speak of such things as degrees of vocal tension, use of vibrato or tremolo, presence or absence of sharp accentuation of tones, volume, ornamentation such as trills and grace notes, nasality, and so on. It is interesting to find that in many cultures, the sounds of instruments have characteristics similar to those of the singing style. Thus the violin playing of India sounds very much like Indian singing, and very different indeed from European violin playing.

The overall sound of music characterizes a musical culture in other ways as well. Sub-Saharan Africa, for example, may be characterized by a multiplicity of simultaneous sounds, and we find polyphony, that is, part-singing or ensemble music. But in addition we also find attempts by single musicians to produce several simultaneous sounds even when the means to do so are limited, and we find that there are always attempts to make these simultaneous sounds contrast with each other, as in the use of unrelated instruments in an ensemble or in the simultaneous use of widely divergent rhythms. In contrast, the music of South and West Asia is usually soloistic, and when several instruments play together, they tend to approximate each other in their tone colors.

It is important to realize that although the musical style of a culture may change rapidly, its singing style and overall sound patterns change very slowly; thus this is one of the traits of music that is most characteristic of a culture and that is closely tied to the value structure of other aspects of life.

The relative stability of singing style and sound ideals in a culture may lead some to believe that these are tied to heredity and race, to assume, for example, that the way in which the voice is used by Indians or Africans is related to the pecularities of their race, their appearance, the color of their skin. But the evidence contradicts this view. Africans and Indians can learn to sing in the styles of other cultures, and indeed, Europeans and Americans, with sufficient effort, can learn to sing in Indian, African, and Chinese styles. The integrity of national or tribal singing styles has other roots. Every people has musical traits which are of great importance for maintaining its cultural identity, whether the musicians are able to verbalize about this or not, and singing styles and sound ideals in music are evidently among these traits. On the other hand, all aspects of music are definitely parts of culture, and the cultural and racial boundaries of the world do not coincide precisely, if at all.

FORM

Having noted the general character of the sound of a music, perhaps the best way to begin analyzing it, whether one hears it or sees it written out, is to find the large subdivisions and the broad tendencies of formal design. Is it made up of several large sections which contrast markedly? Are the sections of equal length? Does the tempo change considerably or suddenly in the course of the piece? Are any of the sections repeated? Is the whole piece repeated several times? If so, are the repetitions more or less exact, or are they variations of the first rendition? Do the sections correspond to sections or lines of the same length in the verbal text? These are the kinds of questions an intelligent listener must ask.

At the same time, we should note the arrangement of the performance, and this is especially important in studying music from a recording. We want to know whether the piece is performed by a single performer or a group, and whether there is alternation. Do several performers sing or play in unison, or does each have his or her own part?

Having identified the several sections of a piece, we must try to establish the relationships among them. One way to do this is to give each of them a letter, and to repeat the letter when the section is repeated. When one section is a variation of a previous one, we give it a superscript number, thus A^1 is a variation of A. When a section is new but seems somewhat reminiscent of a previous one, we can indicate this by a superscript letter so that B^a is a section reminiscent of A. For example, the form of the song in Example 2-1 could be indicated with the following letters: AA^1BA^1.

Sometimes the interrelationship is more complex, as in Example 2-2, where a section reappears at different pitch levels. It could be described

EXAMPLE 2-1. German folk song, "O du lieber Augustin," learned by Bruno Nettl from oral tradition.

by letters $AA^1{}_5A^2{}_5A$, A_5 being a transposition, a perfect fifth higher, of A.

Forms such as AABB, ABBA, and ABCA appear frequently in European folk music. All these forms have in common the use of four musical lines, perhaps of equal length. But the internal differences are significant. Example 2-1 presents a theme, then a contrasting line, and returns to the theme. Example 2-2 is based on a single melodic phrase which, perhaps for the purpose of providing variety, is presented at different pitch levels. But they both share a quality of being rounded off (that is, the opening line returns at the end), which most typically forms the basis of *strophic* songs, in which an entire melody is repeated several times with different words.

EXAMPLE 2-2. Hungarian folk song, from Zoltán Kodály, *Folk Music of Hungary* (London: Barrie and Rockliff, 1960), pp. 61–62.

Tempo giusto

In the music of some non-Western cultures, songs don't have clearly marked endings or forms that are precisely predetermined. The following Navaho song (Example 2-3) is made up of an occasionally regular, but sometimes irregular, alternation of three sections (marked A, B, and C in the transcription). The sequence of the sections is AABBCBABBCBAABABBCB, and so on.

EXAMPLE 2-3. Navaho Indian song, from Bruno Nettl, *North American Indian Musical Styles* (Philadelphia: Memoir 45 of the American Folklore Society, 1954), p. 47.

In the discussion of musical styles of tribal and folk cultures, we must keep in mind the limitations that are imposed by the lack of a musical technology (i.e., notation and music theory) and the absence of intensive training of the musician by professionals. Thus we are apt to find relatively simple forms used, as well as strong unifying factors which act as mnemonic devices. A drone (as in the lowest pipe of the bagpipes), the use of the same musical material in each voice of a part-song, the reappearance of a musical motif at different pitch levels throughout a song, a repeated rhythmic pattern, a simple tonal structure with clearly marked *tonic*, or "home" pitch, and reciting tones—all of these are devices that are arrived at unconsciously but are accepted eagerly by the folk community because they help the folk singer and the listener to organize the musical material in their minds and clarify its structure, thus making oral tradition a more feasible process.

POLYPHONY

Most of the music we deal with in this volume is *monophonic*, which means that only a single tone is heard at a time, and there is no accompaniment except that of drums, rattles, or other percussive sound. But there is a good deal of European, American, and Latin American folk music, and a great deal of African music, which has more than one tone sounding at a time or more than one melody at a time; or it may be accompanied with chords. Several terms have been used to describe such music; perhaps the most satisfactory one is *polyphony*, which we will use here to include all music that is not monophonic, whether is consists of a singer's own simple accompaniment with guitar or of a chorus or of a group of different instruments playing a complex interrelationship as in chamber music.

In a style of polyphonic music that is strange to one's ears, it may be difficult to describe just what is going on. There is not much point, when describing folk music from Russia or from South Africa, in trying to apply labels used for Western art music, such as organum, fugue, conductus, and the like, to music that developed quite outside Western European musical culture.

A better way to begin describing a polyphonic piece is to decide whether the various parts being sung or played at the same time are of equal importance, or whether one stands out as the leading or solo part. Then one can try to describe the melodic relationship among the parts. For example, do they use material based on the same tune or theme, or do they have more or less independent tunes? If the latter is the case, one should decide whether the relationship among the different voices or instruments produces imitation or *canon*, the most common manifestation of which is the *round* (the same tune performed at different time intervals); or *parallelism* (the same tune performed at the same time at different pitch levels); or *heterophony* (something like variations of the same tune played or sung simultaneously). At this point, also, one would like to know how much of the music is composed, and what aspects of it, if any, are improvised. It would also be important to know which aspects of the music had to be performed the way they are, and in which the performer had a choice and the right to make changes according to his or her wishes.

A further point to be considered is the way in which the musicians and listeners in another culture perceive polyphony. Do they concentrate on the effects of the simultaneities, such as chords, and on their progression, or do they listen to the progression of the individual melodies as they proceed side by side? We can hardly make judgments about this on the basis of simple listening, and extensive field research is necessary in order for us to be sure of our ground. But we must at least be aware of the fact that different cultures may perceive the same music differently, and that our own perception of a culture's musical style may or may not accord with that of the members of that culture.

RHYTHM AND TEMPO

We can learn a good deal about the rhythmic character of a culture's music, or of a single piece of its music, also simply by listening. We want to determine, for example, whether the music is organized in measures that recur more or less regularly throughout, and where exceptions occur. If we can perceive a repeated unit of beats and accents, we may conclude that the music is *metric*. We can check this by tapping our foot regularly and seeing whether the tapping fits the music. We also want to know whether a drum or rattle accompaniment, if any, coincides with the rhythmic units of the melody. Then, quite aside from the meter, we may also describe *rhythm* in terms of the lengths of the notes found in a piece. This is something that cannot be found out quite so easily by listening; but it can be indicated, at least approximately, with the use of written notation.

We want to find out, for example, whether most of the notes are of one length, whether two note lengths predominate (as, for instance, quarters and eighths, in Example 2-4), or whether perhaps there are notes of various lengths, from half notes to sixty-fourths.

The *tempo* of a piece is also important here. Is it fast or slow? Here our intuitive judgment cannot always be trusted. A piece that a Western listener considers fast (perhaps because of the speed of the drum accompaniment) may be considered slow by a person from the culture that produced it. One way to measure tempo more objectively is to divide the number

EXAMPLE 2-4. Shoshone Indian Peyote song, from David P. McAllester, *Peyote Music* (New York: Viking Fund Publications in Anthropology, no. 13, 1949), song no. 73. Reprinted by permission of David P. McAllester and Wenner-Genn Foundation for Anthropological Research.

of notes in a melody by the number of minutes the piece takes; this would express the tempo in terms of average number of notes per minute. Another way is to ascertain the speed of the pulse or *beat*, if there is one; it may be the most frequently used note length in the melody, or the length of stroke of the percussion accompaniment.

There are many other factors that make up the rhythmic character of music. The degree of accentuation of stressed notes, mentioned earlier as an aspect of singing style, is a characteristic feature of rhythmic style. The very presence or absence of meter, the degree to which performers deviate from it, the use of different meters simultaneously, the amount of contrast between the longest and shortest notes, and typical rhythmic motifs,

such as dotted rhythms (♪. ♫ ♫. ♫) or more complex patterns that recur,

are examples of things to look and listen for.

MELODY AND SCALE

We come now to the aspect of music that has been of greatest interest to students of folk and nonliterate cultures—melody. This aspect is probably the most difficult to study or describe. A simple approach to an understanding of melody involves consideration of the melodic contour. Does the melody of a piece generally rise, fall, remain at the same level, or proceed in a curve? Does it move in large leaps or primarily stepwise? We are also interested in the *range*, of a tune—that is, the distance, in pitch, between the highest and lowest tones. This can be found with little difficulty by listening.

Then we come to consideration of the *scale*. The uninitiated listener to non-Western musics and to the folk musics of Eastern Europe and even perhaps some of Western Europe, is often struck by the curious, possibly unpleasant sound of it. It may sound out of tune and the listener may have trouble reproducing the tones and intervals vocally. Also, it will not be possible to reproduce the tones correctly on a piano. The reason for this is that the tone systems and scales of many non-Western musics do not conform to the scales used in the music of Western civilization. Under no circumstances should this statement be taken to imply that the Western system of music is somehow a world standard, that it is more natural or more rational than other systems. Although certain musical systems may appear to correspond more closely to natural laws (e.g., acoustical, biological, or psychological), we must assume that all musics are man-made to an equal extent, and that all of them are in some way based on the rules of nature. In this respect, all of them are equally worthy of independent study, and the fact that some seem to us more unusual than others is not to be the basis of value judgments. What we perceive as the peculiarity of certain scales or tone systems is due to the particularity of the tone system with which we have grown up.

A *scale* may be defined as the pitches used in any particular piece of music. A *tone system*, on the other hand, is all the pitches used in a whole body of songs or pieces in the same style. One way to describe a scale is to count the number of different pitches or tones that appear in it. From this kind of description are derived such terms as *pentatonic*, which denotes a scale consisting of five tones; *tetratonic*, a scale of four notes; *tritonic* (three tones); *hexatonic* (six); and *heptatonic* (seven). The mere number of tones, however, doesn't really determine the character of a scale to any great extent; the reason for the curious sound of some non-Western music is not to be sought in the number of tones used.

The distance in pitch between the tones is probably a more important indicator of tonal character than their number. Thus we may find one pentatonic song that uses the scale, A-B-D-E-G and another one that uses the tones, A-B♭-B-C-D. Each uses five tones, but one uses large intervals, the other very small ones. The number of interval arrangements that can be found in folk music is almost infinite, but the listener should decide whether the intervals used are, on the whole, large, small, or medium, and get an idea of the character of the scale being used.

In some cultures there are intervals smaller than the half tone, that is, smaller than anything that can be produced on the piano. More commonly we find intervals intermediate in size between those used in the Western tempered system. Thus the *neutral third*, an interval found in various cultures, is halfway between a major and a minor third. Of course, in Western civilization we use several different pitch standards. The intervals on the piano are somewhat different from those produced on the violin. But we have a range within which an interval is considered in tune. Although "A" is normally supposed to be 440 vibrations per second, a pitch of 435 or 445 would still, by most persons, be considered "A." Presumably a similar range of acceptability exists in the musical system—expressed, or unconsciously taken for granted—of each culture. And one may deviate from pitch more in some musical styles than in others and still operate within the acceptable norm.

Another important feature of musical scales is the hierarchy in importance and function of the individual tones. Most frequently there is one tone which is the basis of the scale; it is apt to appear at the end of a piece and is called the *tonic*. Another tone, often higher and used with great frequency, may be called the *dominant*. Other tones may appear with average frequency, and still others may be rare. Individual tones may also have particular functions, such as appearing typically just before or after certain other tones, thus providing the listener with signals indicating points of the musical structure. In short, the scale of a composition can and should be a capsule diagram of its melodic materials and rules.

In many ways, the music of non-Western and some folk cultures may sound strange, confusing, and even unacceptable to the uninitiated listener. There is a tendency in earlier writings on music, and in present-day remarks of the uninformed, to assume that such music has no structure and no laws, that it is chaotically improvised. One still hears this music characterized at times as "chant," indicating an assumption that the music is simply a vehicle for ceremonial words, and that it has little interest of its own. Nothing could be further from the truth. The intricacy of much of this music—its consistent and logical structure—makes much of it a marvel of artistry. Its simplicity is dictated by the fact that it must be memorized, and by the lack of notation available to the composer. Careful listening can, however, clear up much of the apparent confusion. Intervals that sound out of tune will not sound so harsh once they are heard recurrently in several songs of one group. Of course, all non-Western and folk music is not alike, so that learning one musical language, such as that of the Plains Indians, does not by any means assure understanding of another, such as West African. But as in learning languages, so in learning musical styles, each new style is easier to assimilate than the previous one.

DESCRIPTION OF A CULTURE'S MUSIC

The sections just completed—dealing with sound, form, texture, rhythm, and melody—have concentrated on understanding the musical style of an individual piece of music. We find it perhaps even more necessary to describe the style of a whole body of music—all Sun Dance songs of one Plains Indian tribe, or all music of the Basongye tribe, or even the whole body of music in the Plains, or of one European folk culture such as the Romanian. Of course, we cannot assume that all music in a culture will sound like the one example included on a single recording, or even that all songs of a given tribe exhibit the same characteristics. Nevertheless, we frequently hear statements such as "The Ibo have this kind of music" or "Spanish folk music sounds like that." Fortunately for the student of folk music, there is a good deal of stylistic unity in the folk music of each culture. Such unity is probably greatest in the world's simplest cultures and gives way to increasing diversity as the cultures get more complex.

There are a number of traits of music that occur at least to a small degree in all or nearly all cultures. A short list of universals and near-universals of music would include the following. In all cultures, music consists of discrete artifacts, each with a beginning and end, and with a balance of internal repetition and variation. Most musical utterances descend at the end. All possess a rhythmic structure based on distinctions among note lengths and among dynamic stresses. All cultures have at least some dance with musical accompaniment and some songs with texts made up of words. Music is regularly associated with the supernatural and with religious activity. Features shared by a healthy majority of musics, though by no means all of them, include tetratonic and pentatonic scales composed of unequal intervals, often major seconds and minor thirds; singing in octaves; division of songs and pieces into stanzas and strophes; and the use of *idiophones* (instruments whose bodies vibrate to produce sound) and of sound tools (believed to constitute the oldest layer of man's musical instruments). Each repertory seems to have a mainstream, a unified style clustering in the center, composed of a large number of songs or pieces that are very much alike (though it is often the exceptional material at the borders of a repertory that is valued most highly). And most cultures have some sense of a musical specialist who, for whatever reasons—religious, aesthetic, social—knows music better and is able to produce it more adequately and in larger quantity than others.

The description of the musical style of a given specific whole culture is bound to be essentially a statistical statement. When we say, for example, that most of the scales of the Arapaho Indians are tetratonic, we must add that there are also many songs with five or six tones, some with three, and a few with seven. When we say that English folk songs are essentially *modal*, that is, they use one of several arrangements of seven tones, we must realize that all sorts of other scales also appear. We also face a problem in distinguishing among several kinds of music in a culture: the oldest and perhaps most authentic music, the recent imports and the results of outside influences, and the atypical creations which seem not to belong, if, indeed, such a judgment can be made.

In the past few decades there have been great efforts on the part of individuals, institutions, and governments to collect and study folk musics and other oral traditions. A wealth of material has been gathered in archives, and many recordings have been made available. But there is still much to be done in the way of analyzing the music and describing the styles in scholarly terms. The statements that will be made in this volume will sometimes have to be impressionistic, based on knowledge of only a small segment of a people's music. We can only indicate examples of the kinds of things that occur. We cannot give a complete picture, but we hope that the partial picture presented will stimulate you to strike out on your own in order to learn more.

RESEARCH IN TRADITIONAL MUSIC: ETHNOMUSICOLOGY

Perhaps a few words about the way in which research in folk and non-Western musics is done will help you understand some of the procedures and statements in the following chapters. The field that provides research in this area is now known as *ethnomusicology*. Before about 1950 it was commonly called comparative musicology, and it overlaps with the fields of musicology (the study of all aspects of music in a scholarly fashion) and anthropology (the study of man, his culture, and especially the cultures outside the investigator's own background). Research in ethnomusicology consists essentially of two activities: field work and desk or laboratory work. In past decades it was customary to keep these activities quite distinct. Those who went into the field—to villages, reservations, or colonies, to make recordings—were not necessarily trained in the techniques of analysis and description that form the main part of the desk work. Conversely, the armchair ethnomusicologists rarely went into the field. In recent times it has been assumed that the best work would result if the same person did both the field research and the analytical work. It is now taken for granted that almost every ethnomusicologist is, at various times, both a field and a desk worker.

The distinction between the field worker who is interested only in recording music and the one who is interested in music as an aspect of culture and as a form of behavior is also disappearing. Ethnomusicologists have come to realize that one cannot record and study the music of any people effectively without understanding the cultural context in which the music lives. At the same time, they realize that discussing the uses that a culture makes of music, its attitudes toward music, and the way in which music reflects the values of the society is likely to be meaningless without a knowledge of the music itself. Thus it is true that ethnomusicology has two sides, or two approaches, the musicological and the anthropological, but they are both essential, at least to some degree, for each individual scholar and student.

There are many different types of field projects that an ethnomusicologist may undertake. He or she may go to study the music of an entire people, such as the Yoruba of Nigeria or the people of Afghanistan, but aside from providing an introductory survey, such a project would be useless in the context of the amount of knowledge available today because it would be superficial. More fruitful is the study of a particular type of music or the musical culture of an individual community, of a particular group (such as a minority) in a community, or even of an individual musician. A field worker's approach varies with the project and the emphasis. He or she may simply record music and take down, from the statements of informants, the necessary information on its cultural background. Or musical events may be observed as they occur. The field worker may learn aspects of the musical system by learning how to perform the music; this can be done particularly effectively in those cultures which have established formal musical training. Techniques may be devised, such as musical aptitude tests based on the people's own music, questionnaires, or various approaches involving statistics. In general, we may divide field research into several categories: (1) eliciting material (music and information about it) from informants in special recording or interviewing sessions; (2) observing culture as it operates from the field worker's view as an outsider; (3) participating in the culture as a student and performer; and (4) gaining insights from special tests that oblige the informants to think about their culture in ways to which they are not accustomed.

Obviously, the complexity and difficulties of ethnomusicological field work are considerable and not to be underestimated by the novice who may wish to attempt it. The person who goes off to record the music of an African tribe or a Balkan village must know in advance a good deal about the culture of the people to be visited. Once there, certain techniques must be used to be sure of gaining access to the individuals who know songs, and to ensure that samplings made of the music are representative. The field worker should not try to record only one kind of song. A collector of folk songs in the Virginia mountains should not try to record only old English ballads, for example. This approach will not only cause much other valuable material to be missed, but may also alienate the singers, because they will probably consider other songs equally valuable; thus the collector may not even succeed in hearing as many old English ballads as he or she would if a more broad-minded approach had been taken. A field worker must get to know people in the community very well. A three-day field trip is usually not very successful; ideal field work requires months or even years of stay, with follow-up visits to see how songs as well as attitudes toward music have changed.

Whatever the field worker's specific approach, he or she should take a broad view of the task. Turning on the tape recorder or learning how to play an instrument is only a small part of the job. It is also important to find out what informants think about the songs they sing; what they consider a good song or a bad one, and why; how they learn songs; how they compose; who the good musicians are and what makes them good musicians; what kinds of songs the culture has (according to the tribe's own classification); what kinds of terms they use, if any, to talk about music; what kinds of music outside their own they have had contact with; what activities each song is designed to accompany, if any; what the status of the musician in the society is; and so on. The field worker may have to use special eliciting techniques. David McAllester, for example, widely known for his collecting of Navaho music, said that he persuaded the Indians to sing for him by singing folk songs or even Indian songs to them.[1] It may be useful to find an informant who will assume the role of teacher to the field worker. It is necessary to record the same song as it is sung by different people in a community, or by the same person at different times, in order to find out what aspects of a song remain stable and which ones are subject to change; also how much a song changes in a given period of time. But no matter how much an ethnomusicologist prepares for a field trip and how much he or she learns from books and records, it will become apparent in the first week in the field that somehow everything is different from what was expected, and that there is no substitute for seeing the situation at first hand.

TRANSCRIPTION AND ANALYSIS

The job of analyzing and describing music may be done simply by listening with techniques something like those described in the first pages of this chapter. More likely the ethnomusicologist will want to set at least some of the music down on paper in notation. This process is called *transcription.*

Because our ordinary system of notation was devised essentially for the music of Western civilization, and because its purpose is to help a performer carry out the composer's intentions rather than to describe the musical actions of the performer, it is not surprising that the system is rather imperfect for the descriptive use to which it is put in ethnomusicological transcription. The fact that the rhythms and scales of non-Western and folk musics do not always fit into the Western system makes it all the more difficult to reproduce such music in conventional notation. Yet, although various special systems have been devised, most scholars have returned to the conventional one despite its shortcomings. It is one, after all, that can be easily mastered and that is already understood by individuals who are acquainted with Western music. It can be used in folk song collections that serve the double purpose of being scholarly descriptions of music and anthologies for performance. Some transcribers have added special symbols where the conventional system of notation is wanting. For example, intervals smaller than a half step are frequently indicated by placing a plus (higher) or a minus (lower) sign above a note.

Careful listening to even a simple folk tune indicates that a considerable number of musical events take place in every second of singing. The

---

[1] David P. McAllester, *Enemy Way Music* (Cambridge, MA: Peabody Museum of Harvard University, 1954).

question is whether we should try to capture each of these or whether we should restrict our notation to the main lines. The ethnomusicologist, careful and thorough, would like to capture all. If he or she has a talented ear and enormous patience, a very intricate notation will be produced. This procedure was followed by Béla Bartók, not only a great composer but also one of the most important scholars of folk music, who collected vast numbers of Hungarian, Slovak, Yugoslav, and Romanian folk songs. Example 2-5 shows one of his transcriptions of Yugoslav folk music. Below the melody in all its detail is a less complicated version of the song that gives only the main notes.

Of course, the important thing in transcribing is to be objective, to discover what actually occurs. And make no mistake about this: What one

EXAMPLE 2-5. Serbo-Croatian folk song, with complex and simplified transcriptions by Béla Bartók and Albert B. Lord, *Serbo-Croatian Folk Songs* (New York: Columbia University Press, 1951), p. 154.

hears is conditioned by one's own musical experiences and also by one's expectations concerning the music being heard. An example of how expectations may actually interfere with an understanding of musical structure is provided by Timothy Rice in his account of field work carried out in southwestern Bulgaria.[2] The prevailing assumption among Bulgarian scholars that the people of this region sang in two parts (and not three) at first caused Rice to disbelieve his own ears and even to question the singers' competence and reliability. His attempts to transcribe the music were unsuccessful until, finally, close listening to each singer individually and recording of the singers using three separate microphones verified the existence of three distinct lines (two of which coincided through much of a song).

In order to save time and increase accuracy and objectivity, several attempts have been made to devise machinery that would measure pitch and transcribe music. These range from a monochord—simply one stretched string with a graduated table to show vibration rates—invented by Jaap Kunst, to elaborate electronic devices based on the oscilloscope and on computers. In the 1950s instruments called *melographs* were developed— by Charles Seeger at the University of California at Los Angeles, by Dalia Cohen and Ruth Katz in Jerusalem, and by a group of Norwegian scholars headed by Olav Gurvin—to graph music electronically;[3] melographs are manufactured commercially today. Melographs produce detailed graphs like the one shown in Example 2-6 (in which the top section indicates amplitude or rhythm, which is derived from volume; the series of dots in the middle indicates the time, the space between two dots equaling one second; and the bottom section indicates pitch movement or melody). It is often necessary to retranslate such graphs into a more musically meaningful form—like conventional notation with all its deficiencies. Even so electronic transcription has contributed to our understanding of folk and non-Western styles, and has been particularly valuable to the analysis of musical features that cannot be expressed adequately using conventional Western notation—for example, intonation and fluctuation in volume.

Transcription of the musical sound into some kind of notation system is only one of the techniques used by ethnomusicologists to prepare their material for analytic conclusions. Processing musical data with computers,

---

[2] Timothy Rice, "Understanding Three-Part Singing in Bulgaria: The Interplay of Theory and Experience," UCLA *Selected Reports in Ethnomusicology*, VII (1988), 43–57.

[3] Charles Seeger, "Prescriptive and Descriptive Music Writing," *Musical Quarterly*, LXIV (1958), 184–95; Karl Dahlback, *New Methods in Vocal Folk Music Research* (Oslo: Oslo University Press, 1958); and Dalia Cohen and Ruth Katz, "Remarks Concerning the Use of the Melograph in Ethnomusicological Studies," in *Yuval: Studies of the Jewish Music Research Centre*, ed. Israel Adler (Jerusalem: Magnes Press, 1968). See also the collection of studies carried out with the help of Seeger's Melograph Model C in the UCLA *Selected Reports in Ethnomusicology*, Vol. II, no. 1 (1974).

EXAMPLE 2-6. Graph of an automatic transcription of part of a Norwegian folk song; from Karl Dahlback, *New Methods in Vocal Folk Music Research* (Oslo: Oslo University Press, 1958), p. 127.

counting various kinds of intervals and note values, tracing the development of a musical motif from the beginning to the end of a performance, comparing various versions of one song, classifying a repertory in groupings that are internally related, comparing the structure of a melody with that of its accompanying verbal text—all of these are examples of the kinds of things that are frequently done together with, or in some cases, instead of, transcription.

All of these techniques are, however, only stepping stones for the ethnomusicologist to get at the central questions of the field: What is the nature of music throughout the world? What does music accomplish in culture generally? Why do different cultures produce different musics? And for each individual culture: What are the conditions under which music changes? By what processes does it change?

BIBLIOGRAPHICAL NOTES

Methods of analysis and approaches to describing musical styles are set forth in Curt Sachs, *The Wellsprings of Music* (The Hague: Martinus Nijhoff, 1962) and Alan Lomax, *Folk Song Style and Culture* (Washington, DC: American Association for the Advancement of Science, 1968) and *Cantometrics: An Approach to the Anthropology of Music* (Berkeley: University of California Extension Media Center, 1976); several articles by Mieczyslaw Kolinski, especially his "Classification of Tonal Structures," *Studies in Ethnomusicology*, I (1961), 38–76; Bruno Nettl, *Theory and Method in Ethnomusicology* (New York: Free Press, 1964); and Marcia Herndon, "Analysis: Herding of Sacred Cows?," *Ethnomusicology*, XVIII (1974), 219–62. Volume VII (1988) of the UCLA *Selected Reports in Ethnomusicology* is entirely devoted to studies dealing with the issue of conceptualization in music. Many publications deal with methods of analyzing individual aspects of music. Among them are Sirvart Poladian, "Melody Contour in Traditional Music," *J-IFMC*, III (1951), 30–35; Mieczyslaw Kolinski, "Consonance and Dissonance," *Ethnomusicology*, VI (1962), 66–74 and "Reiteration Quotients: A Cross-Cultural Comparison," *Ethnomusicology*, XXVI (1982), 85–90; and Curt Sachs, *Rhythm and Tempo* (New York: Norton, 1953), Chapters 1 and 2. The question of universals has been widely discussed. See, for example, essays on the subject in *Ethnomusicology*, Vol. XV, no. 3 (September 1971); and in *World of Music*, Vol. XIX, nos. 1–2 (1977), and Vol. XXVI, no. 2 (1984). Other specialized studies dealing with topics discussed in this chapter include Edward O. Henry, "The Variety of Music in a North Indian Village: Reassessing Cantometrics," *Ethnomusicology*, XX (1976), 49–66; George List, "The Reliability of Transcription," *Ethnomusicology*, XVIII (1974), 353–77; and Nazir A. Jairazbhoy, "The 'Objective' and Subjective View in Music Transcription," *Ethnomusicology*, XXI (1977), 263–74. The UCLA *Selected Reports in Ethnomusicology*, Vol. II, no. 1 (1974), is entirely devoted to melographic studies. *Ethnomusicology*, Vol. VII (1964),

223–77, contains a detailed symposium on transcription and analysis on the basis of a single Bushman song.

General works about the field of ethnomusicology, its history, and its theories are Jaap Kunst, *Ethnomusicology*, 3rd ed. (The Hague: Martinus Nijhoff, 1959); Mantle Hood, "Music, the Unknown" in *Musicology* (Englewood Cliffs, NJ: Prentice-Hall, 1963) and *The Ethnomusicologist* (New York: McGraw-Hill, 1971); and Bruno Nettl, *Theory and Method in Ethnomusicology* and *The Study of Ethnomusicology: Twenty-nine Issues and Concepts* (Urbana: University of Illinois Press, 1983). The last-cited book addresses many of the issues surveyed in this chapter. Other discussions of research methods appear in Alan P. Merriam, "Ethnomusicology, Discussion and Definition of the Field," *Ethnomusicology*, IV (1960), 107–14, and "Ethnomusicology Revisited," *Ethnomusicology*, XIII (1969), 213–29. *Ethnomusicology*, Vol. XXXI, no. 3 (Fall 1987), presents a provocative essay by Timothy Rice, "Toward the Remodeling of Ethnomusicology," followed by responses by five other scholars.

Ann Briegleb, *Directory of Ethnomusicological Sound Recording Collections in the U.S. and Canada* (Ann Arbor: Society for Ethnomusicology, 1971) is an important research tool. *Indiana University, Archives of Traditional Music, Catalog of Phonorecordings of Music and Oral Data* (Boston: G. K. Hall, 1975) is an inventory of one major collection. Collections of musical instruments are identified in William Lichtenwanger, *A Survey of Musical Instrument Collections in the United States and Canada* (Ann Arbor: Music Library Association, 1974), and in Jean Jenkins, *International Directory of Music Instrument Collections* (Buren, Netherlands: Frits Knuf, 1977); the latter volume excludes collections in the United States and Canada.

The standard work on musical instruments is Curt Sachs, *The History of Musical Instruments* (New York: Norton, 1940). René T. A. Lysloff and Jim Matson, "A New Approach to the Classification of Sound Producing Instruments," *Ethnomusicology*, XXIX (1985), 213–36, offers an alternative approach to instrument classification. Important dictionaries of musical instruments are *The New Grove Dictionary of Musical Instruments*, 3 vols. (London: Macmillan Press, 1984), Curt Sachs, *Real-Lexicon der Musikinstrumente* (New York: Dover, 1964), and Sibyl Marcuse, *Musical Instruments: A Comprehensive Dictionary* (Garden City, NY: Doubleday, 1964). Several volumes of the *Handbuch der europäischen Volksmusikinstrumente*, an encyclopedia of European folk instruments, have appeared; these are cited later in the relevant chapters. The basic book on dance, despite its considerable age, is Curt Sachs, *A World History of the Dance* (New York: Norton, 1937). An excellent survey of research in non-Western dance to 1960 is Gertrude P. Kurath, "Panorama of Dance Ethnology," *Current Anthropology*, I (1960), 233–54. Studies of dance, body movement, and musical sound in various cultures are collected in *The Performing Arts: Music and Dance*, ed. John Blacking and Joann W. Kealiinohomoku (The Hague: Mouton, 1979), and in *The Anthropology of the Body*, ed. John Blacking (New York: Academic Press, 1977).

THREE

THE GENERAL CHARACTER
OF EUROPEAN FOLK MUSIC

Each country in Europe—in some cases each region, each district, and each community—has its own folk music and its own style. But the various traditions also have much in common; in some ways, European folk music is indeed a single corpus of musical style. In this chapter we will explore the unity of European folk music. In Chapters 4, 5, and 6 we will discuss the special characteristics of regions and countries.

We have pointed out that it is very hard to state concretely just how much difference there is between one kind or style of music and another. One way of telling that a musical style is similar to another one, the second of which you already recognize, is that the first of the styles also appeals to you. If this is true, and a person who is acquainted with British folk music finds Russian folk song more appealing than the music of Polynesia, then Russian and English folk song are indeed more similar to each other than are the English and the Polynesian. This has to do with the fact that folk music styles, like languages, exhibit greater or lesser degrees of relationship. Just as it is usually easier to learn a language that is closely related in structure and vocabulary to one's own, it is easier to understand and appreciate a folk music style similar to one that is already familiar. (Of course, this hypothesis does not explain the fascination that an utterly strange music may immediately hold for a previously unexposed listener, but obviously there are many things that determine what kind of music will speak to an individual. Familiarity, however, is one of the strongest criteria.)

If we use this only very moderately reliable measuring device, we find that most of the European styles are rather similar to each other. And, on the whole, those that are geographically close to each other are also the most closely related in terms of musical style. There are a number of characteristics which we find to be present throughout Europe—with the usual pockets of exception, of course—and throughout that part of the world inhabited by descendants of Europeans.

We really know very little about the history of European folk song. We have little evidence as to the age of individual songs, although some idea can be gained from the notations of folk songs made by composers from the Renaissance on. But in such cases we don't know as a rule whether a song was really part of the folk tradition, or whether it was an art or popular song that later moved into the realm of folklore. We also know little about the age of the various styles of folk music in Europe. Still, we are sure that for centuries there has been a close relationship between the art music of the continent and its folk music. How could it be otherwise? Villages and cities could not live without some mutual contact. In the early Middle Ages, wandering minstrels carried their tunes from court to village and from country to country. The villagers of the Middle Ages attended church and heard plainsong. The composer at the court of a minor duke in seventeenth-century Germany drew his performers from the village musicians living on his lord's estate. We have ample evidence for assuming a constant relationship between folk musicians and their counterparts.

Contact among musical styles was accelerated by the invention and rapid dissemination of printing after the fifteenth century, especially in Western Europe. We tend to think of the folk and the art music traditions as living essentially separate lives, but this is surely erroneous not only in a consideration of European culture but also in the case of those Asian civilizations that have similar stratification. The folk musics of China, India, the Islamic world, and elsewhere all bear important similarities to the art musics of their countries. And in Europe, where printing provided a particularly good and rapid method of dissemination, especially of the words but to an important extent also the music of song, the relationship has been especially close.

Of course, one can speak about the effects of art music on folk music only for those periods in which a well-developed fine-art tradition in music existed. Such a tradition evidently did not exist to a large degree before the Middle Ages, and it did not come to Eastern Europe until even later. There are those who believe that the styles of European folk music evolved to a state similar to their present one before the time (perhaps a thousand years ago) when art music composers first began to influence folklore, and that the folk styles are an invaluable remnant of precultivated times, even of prehistoric eras. This belief can be neither substantiated nor negated. But we are probably safer in believing that the styles of European folk music developed sometime in the Middle Ages, and that this happened to some extent under the influence of the art music that was also developing at the time. This, after all, might account for the rather considerable degree of homogeneity in European folk music.

THE STROPHIC FORM

The most characteristic trait of European folk songs is their *strophic* structure. We tend to accept as normal a structure in which a tune with several lines is repeated several times, each time with different words. But this kind of arrangement is not so common elsewhere in the world, and it ties the European nations together as a musical unit. The length of a strophic song, or a song with stanzas can vary greatly, from a short bit (see Example 3-1) to a relatively elaborate piece (see Example 3-2).

It is important to realize, however, that strophic songs are found also in other parts of the world. They appear in some North American Indian cultures, in the Middle East, and in Asia and Africa. Their basic principle is that a tune, or a portion of a tune, can be sung more than once, with different words. This principle is accepted at various levels in a multitude of musical styles. Indeed, in some of the world's simplest styles, the repetition of a single musical motif, with slightly or completely different words, is common. But the more or less exact repetition of a fairly detailed musical organism with several different sets of words as the basic and by far predominant type of organization sets Europe apart, and, interestingly, it is important in all types of European music—folk, art, and popular music, and in all areas—East and West, North and South.

The special character of the strophic song is derived from a peculiar trait of European poetry—folk poetry as well as that of the more learned poets. This is the tendency for poems to consist of units of two, three, four, five, six, or more lines. Such units, called *stanzas* or *strophes*, have a form that is repeated; the interrelationship of the lines is repeated, but the words—or at least most of them—are not. The lines may be interrelated by the number of syllables or of poetic feet in each, or, more commonly,

EXAMPLE 3-1. Slovak folk song with short stanza, learned by Bruno Nettl from oral tradition.

EXAMPLE 3-2. Irish folk song, "Patty McGinty's Goat," collected in Newfoundland by MacEdward Leach, transcribed by Bruno Nettl.

by a rhyme scheme. But in any event, some sort of structure is given to the stanza quite aside from the meaning of the words. Whereas the words themselves progress through the poem, telling a story or expressing the poet's feelings about practically any subject, the structure of the stanza is repeated. We don't know whether a strophic structure in the poetry inspired a corresponding structure in the music, or whether the reverse occurred. But logically, it is a simple transition from a repeated poetic structure to a repeated melody, with the words and their content changing from stanza to stanza.

The following stanza of the famous English ballad, "Barbara Allen," shows us some of the traits of the poetic unit typical in European folklore:

> Oh yes I'm sick, I'm very sick
> And death is in me dwelling;
> No better, no better I ever shall be
> If I can't have Barb'ry Allen.

Even if we saw the complete poem without music and without the printer's divisions into stanzas, we could easily figure out that it is arranged into stanzas, because (1) lines 2 and 4 rhyme at least approximately (also lines 6 and 8, lines 10 and 12, and so on), and (2) every fourth line ends with the words "Barb'ry Allen." In other songs and in other languages, there are different characteristics of the stanza, different ways of identifying the stanza as a unit. But the same kind of musical structure, strophic, with its repetition of a few musical lines, is found throughout Europe (if not in all songs) and is an accompaniment to and analogue of the poetic structure.

The close relationship between the words and music of European folk song is exhibited in other, more intimate ways as well. The lines of music and text usually coincide, and the points at which the music comes to a temporary rest are also those at which a sentence, phrase, or thought in the text is completed. There is, moreover, a close relationship between the smaller segments of musical and linguistic structure, for example, between stress and accent, and between the length of tone and of syllable, although the nature of this relationship varies from nation to nation because of the differences in structure among the various languages. In art song, this relationship has often been refined, and rough edges of the sort that may result from oral tradition are smoothed out.

CHARACTERISTICS OF EUROPEAN SCALES

We have mentioned the basic strophic structures of European folk music as a reason for our belief that it is essentially a stylistic unit. Let us also briefly discuss the unity of these styles with regard to individual elements of music—scales, meter, intervals, and manner of singing.

The scales of European folk song exhibit great variety. Most typically, there are songs with only two or three different tones (these are most frequently children's ditties or game songs), there are songs with five tones (pentatonic scales), and others with six or seven tones. But the kinds of intervals (the distances in pitch) among the tones are not quite so diverse. The tendency is for European folk songs to use intervals that fit into the *diatonic system*, a system of tones that we can hear by playing the white keys of the piano. The diatonic system consists of major and minor seconds and of intervals produced by adding seconds. Throughout Europe, it seems that the most common intervals in folk music are the major seconds and the minor thirds. Unfortunately, we do not yet have statistics to prove this definitively, but a thorough inspection of a few representative song collections would be convincing. Other intervals are also found, of course, and occasionally there are intervals that do not fit into the diatonic system and which could not even be reproduced approximately on the piano. Also, in folk singing the intervals generally are not sung with the degree of precision found on the piano, and deviation from a standard norm seems to be somewhat greater in folk than in concert music. Nevertheless, adherence to the diatonic intervals seems to be one of the great general characteristics of European folk music.

Of course, other cultures also use scales which fit into the diatonic system. In some Asian civilizations, music theory that is almost parallel to that of Europe (so far as the arrangement of pitches in a scale is concerned) has developed, and intervals approximately the size of a major second are probably found in the vast majority of world musics. Nevertheless, the almost perfect adherence of European folk song to this diatonic system is one of its chief characteristics.

Going into a bit more detail, we find that a great many of the songs that use seven tones can be explained, as far as their tonal material is concerned, in terms of the modes (Dorian, Phrygian, Lydian, Mixolydian, Aeolian, Locrian, and Ionian) that are used to classify Gregorian chant (in slightly different form) as well as other medieval and Renaissance music. This fact has led some scholars to believe that the styles of European folk music actually originated in the music of the church, and indeed we must concede the possibility of a great deal of influence of church music on folk song. But quite apart from that, these modes are useful as a system for classifying folk music. As such, it can be used to classify only those songs and pieces which actually have seven tones. For instance, Example 3-3 could be considered a Mixolydian tune transposed up a fourth.

We might be tempted to classify tunes that have only five tones according to the same system of modes, pretending that two tones of the mode are simply absent. The trouble is that we could not prove which tones are lacking. A song with the scale A-C-D-E-G that ends on A could

EXAMPLE 3-3. Russian folk song in the Mixolydian mode, from Elsa Mahler, *Altrussische Volkslieder aus dem Pečoryland* (Basel: Bärenreiter-Verlag, 1951), p. 43.

be considered Aeolian (or minor), if the missing tones were B and F. But if they were B-flat and F the tune would have to be classified as Phrygian. And if the missing tones were B-flat and F-sharp the scale would not fit any of the above-mentioned modes at all. (See Example 3-4 for the various modes that can be fashioned out of a nucleus of five tones in the diatonic system.) Thus we can hardly accept the blanket statement that frequently has been made that folk music is modal in the sense of the Gregorian modes. But a great many European folk songs do fit into that system.

Pentatonic songs make up a large proportion of the European body of folk song; their scales are usually composed of major seconds and minor thirds, as in Example 3-5. Pentatonic songs cannot, however—even with the special kind of pentatonic scale illustrated here—be considered as primarily a European phenomenon. This type of scale is one that Europe shares

EXAMPLE 3-4. Diatonic modes based on a single group of five tones.

Anhemitonic Pentatonic

Not in the traditional diatonic mode system

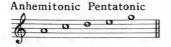

with a large part of the world, particularly with Northern Asia, with the American Indians, and with sub-Saharan Africa.

The same is true of the songs with two or three tones, illustrated in Example 3-6. This very limited kind of scale is found in repertories throughout the world. There are some tribal cultures, particularly in the Americas and in Northern Asia, whose music hardly goes beyond it. This is true, for example, in the music of the Vedda of Ceylon (a people whose traditional music is now extinct, but whose songs were recorded, in rather small number, around 1900), and the songs of the last member of the Yahi Indians, the famous Ishi. In these cultures, however, an occasional fourth or fifth tone appears as well. Of course, musics using a limited number of tones need not be simple in every way. The songs of Ishi, for example, exhibit considerable sophistication in other respects.

EXAMPLE 3-5. English folk song with a pentatonic scale, from Jan P. Schinhan, ed., *The Music of the Ballads* (Durham, NC: Duke University Press, 1957. *The Frank C. Brown Collection of North Carolina Folklore,* IV), p. 184.

EXAMPLE 3-6. Tritonic children's ditty, found in various nations with different sets of words.

Cultures with more complex scale systems also tend to have some songs with only two or three tones, and this is true of European folk cultures. In most cases (in Europe and elsewhere) these are children's songs, game songs, lullabies, and old ritual melodies. The melodies of epic poetry also frequently have few tones. The widespread geographic distribution of these scales, coupled with the simplicity of the songs which they usually accompany, has led some folklorists to believe that in Europe they constitute a remnant of an ancient musical culture. These scholars believe that all music must at one time have been as simple as this, and that such songs were driven into a corner of the repertory, just as those cultures which use only such songs were driven into the geographical corners of the world as newer, more complex music was invented. But this is only one of several possible explanations. The simple children's ditties of Europe may have nothing to do with the limited scales of the Yahi Indians, whose history may have included, in earlier times, more complex scales which gradually become more and more restricted in order to make possible the greater development of other aspects. It would be a mistake to take for granted the assumption that music everywhere moves consistently from simple to more complex forms. Thus the simplest songs of Europe may be the most archaic, but they are probably not representative of a stage in world music in which all music was based on two-tone and three-tone scales. If ever there was such a stage, it must have occurred many millenia ago, for we know that human culture, in many varieties, has been present in sophisticated forms for that long.

In summary, then, the seven-tone scales, with their modal arrangements, are a hallmark of European folk music, but they are not really limited to Western culture. The pentatonic scales are important in most if not all European traditions, but they are equally important in a large variety of non-Western cultures and constitute the dominant scale type in some of them. The restricted two- and three-tone scales are found throughout the world, but except in a few isolated cultures, they constitute a small minority of the repertory.

METER AND SINGING STYLE

Most European folk music adheres to the concept of *meter*. This means that there is some regularity of recurrence in the accent pattern of the music, though such regularity does not by any means imply the predomi-

EXAMPLE 3-7. English folk song, "Lady Isabel and the Elf Knight," from Cecil Sharp, *English Folk Songs from the Southern Appalachians* (London, New York: Oxford University Press, 1952), I, 7.

nance of common or triple meters without deviation. A large proportion of European folk songs and pieces can indeed be classed as *isometric*, that is, dominated by a single metric pattern, such as 4/4, 3/4, 6/8 (or even 5/8, 7/8, etc.). When several meters are used, these tend to appear in recurring sequences; thus a song, particularly one in Eastern Europe, may have a meter consisting of the regular alternation of 3/8, 4/8, and 5/8 measures (see Example 5-3). Music in which no metric pattern can be detected is not common in European folklore. Deviations from a metric pattern—for example, the elongation of tones at points of rest, near the endings of lines or of phrases—are common (see Example 3-7), but these deviations tend to reinforce the metric character of the music rather than to negate it. Thus another trait, found also, to be sure, elsewhere in the world, ties European folk music into a homogeneous unit.

The metric character of European folk music is closely related to the metric organization of much of the poetry. Those peoples that have well-developed metric poetry are also those whose music most typically adheres to a simple meter. Those peoples in Europe (mainly in Eastern Europe) whose poetry is organized in terms of syllable count rather than metric-foot count are also those that have a certain amount of nonmetric music and more complex and more varying metric patterns in their folk music.

The manner of singing—use of the voice, movements and facial expressions, types of tone color—is another important feature. We have few guidelines for describing this phenomenon. Alan Lomax[1] is one of the few scholars who has paid attention to this important aspect of music. Lomax has claimed that it is possible to divide the world into relatively few areas, each of

[1] Alan Lomax, "Folk Song Style," *American Anthropologist*, LXI (1959), 927–54. See also his *Folk Song Style and Culture* (Washington, DC: American Association for the Advancement of Science, 1968) and *Cantometrics: An Approach to the Anthropology of Music* (Berkeley: University of California Extension Media Center, 1976).

which has a particular manner of singing that exists independent of the geographic distribution of other aspects of musical style such as melody, rhythm, and form. Europe, he has found, is rather complicated, for it possesses a number of singing styles that do not have contiguous distribution.

What we are interested in assessing, in a discussion of singing style, are those things that go into the singing of almost every tone, the things that make the sound of a singer and of the entire culture distinctive and recognizable immediately. Among the parameters of singing style are: (1) degree of tension, or its opposite, called by Lomax "vocal width"; (2) amount of ornamentation; (3) raspiness; (4) accentuation, that is, degree of strength with which individual tones are attacked, and degree to which stressed tones are distinguished in loudness and sharpness from the unstressed ones; (5) nasality; (6) pitch level, that is, the level of singing within the singer's natural vocal range; (7) vocal blend, that is, the degree to which singers in a group blend their voices; and (8) ornamentation. Before Lomax, the Hungarian composer and folk song scholar Béla Bartók divided Hungarian and other European folk singing into two basic singing styles, *parlando-rubato* and *tempo giusto*. The first of these is a singing style in which emphasis is on the words, there is not much strict adherence to tempo and meter, and there is a substantial amount of ornamentation. Tempo giusto implies greater stress on musical meter and tempo, and less on the words. Bartók found both of these singing styles in Hungarian folk music, and both appear to be present in many European countries, although their definition must generally be adjusted for each culture. According to Lomax, however, there is in each culture one dominant singing style, and it can be identified rather easily in any small sampling of singing. Moreover, the main singing style of each culture is determined by the character of that culture, and in particular by the types of relationships among people that are typical of that culture.

Lomax assigned three singing styles to European folk music: " Eurasian," "Old European", and "Modern European". The Eurasian style, which is found primarily throughout most of the high cultures of Asia, is represented in Europe in parts of the British Isles and France, in southern Italy, and in the Mohammedan parts of the Balkans. The singing is high-pitched, strident, and harsh, and the singers' facial expressions are rigidly controlled or sad. The style lends itself well to long, ornamented tones and passages, and the character of the music is sweetly melancholy. As for Lomax's characterization of social structure, the Eurasian area is one in which the position of women is below that of men; they may be put on a pedestal, but they do not have equality.

The Old European style is found in the Hebrides, northern England, Scandinavia, the Pyrenees, Czechoslovakia, western Yugoslavia, northern Italy, Germany, parts of the Balkans, the Ukraine, and the Caucasus. Here singing is done with the throat relaxed, and the facial expressions of the singers are lively and animated. The tunes are simple and unornamented, and group singing is common. Cooperation among the singers in a chorus seems to have allowed polyphony to develop, and possibly some of the polyphonic types of folk music antedated the development of polyphony in European cultivated music. In these areas, in any event, harmony was easily accepted. The idea of cooperation in music seems to have something to do with social cooperation, for the position of women in the Old European areas, according to Lomax, has been one of equality with men.

The Modern European style is a later layer which seems to have been superimposed on some of the other styles, perhaps as a result of urban influence. It is found in most of England and France, in Hungary, central Italy, and colonial America. This is the area of ballads and lyrical love songs. Singing, in contrast to the Old European style, is normally done by soloists or in unblended unison. The vocal quality is harsh and strained, and interest is more in the words than in the music.

Although Lomax's observations are controversial, they are certainly stimulating. They are based on the assumption that the way in which people sing is more likely to remain constant than the musical content of their songs, and on the belief that a small sample of singing from a particular area or country will indicate the total singing style of that area. Lomax's approach seems to imply, accordingly, that each culture can sing in only one way (a theory that has been proved incorrect in various cultures, as for instance among the North American Indians). His observations lead us to conclude that Europe is not a unit as far as singing style is concerned, but that two or three styles of singing and voice production are found, and that each of these is supranational in character and cuts across the boundaries of politics, culture, and language. He also shows that the two main European singing styles are not found to a great extent on other continents (except among descendants of Europeans).

WANDERING MELODIES

Quite aside from the characteristics of the elements of music, the actual tunes found in different parts of Europe indicate that Europe is a historical unit. In the nineteenth century, some scholars began to be intrigued by what they came to call "wandering melodies," that is, by tunes whose variants were found in the folk traditions of widely separated countries. The existence of these melodies, or melody types, is also proof of the close relationship of art, church, and folk music. Melody types found in European folk music are also frequently found in hymns and art songs, particularly of the periods before 1700. They are probably not simply quotations of folk songs, in the sense of "quoting" something strange or exotic, as in nineteenth- and twentieth-century art music, but part and parcel of the basic material of art music.

Example 3-8 illustrates the phenomenon of wandering melodies. More extensive examples of related tunes found in larger numbers of countries, and including art music, can be found in various publications, particularly in Walter Wiora's *Europäischer Volksgesang*.[2] In a good many cases, it is quite likely that the similar tunes found in several nations are indeed wandering melodies or, rather, variants of a single wandering melody. Whether or not the three tunes in Example 3-8 are genetically related we cannot say. Curiously, the variants of a tune found in separated countries are usually accompanied by widely varying verbal texts. An English ballad tune that has related forms in other countries will hardly ever be found outside England with a translation of the same ballad story. This very fact may lead us to suspect that the existence of similar tunes in different countries is not always, and perhaps not even frequently, simply the result of a tune's migration. In any event, we cannot *prove* in most cases that the tune has actually migrated. It is likely that traveling singers of the early Middle Ages (their existence is documented) taught peoples of different lands the original forms of many songs which developed into groups of melodies related in the manner of Example 3-8.

Another way of explaining the phenomenon of wandering melodies is that the musical characteristics of European folk song have been so homogeneous and have developed so much in the same direction throughout the continent that similar tunes were composed independently in several countries. Given a certain restricted set of musical characteristics—for the sake of argument, let's assume melodies composed of five tones with seconds and thirds predominating, regular metric structure, the tendency for the final sections of songs and of phrases to be lower in pitch and more drawn out rhythmically than the rest, and a range of about an octave—it is conceivable that similar tunes might spring up independently in several places at various times. Thus the fact that there are some obvious similarities among the tunes in the forgoing examples does not in itself prove that all of them are descended, through the use of communal recreation, from a single parent tune. But whichever explanation is the correct one (and we may never know in many specific cases), the existence of similar tunes throughout the continent again shows us that Europe is an entity as far as its folk music is concerned.

[2] Wiora, *Europäischer Volksgesang*, p. 5f.

EXAMPLE 3-8. Tunes from Spain, Romania, and England similar in structure and possibly genetically related, from Walter Wiora, *Europäischer Volksgesang* (Cologne: Arno Volk Verlag, 1950), pp. 50–51.

SOME SONG TYPES FOUND IN EUROPE

Europe is a unit not only in the purely musical aspects of folk song. The cultural background and context as well as the words of the songs also indicate the essential integrity of the continent. There are certain types of songs that are found throughout Europe, though they are not present everywhere in the same proportion of quantity and importance.

One important song type is *narrative song*. Two main styles of songs that tell a story have been developed in Europe: *epics* and *ballads*. Narrative songs, particularly epics (distinguished from ballads by their length and heroic quality), are found outside Europe, in areas as divergent as the Great Basin of North American Indian culture, Iran, Borneo, and Japan, but only in Europe do they constitute one of the most important, perhaps the preeminent, folk song type.

The ballad was developed in Europe in the Middle Ages—first, presumably, by song composers of city and court—and evidently passed into oral tradition and the repertories of folk cultures thereafter. The musical characteristics of the ballad are not different from those of most other kinds of folk song. Usually there are three to six musical lines and a number of stanzas. The ballad tells a story involving one main event. In contrast to the ballads, the epic songs are long, complex, and involve several events tied together by a common theme. Typically, the epic, as exemplified perhaps by the heroic songs of the southern Slavs, does not have a strophic arrangement but tends rather to use a line which, with variations, is repeated many times. But there are subtypes of these genres and it is at times difficult to distinguish between them. (See Chapter 4 for more detail about ballads, Chapter 6 for epics.)

Love songs are important in many European countries (they are relatively rare in the folklore of other continents). They are more common in Western Europe than in the East, and characteristically they express love for another person in a melancholy or tragic setting. The music of love songs does not, on the whole, differ in style from that of other folk songs.

A number of ceremonial song types are common throughout Europe. Of course, the use of folk songs in an ecclesiastical setting is found. There are areas in which genuine folk hymns are sung; in Germany, a body of spiritual folk song became a partial basis of the Lutheran hymn, and the singing of "Kyrieleis" (a corruption of "Kyrie Eleison") in the rural communities was reported in medieval sources. But more typical are songs involving ceremonies that may have been practiced long before the advent of Christianity in Europe. Thus there are songs which revolve around important events or turning points in a person's life: birth, puberty, marriage, and death.

In some countries these proliferated, as in France, where special songs for various events in a child's life (first words, first walking, etc.) were developed. The French have songs to urge a child to eat, to teach him to count, and so on. These are songs accompanying the so-called rites of passage which are important in practically every culture.

There are also songs involving the turning points in the year, such as the advent of spring, the summer and winter solstices, and the equinox. These have frequently been associated also with agriculture, and some have been attached, since the introduction of Christianity, to Christian festivals. Thus some pre-Christian winter solstice songs have become Christmas songs, as may have been the case of the popular German "O Tannenbaum." Pagan spring songs have sometimes become Easter or Whitsuntide songs. These calendric song types are common in several nations of Europe.

Songs involving agriculture are also common, more so in Eastern than in Western Europe. Perhaps these songs should be generally regarded as work songs, because some of them actually aid in the rhythm of work, whereas others, such as the short tunes used by the Lapps to call reindeer, are functional in labor but not in a rhythmic sense. Another type of agricultural song, simply describing the work, is not sung during work but perhaps at social gatherings in the evening. Again, work songs are found also on other continents, but they are more common in Europe than in most other areas. As before, we cannot say that their style differs appreciably from the styles of European folk songs at large, although a few types of work songs do have special musical styles. Thus the *tribbiera* of Corsica (Example 3-9), a type of song sung while driving oxen around a small enclosure in which threshing is done, always has a form consisting of two sections with words, followed by a long, *melismatic* call (that is, with several tones sung to each syllable).

Another characteristic type in European folk music is the humorous song. Musically this type does not differ especially from other songs, and

EXAMPLE 3-9. Corsican tribbiera, from Wolfgang Laade, "The Corsican Tribbiera: A Kind of Work Song," *Ethnomusicology*, VI (1962), 185.

of course humorous words can be associated with all sorts of songs—ballads, work songs, children's songs, and so forth. One special type of humorous song found in many countries is the cumulative song. These are songs in which each stanza, while presenting something new, also incorporates elements from the previous stanzas. Although they are not always uproariously funny or even mildly amusing, some elements of humor are usually found, and perhaps even the process of cumulation can be considered as having a humorous effect. Among the best known songs are "The Twelve Days of Christmas" and "Alouette."

Dance music is one of the main types of traditional music throughout the world. In Europe it is an important genre, and accompanies two main types of dance. It has been assumed that the older dances are those involved with rituals and ceremonies (round dances are especially characteristic here); these tend to be accompanied by relatively simple music.[3] Dances that came into the European folk repertory at later times–and these include most couple dances and many of the other kinds of social dances—have more complex music which shows, as does the dance itself, the influence of more sophisticated musical cultures. However, although we can in good conscience make such broad generalizations about folk dance and dance music, we must also stress the tremendous variety of European dances. The dance seems to be one area of culture in which European trends are similar or closely related to those in other continents. Possibly this means that the older layers of European culture, those which antedate the introduction of Christianity and stem from a time when the European folk cultures would have been classed as primitive or nonliterate, have remained present in the dance more than in some other aspects of culture.

At any rate, *mimetic dances* (those which choreographically represent actions, events, feelings, persons, or animals) are found throughout European folk culture and in other continents as well. The same is true of dances with weapons (sword dances, for instance, performed in Scotland, Central Europe, and India), dances having sexual symbolism, and acrobatic dances, to name just a few. Gertrude Kurath[4] made a survey of European folk dances and divided the vast array into several types, according to the form and style of dancing. For example, she distinguished among circle, longway (line), and quadrille (square) dances, according to the formation used by the dancers. The point is, again, that each of these forms is found all over Europe, and that similar dances are performed in areas and countries with sharply contrasting cultures. The maypole is used in dances of Spain, England, Germany, and Hungary; the "hey," a technique in which two lines

[3] On this point see, for example, George Herzog, "Song," Funk and Wagnalls *Standard Dictionary of Folklore, Mythology, and Legend* (New York, 1949–50), II, 1035.

[4] Gertrude P. Kurath, "Dance," Funk and Wagnalls *Standard Dictionary of Folklore, Mythology, and Legend* (New York, 1949–50), I, 276–96.

of dancers wind in and out of a circle, is found in England, Germany, Czechoslovakia, and Spain. Thus, in spite of national and regional peculiarities, we see again the basic unity of European folklore.

INSTRUMENTS AND INSTRUMENTAL MUSIC

Although singing accounts for a preponderance of music making, formal and informal, in the European folk music tradition, musical instruments are important, and instrumental music is of very great interest. The participation of a population in singing is quite general, that is, most people in a folk culture can sing some songs and recognize many more, but instruments are to a much larger extent the property of specialists. As we have pointed out, professional musicians, who have theoretical training and who make their living entirely through music, are not common in folk cultures. When they are found, they are usually instrumentalists. Instruments are typically played by only a small number of persons in a folk community, and these are usually professionals at least in the sense that they are recognized for their skill and called upon to perform on special occasions.

According to Curt Sachs[5] and others, the primitive instrumental styles of the world did not come about through simple imitation, on instruments, of vocal melodies. To be sure, vocal music must have come into existence before instrumental. But instrumental music presumably came about through the elevation of noise-making gadgets to really musical artifacts, through the coincidences of accidentally discovered acoustic phenomena, and through visual criteria used by craftsmen. For example, the maker of a flute may, in positioning the finger holes, be guided by the visual effect of the design more than by the pitches and intervals which a particular arrangement of these holes will produce. This line of reasoning could, in fact, help to explain the fact that the instrumental music of European folk cultures often seems quite unrelated to the songs found in the same area and sung by the same people. Also, there seems to be more stylistic variety in the instrumental music of Europe than in its vocal music, perhaps because of the limitations of human voice and ear as compared with the relative freedom allowed instrumentalists who need to know the right motions to make, but not necessarily how the music will sound before they play it. Random improvisation and toying with an instrument may have a considerable effect on developing the styles of instrumental folk music.

Regarding the instruments themselves, we can make very few general-

---

[5] Curt Sachs, *The Wellsprings of Music* (The Hague: Martinus Nijhoff, 1962), p. 110f.

izations. They vary enormously in type, design, and origin, to say nothing of the sounds they produce. Insofar as their origin is concerned, we can divide them roughly into four classes. (1) Among the simplest instruments are those which European folk cultures share with many of the simplest tribal cultures throughout the world, including rattles; flutes (with and without finger holes) usually made of wood; the bullroarer, a piece of wood or other material tied to a string and whirled in the air; leaf, grass, and bone whistles; and long wooden trumpets such as the Swiss *alphorn*. These (like the songs with the most restricted scales) tend to be associated with children's games, signaling practices, and remnants of pre-Christian ritual. Many of them actually function as toys, much as do their counterparts in simpler cultures. They are evidently archaic and became distributed throughout the world many centuries ago, but the fact that they are used as toys and for pre-Christian ritual does not necessarily mean that these rituals were, in earlier times, accompanied only by the simplest of musics. (2) A second group consists of instruments that were brought to Europe from non-European cultures in more recent times. They are much more complex, and evidently many of them were changed substantially after they were brought to Europe. Among them are bagpipes, simple fiddles such as the Yugoslav one-stringed *gusle*, the folk oboes and double-oboes of the Balkans, the banjo, and the xylophone. In general, the sources of these instruments were the Middle East and Africa. (3) Another group consists of instruments developed in the European folk cultures themselves, usually made from simple materials. A characteristic example is the *dolle*, a type of fiddle used in northwestern Germany, made from a wooden shoe. A more sophisticated one is the bowed lyre (sometimes also called the bowed harp), once widespread in Northern Europe and the British Isles, but now mainly confined to Finland. (4) A final, and perhaps the most important, group includes the instruments that were taken from urban musical culture and from the traditions of classical and popular music, introduced into folk cultures, then sometimes changed substantially. Prominent among these are the violin, bass viol, clarinet, and guitar. Some instruments used in art music during the Middle Ages and other early periods of European music history continued to be used in folk music into the twentieth century. Examples are the violins with sympathetic strings, related to the *viola d'amore* and still used in Scandinavia, and the hurdy-gurdy, related to the medieval *organistrum* and still played in France.

In Chapters 4 through 6 we will explore European folk music in somewhat more detail. Unfortunately, even if comprehensive information were available we could not give the whole story on these pages. We cannot even give samples of the music of each nation. All we can do is to give some examples of what is typical, what is common, and what is particularly noteworthy, and then hope that you will continue delving into the specialized literature and, above all, proceed with listening in order to gain a broader understanding of this fascinating area of European culture.

BIBLIOGRAPHICAL NOTES

The only general and comprehensive book on European folk music is in German, and it approaches its field from a very special viewpoint, attempting to show various historical layers evident in modern traditions. Nevertheless, it is worth reading: Werner Danckert, *Das europäische Volkslied* (Bonn: Bouvier, 1970). Several collections of European folk music that make it possible to compare the various styles are Leonhard Deutsch, *A Treasury of the World's Finest Folk Song* (New York: Howell, Siskin, 1942); Maud Karpeles, *Folk Song of Europe* (London: Novello, 1956); *Europäische Lieder in den Ursprachen* (Berlin: Merseburger, 1956), a collection published under the auspices of UNESCO; and Walter Wiora, *European Folk Song; Common Forms in Characteristic Modification* (Cologne: Arno Volk, 1966), a collection that illustrates the unity of European folk song by presenting variants of the same tunes or tune types from many countries. James Porter, "Prolegomena to a Comparative Study of European Folk Music," *Ethnomusicology*, XXI (1977), 435–51, considers the usefulness of the comparative method in the study of the folk music of Europe.

Important general bibliographies of European folk music are Karel Vetterl, *A Select Bibliography of European Folk Music* (Prague: Czechoslovak Academy of Sciences, 1966), and *Annual Bibliography of European Ethnomusicology*, ed. Ivan Mačák (Bratislava: Slovenské národné múzeum, 1966–). More specialized bibliographies are cited in later chapters. Walter Wiora, *Europäische Volksmusik und abendländische Tonkunst* (Kassel: Hinnenthal, 1957), surveys the role of folk music in the history of European art music. Publications dealing with European folk instruments are cited in the bibliographical notes for Chapter 2.

Introductions to the field of European balladry are Gordon H. Gerould, *The Ballad of Tradition* (Oxford: Clarendon Press, 1932) and William J. Entwistle, *European Balladry* (Oxford: Clarendon Press, 1939). The many variants of a single ballad text in several European nations are studied in Iivar Kemppinen, *The Ballad of Lady Isabel and the False Knight* (Helsinki: Published by thé author, 1954). A short discussion of European epics is Felix Hoerburger's "Correspondence Between Eastern and Western Folk Epics," *J-IFMC*, IV (1952), 23–26. The entire epic tradition is discussed, but with emphasis on the Yugoslav forms, in Albert B. Lord, *The Singer of Tales* (Cambridge: Harvard University Press, 1960). Hungarian ballads are the focus of Lajos Vargyas, *Hungarian Ballads and the European Ballad Tradition*, 2 vols. (Budapest: Akadémiai Kiadó, 1983). Finally, a classic on folk song as a living artifact is Phillips Barry, "The Transmission of Folk Song," *Journal of American Folklore*, XXVII (1914), 67–76.

FOUR

THE GERMANIC PEOPLES

The Germanic peoples—that is, those peoples that speak Germanic languages—can be divided into three groups on the basis of their folklore: (1) the British, including the Scots and Irish; (2) the Scandinavians; and (3) the Dutch and the German-speaking peoples of Germany, Austria, most of Switzerland, and other areas in Eastern Europe. Although these three groups of peoples speak related languages, their cultures cannot be considered particularly similar, and this is also true of the styles of their folk music. Of course, the folk music of the Germanic peoples is known in different phases and varying degrees. For the English-speaking peoples there exists a vast body of ballads, collected in America as well as in Britain, and the study of ballad variants, their interrelationship, structure, and origin, has been carried further for British material than elsewhere. Of German folklore we know best the songs that have come into the repertory rather recently. Swedish and Norwegian folk music happens to have available a large collection of fiddle tunes, because some Swedish and Norwegian collectors have concentrated on this aspect of music. Also, the Germanic peoples have been strongly influenced by their neighbors. For example, British folk song shows considerable relationship to that of the Low Countries and France, and German folk music is at times similar to that of its neighbors to the east—Czechoslovakia, Poland, and Hungary; Austrian folk songs have some common features with those of Italy. Thus, although we are treating the Germanic peoples as a group in this chapter, it should not be assumed that their folk music is necessarily a stylistic unit. We should avoid the corresponding conclusion that the style of Germanic musics goes back to the time when all Germanic peoples were one and spoke one tongue, and the equally erroneous assumption that the Germanic-speaking peoples possess a psychic unity. The heritage of Germanic languages goes back much further than the style of present-day folk music, and whatever musical similarities are found are due almost certainly to cultural contact in more recent times, that is, from the early Middle Ages on.

THE BRITISH CHILD BALLADS

The most characteristic type of British folk song is the *ballad*, and the most famous ballads are the Child ballads. These bear the name of Francis James Child (1825–96), who organized, published, and classified those ballads which he assumed were of popular (that is, rural and truly anonymous) origin. He avoided, in his classification, those ballads in the folk tradition which could be traced to the cities or to professional songwriters, and those which he thought did not have high literary quality. It is now possible to trace many of the Child ballads, to various sources; still, as a whole, these ballads are, textually and to an extent musically, a stylistic unit which contrasts with other bodies of English-language song. Because the different variants of each ballad do not bear identical titles or first lines, Child gave each ballad (or group of variants) a number, and for this reason the most famous ballads are known by their "Child numbers."

The stories of some of the most famous ballads are widely known to students of literature. Child 10, "The Two Sisters," deals with jealousy between two girls over a lover; the man chooses the younger sister, who is thereupon drowned by the older one, who in turn is punished for her crime. In an epilogue, various parts of a musical instrument are made from the younger sister's body. "Lord Randall" (Child 12), perhaps the best known of the Child ballads, tells in a dramatic retrospective dialogue the story of a young man who is poisoned by his sweetheart. This type of dialogue is also used in "Edward" (Child 13), in which a young man confesses that he killed his brother and that he will now leave his family. "The Maid

Freed from the Gallows" (Child 95) finds that no one in her family is willing to rescue her from punishment by paying her fine, until her lover arrives.

Love ballads, especially tragic ones, are important among the Child ballads. "Mary Hamilton" (Child 173) is an historically based story of a lady-in-waiting at the English court who is condemned to death because she becomes pregnant by the king. "Little Musgrave" or "Little Mathy Grove" (Child 81) is seduced by a noble lady; they are discovered by the husband, who kills Musgrave in a duel. In "The Gypsy Laddie" (Child 200) a noble lady runs off with a gypsy, and when her husband finds her, she tells him that she prefers to stay in poverty with the gypsy band. Some of the ballads have very simple stories. This is true of "Barbara Allen" (Child 84), in which a girl who has spurned her lover has second thoughts when she hears that he is sick with love, but arrives too late to save him from death. The eternal triangle is exemplified in Child 73, "Lord Thomas and Fair Elinor," in which a man jilts his fiancée to marry another; the unhappy girl comes to the wedding, kills her rival, and is in turn killed by her former lover, who ends the story by committing suicide. "Lord Lovel" (Child 75) is one of a number of ballads in which separated lovers are reunited in a meeting resulting from an outrageous coincidence.

Ballads of the sea are common. They can be exemplified by Child 286, "The Golden Vanity," in which a cabin boy is promised the hand of the captain's daughter if he will swim to and sink an enemy ship, but when his mission is accomplished, the captain leaves him to drown in the sea. "Lord Bateman" (Child 53) is imprisoned by the Turks but aided in his escape by a Turkish lady, whom he promises to marry; seven years later, she seeks him out just as he is about to marry another, and he finally keeps his word. In the "House Carpenter" (Child 243) we see remnants of the supernatural elements which once were common in ballad texts. A married woman is persuaded to run off with a former lover who, it turns out, has become a demon and destroys his ship and her when he finds that she wants to return to her husband and child. Remnants of medieval superstitions are also found, for example, in Child 155, "Sir Hugh," in which a young boy happens into the garden of a Jewish family and is sacrificed by the Jew's daughter in a satanic ritual. Humorous ballads are also known, as for example Child 277, "The Wife Wrapped in Wether's Skin," in which a man, afraid to beat his aristocratic wife, wraps her in a sheepskin, which he is able to whip. "Our Goodman" (Child 274) comes home drunk and finds his wife in bed with another man, but she insists that the evidence— the man's horse, hat, and head—are ordinary things he should expect to find in the house: a cow, a chamber pot, and a cabbage.

A few of the ballads, as they are found in tradition today, consist of only a vestige of the original story, or of a set of formulas which accompanied the story. Child 2, "The Elfin Knight," is a dialogue between two lovers who ask each other to prove their love by committing extraordinary feats, such as making a cambric shirt without any needle or needlework. Religious stories are also found. The best known is the "Cherry Tree Carol," an apocryphal story in which the unborn baby Jesus commands a cherry tree to bow down and to give cherries to his mother, after which he announces his birth and identity from the womb.

There are about three hundred Child ballads, but for only about two hundred has any music been collected; for the rest, only words survive. The famous ballads we have enumerated share some characteristics, and they are representative of the whole Child group (with the exception of a number dealing with Robin Hood), although most of the ones mentioned here are tragic, whereas the majority of the whole group of Child ballads actually do not have unhappy endings. The stories of these ballads are easily available in most of the large array of folk song collections made in the United States, and in Child's own collection, which dates from the late nineteenth century.[1] The stories usually revolve around one incident, names of places and characters change from variant to variant, and setting and background are only briefly stated. The narrator does not take an active part in the story but tells it dispassionately. There is some dialogue, and there is also a tendency for whole verses to be virtually repeated, as in the following excerpt from Child 200:[2]

(He says):   Take off, take off those milk-white gloves,
                                     Those shoes of Spanish leather,
                                     And hand you down your lily-white hand,
                                     We'll bid farewell together.

(Narrator says):   Oh she took off those milk-white gloves,
                                     Those shoes of Spanish leather,
                                     And she handed him down her lily-white hand,
                                     They bade farewell forever.

Other characteristics of ballads are also found in this example. We see the use of conceits, that is, of descriptive phrases which appear repeatedly as if they were formulas. Thus hands are often described as "lily-white" (as are gloves), horses are "milk-white," and so on. Many ballads have refrains, the origins of which are sometimes obscure. Flowers, plants, and spices are sometimes mentioned, as in Child 2,[3] which was made famous in another variant, by Simon and Garfunkel.

[1] Francis James Child, *The English and Scottish Popular Ballads*, 5 vols. (Boston and New York: Houghton Mifflin, 1882–98; reprint New York: Folklore Associates, 1956).

[2] Cecil J. Sharp, *English Folk Songs from the Southern Appalachians* (London: Oxford University Press, 1952), I, 235.

[3] Sharp, *English Folk Songs*, I, 1.

(Verse) Go tell her to make me a cambric shirt
(Refrain) Setherwood, sage, rosemary and thyme,
(Verse) Without any needle or needle's work,
       And then she'll be a true lover of mine.

Refrains, incidentally, are a feature of song shared by all regions of Europe. Some refrains mention dancing or movements that can be interpreted as parts of a dance. Here is an excerpt from "The Two Sisters" (Child 10):[4]

       There lived an old lord in the North countree
(Refrain) Bow down, bow down.
       There lived an old lord in the north countree
(Refrain) Very true to you. . . .

"Bow down" is thought to be derived from dancing. This is interesting in light of the theory that the ballad, narrative though it is, began as a dance song type. The name may be derived from the Latin *ballare* (to dance), and there is some evidence that ballads were once used as dance songs in medieval Scandinavia. On the Faeroe Islands, between Scotland and Norway, this tradition is still in existence, and lively group dances using the "Faeroe step" (two steps left, one right) may be performed while the dancers sing Norwegian ballads. We know of no ballad dancing in the English-speaking world, but this practice may once have existed there as well.

A look at the collections of Child or of some of the more recent great American collectors makes it obvious that the differences among variants of one ballad can be very great. Take Child 12, the popular "Lord Randall." Randall's name appears in all sorts of variant forms: Randall, Rendal, Lorendo, Durango, William, Tyranty, Nelson, Elson, King Henry, Willie Doo, and so on. The person who poisons him may be his sweetheart, his grandmother, or his stepmother. It has even been established that the children's song, "Oh where have you been, Billy boy, Billy boy?" which ends, "She's a young thing and cannot leave her mother" was derived from one version of the more dramatic "Lord Randall." Thus it would seem that formulas are very stable elements, whereas the details of a story are more subject to change. The lengths of the variants also differ greatly. A story told in one ballad with the use of fourteen stanzas may, in another version, be summarized in four, through elision, omission of events, and omission of stanzas giving background information.

Similar variety is found in the tunes. Bertrand H. Bronson[5] has

---

[4] Sharp, *English Folk Songs*, I, 27.

[5] Bertrand Harris Bronson, *The Traditional Tunes of the Child Ballads* (Princeton, NJ: Princeton University Press, 1958–72).

EXAMPLE 4-1. English folk song, "The Sweet Trinity," from Jan P. Schinhan, ed., *The Music of the Ballads* (Durham, NC: Duke University Press, 1957. *The Frank C. Brown Collection of North Carolina Folklore*, IV), p. 120.

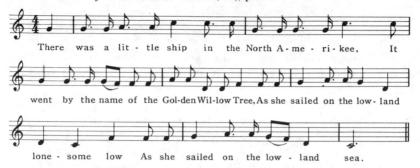

There was a lit-tle ship in the North A-me-ri-kee, It went by the name of the Gol-den Wil-low Tree, As she sailed on the low-land lone-some low As she sailed on the low-land sea.

assembled all of the tunes known to be used for the Child ballads, and has found that for each ballad story there seem to be two or three basic tune types to which all of the variants are sung. For example, most of the tunes of "The Golden Vanity" (Child 286) are related to one of the two in Examples 4-1 and 4-2.

Although ballad stories evidently moved from nation to nation in the Middle Ages, the tunes usually did not accompany them. For example, there is the ballad of "Lady Isabel and the Elf-Knight" (Child 4), in which a knight courts a lady but really intends to kill and rob her; when she discovers his false intentions, she foils him and causes him to drown. This ballad is known throughout Europe except for the Balkan area, but its

EXAMPLE 4-2. British folk song, "The Little Cabin Boy," from Phillips Barry, Fannie H. Eckstrom, and Mary W. Smyth, *British Ballads from Maine* (New Haven, CT: Yale University Press, 1929), p. xxxiii.

♩ = 132

There was a ship in the North-ern Coun-trie, All in the low-lands low; The name of the ship was the Gold Chi-na Tree, All in the Low-land low, low, low, Sail-ing the Low-land low, low, low, Sail__ ing the Low-lands low.

tunes are largely national in origin, and the tunes used with the British versions are evidently not related to those used in Dutch, Scandinavian, German, or other versions. On the other hand, variants of a tune used for one ballad in the British repertory may be found in other British ballads or songs.

BROADSIDE BALLADS

Besides the Child ballads, for which no written original can usually be found, the English-language repertory possesses other types, particularly a group of later origin, the *broadside ballads*. This type, so named because it appeared printed on large sheets of paper called broadsides, became popular throughout Western Europe. Written frequently by professional songwriters, the broadside ballads tend to deal with historical events more than do the popular ballads, and they contrast with the Child ballads also in their concern for detail, in their more complex plots, and in the involvement of the narrator, who frequently appends a moral. The words are often shamelessly sentimental and usually do not have the literary value of the older ballads. But the broadside ballads (which were still being written in the twentieth century) functioned somewhat as newspapers in areas in which illiteracy was common. Not all of them passed into oral tradition of course, but a good many did and have thus become true folk songs. Some of our best-known songs originated as British broadside ballads: "The Foggy Dew," made popular by Carl Sandburg, "Brennan on the Moor," "Devilish Mary," and "Sam Hall." Some of the broadsides are even derived from the Child ballads. A broadside ballad called "The Turkish Lady" is obviously a variant of "Lord Bateman" (Child 53), in which a Turkish lady saves an English prisoner in her father's jail and marries him. The tunes of the broadside ballads are of diverse origin. Many of the printed broadsides did not include music but simply named the tune of this or that popular song, folk song, or hymn. Finally, the practice of printing broadside ballads and their dissemination into folk tradition is found not only in Britain but also in most European countries and in America.

THE STYLE OF BRITISH FOLK MUSIC

As we have pointed out, the music of the British ballads does not differ greatly from that of British folk song in general; thus the following discussion of ballad tunes can be said to apply to British folk song at large. Many of the older tunes have, as one characteristic, a melodic contour

EXAMPLE 4-3. British folk song, "Lord Gregory." Reprinted from *The Traditional Tunes of the Child Ballads*, Vol. 2, by Bertrand Harris Bronson by permission of Princeton University Press, copyright 1962.

which roughly forms an arc, starting low, rising in the second phrase, remaining on the higher level of tessitura in the third phrase, and moving down to the level of the first in the fourth phrase. Four phrases or lines are common, but five (usually through repetition of the fourth), six, and eight are also found, as well as two and three. The three British folk songs printed as Examples 4-3, 4-4, and 4-5 may be considered representative of the whole style to an extent, even though certain song types, such as dance songs, game ditties, children's songs, and humorous songs, are not exemplified. Example 4-3 is a Scots version of Child 76, as sung by Ewan MacColl, the well-known folk singer. Example 4-4 is a variant of the same song collected in southern Indiana. It is essentially the same melody, but is sung in quite a different manner. Example 4-5 is the tune of a broadside ballad, "Girls of Newfoundland," of Irish origin, collected in Labrador. Perhaps we should point out here that much more British folk music has been collected in North America than in Britain, and that, for material collected in Britain itself, published collections with reliable transcriptions are difficult to come by. Thus we must rely to some extent on American versions for a picture of British folk music.

EXAMPLE 4-4. British folk song, "The Lass of Loch Royal," from Bruno Nettl, "The Musical Style of English Ballads Collected in Indiana," *Acta Musicologica*, XXVII (1955), 83.

EXAMPLE 4-5. British folk song, "Girls of Newfoundland," collected in Newfoundland by MacEdward Leach, transcribed by Bruno Nettl.

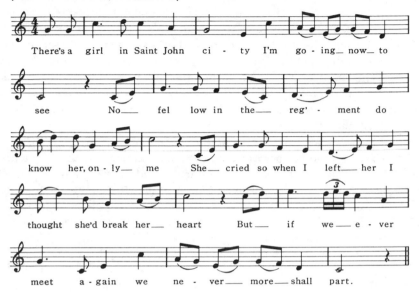

Examples 4-3 and 4-4 use the so-called ballad meter, that is, iambic lines alternating in four- and three-foot lengths (- / - / - / - / ; - / - / - / ; and so forth). This is common, though by no means universal, in British folk song and tends, in music, to be translated into one of three types of rhythm: $\frac{4}{4}$ ♩ | ♩♩♩♩ | ♩♩♩ or $\frac{3}{4}$ ♪ | ♫ ♩· ♪ | ♫ ♩· (with several variants, e.g. $\frac{5}{4}$ ♩ | ♩♩♩♩ ♩ | ♩♩♩ or $\frac{4}{4}$ ♪ | ♫ ♩ ♪♪ | ♫ ♩ ♪) or ♪ | ♩ ♪♩ ♪ | ♩ ♪♩). Example 4-3 uses the first of these, and Example 4-4 a variant of the second. There is, however, a tendency in those songs that are sung in the parlando-rubato singing style to include elongation and shortening of measures, and even a systematically heterometric structure. Thus, in Example 4-4, the measures have, respectively 3, 5, 5, 7, 5, 7, 6, 6, and 5 eighth-note equivalents.

Songs whose words are not cast in ballad meter nevertheless tend to use the same rhythmic types, with minor adjustments, in their tunes. Thus, Example 4-5 has a structure rather similar to that of Example 4-3, but the text has eight lines instead of four. This type of stanza is most frequently set to variants of the first or second rhythmic types given in the previous paragraph; it is more common in the broadsides than in the

Child ballads, and particularly widespread in the English-language ballads
sung by the Irish.

British folk song is frequently said to be modal, but the great majority
of the songs fall into the major or Ionian mode. (Our three examples are
all major.) There are also many songs in the Mixolydian mode (major with
lowered seventh), in Dorian (minor with raised sixth), and in Aeolian (natural
minor). The other modes are not common. Some modulation may occur
(though this is often hard to identify because the music is monophonic) as
in Example 4-3, in which the first two phrases seem to have G for a tonic,
but the last one D.

Much has also been said of the pentatonic nature of British folk
song. A rather large minority of the songs are pentatonic, but the majority
(again, except for the old layer of children's and related songs) seems to
be heptatonic or hexatonic. It is sometimes revealing to examine the functions
of the various tones in a scale, however, for often it will be evident that
the most important and most common tones are indeed five in number,
while the other two are subsidiary or used only in ornaments. Also, the
scale structure of the individual phrases or lines may be pentatonic. For
instance, in Example 4-3, the first half of the song uses a common kind of
pentatonic scale—D, F-sharp, G, A, B; the other tones, E and C-sharp,
are brought in only later. Similarly, in Example 4-4 important tones are
B, C (tonic), E, F, and G. Example 4-6, a version of Child 53, uses six
tones, but one of them, F, appears only in ornaments. This song is a good
example of the kind of pentatonism found in British folk music.

The emphasis on pentatonic structure does not seem to be an ingredient of the newer layer of British song. The tunes that were introduced
into the folk culture more recently, perhaps since the advent of music
printing and the broadside ballad in the sixteenth century, are both more
varied in style and more closely related to popular and art musics. This is

EXAMPLE 4-6. British folk song, "Lord Bateman," from Bruno Nettl, "The Musical
Style of English Ballads Collected in Indiana," *Acta Musicologica*, XXVII (1955), 83.

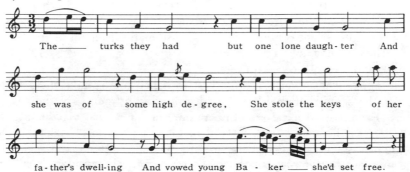

to be expected with regard to the broadsides, because their writers frequently set them to tunes of any sort that were widely current. The later tunes are more frequently in major or harmonic minor, rarely pentatonic, and they do not deviate, as does Example 4-4, from a standard and consistent metric structure.

As we noted earlier (p. 47), Béla Bartók divided Hungarian folk singing into two types, parlando-rubato and tempo giusto.[6] The distinction between these two ways of singing does not always emerge from printed music, because it involves the singer's interpretation of rhythm and tempo. Although the distinction was derived for use in describing Hungarian folk music, it applies also to singing in other countries, especially those of Northern and Eastern Europe. Example 4-3 is a sample of tempo giusto singing, and Example 4-4, a variant of the same song, exemplifies the parlando-rubato. In Hungarian folk music, parlando-rubato is used mainly for ballads and tempo giusto for dance songs, but both styles are found in British ballad singing.

Much of Irish folk song today is in the English language, and, indeed, the songs of Irish origin have contributed greatly to the English-language heritage of the United States, Canada, and Australia. On the whole, their musical style does not differ greatly from that of the English folk tunes of eighteenth- and nineteenth-century origin. Yet, certain minor traits characterize the singing of these ethnic groups. For example, Irish singers will take a conventional major ending (e.g.,) and change it to end on a repetition of the tonic ( ).

There is also a living tradition of Irish song in Gaelic. Love songs are the predominant type, though one also finds lullabies, religious songs, nonsense songs, and even versions of a few Child ballads. Among the Gaelic song traditions of Scotland is that of the *waulking song*, originally sung while shrinking newly woven cloth. In parts of the Outer Hebrides, these songs are still sung by women as a form of communal music-making as they go through the motions of the accompanying task using a piece of dry, machine-shrunk cloth.[7]

The Welsh have developed—partly through their folk heritage and partly because of the influence of hymn singing—a tradition of choral singing of folk songs; this is done largely in the style of nineteenth-century hymns, with conventional chord progressions and triadic harmony. They also preserved, into the nineteenth century, an instrument that evidently was wide-

---

[6] Béla Bartók, *Hungarian Folk Music* (London: Oxford University Press, 1931).

[7] Francis Collinson, "Scotland: Folk Music," in *The New Grove Dictionary of Music and Musicians*, ed. Stanley Sadie (London: Macmillan, 1980), XVII, 72.

spread in medieval art music, the *crwth* or *crowd*, a lyre with six strings—
four over the fingerboard, two as drones—which was usually bowed. It
evidently accompanied the songs of the bards, whose importance among
the Welsh and Irish was very great. A similar instrument, the *tallharpa*,
was used in Finland and Estonia; today, Finland is the only country in
which bowed lyres are still widely used.

BRITISH AND BRITISH-AMERICAN FIDDLE TUNES

Of the several instrumental traditions that flourish in Britain (and
therefore also in the United States and Canada), music for the fiddle is
particularly important. This instrument is essentially the same as the classical
violin, though more varied and flexible both in its physical characteristics
(e.g., the bridge is occasionally flattened slightly to facilitate the playing
of double stops) and in its performance practice. For instance, the bow
may be gripped in any of several ways; the instrument may be held against
the player's chest rather than under the chin; vibrato, if present, is usually
a tight finger vibrato; and on rare occasions, *scordatura* may be employed
(e.g., retuning the fiddle from the usual set of fifths, G-D-A-E, to A-E-A-E).
The repertory played by British and American fiddlers consists of
thousands of tunes bearing an array of titles. Some of these titles associate
tunes with people, places, or events: "Durang's Hornpipe" (Durang was a
dancer); "Marquis of Huntley's Reel" (an example of title as dedication);
"Kentucky Waltz"; "Hull's Victory"; and "Bonaparte's Retreat." Some titles
refer to texts associated with given tunes, for example, "Buffalo Gals," "Old
Joe Clark," and "Cotton-Eyed Joe." (Whether the instrumental or vocal
form came first is rarely clear.) Other titles are colorful, even cryptic: "Devil's
Dream," "Ducks on the Millpond," "Lost Indian," and "You Married My
Daughter (and Yet You Didn't)." But despite the vividness of these titles,
most tunes are not programmatic; a very few tune names refer to playing
techniques, for example, "Drunkard's Hiccups," which features left-hand
pizzicato (plucking of the strings). Most tunes are known by one or a handful
of titles, though some titles can be said to "float," that is, freely associate
with many tunes. The tune illustrated in Example 4-7 is known as "Lord
McDonald's Reel" (or just "McDonald's Reel") in Britain and in New
England, but is called "Leather Britches" in the southern United States.
Each fiddle tune consists of two short strains, each composed of
two balanced phrases. The two strains often (but not always) share quite a
bit of melodic material and an implied harmonization, but contrast in the
ranges explored as they begin. Thus we may speak of a "low" and a "high"
strain. A performance, almost always in tempo giusto, consists of the approxi-

EXAMPLE 4-7. A British-American fiddle tune in two forms. (1) "Lord McDonald's Reel," from William Napier, *Napier's Selection of Dances and Strathspeys* (London: author, c. 1800), p 12. (2) "Leather Britches" (sample strains), performed by Clark Kessinger, transcribed by Chris Goertzen from *The Legend of Clark Kessinger* (County Records 733), recorded in 1964, probably in St. Albans, West Virginia. Used by permission of County Records.

mate alternation of strains or pairs of strains (e.g., the low strain twice, the high strain twice, the low strain twice, and so on). The performance lasts until the dance it accompanies is over (perhaps two to ten minutes), or, in recent times, for the approximately three minutes typical of contest playing.

This repertory coalesced in mid- to late-eighteenth-century Britain. Although many tunes were added much more recently, the style has remained remarkably compact. This fact, as well as the generally stable tune/title linkage, may be due in part to the frequently stabilizing influence of print: The repertory has always retained a modest foothold in popular music. The musical language is much the same as in British ballads. Most tunes are in major, with frequent pentatonic leanings. The fourth and seventh degrees of the major scale are typically avoided except in cadential areas (see Example 4-7). A significant minority of tunes are in the Dorian or Mixolydian mode.

SOME NETHERLANDISH FOLK DANCES

Evidently folk dancing has been a prominent activity in the Low Countries for centuries. An edict of Charlemagne outlawed dancing in churches and ceremonies, indicating the popularity of such activities. The practice of religious dance, including dances on the occasion of death, particularly by young girls, is attested to by various documents from history, and appears to have remained in the folk tradition until relatively recent times. The religious dances are almost always round dances.

In other ways, also, Dutch folk music seems to have had a close relationship to the practices of Christian worship. There are many religious folk songs and carols of various kinds (Christmas and Easter), and the style of a great deal of Dutch folk music reminds us of the styles of Christian monophonic hymns and Lutheran chorales. To a considerable degree this is true of German folk music as well, for in many instances it also adheres to the style of the hymn, with its typical lines consisting mainly of quarter notes except for the final long tone.

Many European folk dances have their origin in pre-Christian ritual dancing. An example from Holland is the "Seven Saults" dance, described by Kunst,[8] and known also in other parts of Western Europe. It was evidently once a sacrificial dance, but after the introduction of Christianity it was danced at harvest festivals, fairs, and wedding parties. These functions are residual of pre-Christian ceremonies involving the life cycle or changes in the year's cycle. Kunst reports seeing the "Seven Saults" still performed on the Dutch island of Terschelling. The dance involves seven motions of a mildly acrobatic nature: stamping with each foot, touching the ground with each knee, then with each elbow, and finally with the nose. It was evidently performed—as are many European folk dances—with the accompaniment of group singing, such as that found in Example 4-8. The tune in this example shows us some of the traits common in Western European folk dance music. Of course, because the music is used for dancing and is sung by a group, it could not easily partake of the parlando-rubato singing style with its fluctuating tempo and emphasis on words. It tends to be rigid in this aspect of music, to have simple rhythms consisting largely of two- or three-note values (as in this case, quarter, eighth, and sixteenth

[8] Jaap Kunst, "On Dutch Folk Dances and Dance Tunes," *Studies in Ethnomusicology,* I (1961), 35.

EXAMPLE 4-8. Dutch folk dance tune, from Jaap Kunst, "On Dutch Folk Dances and Dance Tunes" in *Studies in Ethnomusicology*, ed. M. Kolinski (New York: Oak Publications, 1961), I, 32.

Heb je wel ge-hoord van de zi - za - ze-ven, heb je wel ge-hoord van de

ze ven sprong? Dacht je dat ik die zi za ze-ven, ze-ven sproong niet

dan sen kon? Da's een da's twee, da's drie, da's

vier, da's vyf, da's zes, da's ze ven.

notes). The tune is in major, with an implication of harmony in the Western tradition, based on tonic, subdominant, dominant, and dominant seventh chords. Note also the repetitive refrain, whose words count off the "seven saults."

Holland, being near the center of the Germanic-speaking area, exhibits musical relationships to England, Germany, and Scandinavia. In both dance and dance music, some similarities between Dutch and Scandinavian folk music are striking. Variants of the same tunes and dance movements are found in both areas, as well as in Scotland, which was at one time under strong Danish and Norse influence.

SAMPLES OF SCANDINAVIAN
INSTRUMENTAL FOLK MUSIC

The folk music of Scandinavia is of great interest because in some ways it seems to exhibit very ancient traits, and yet in other ways it has been very much under the influence of the cultivated tradition of the cities. An example of ancient practice frequently cited is the use of parallel fifths in Iceland, where some traits of medieval Norwegian culture evidently have been preserved. For a long time there raged an argument, mentioned in Chapter 3, about the origin of Icelandic "organum," whether it represents a case of medieval church music practice which trickled down to the folk tradition or whether it is an example of ancient and generally forgotten folk practice which in the Middle Ages was taken up by the Western church. Similar historical arguments have been going on for decades about the relationship of other folk polyphony—that of Russia, the Ukraine, Yugoslavia, the Caucasus, the mountains of Italy—to that of medieval art music. The arguments have brought no conclusions, and today the interest in primacy has dwindled, especially as various kinds of polyphony have been discovered in many European folk traditions, but we may still marvel at what must surely be a musical tradition of great age. Aside from simple parallel fifths, Icelandic music seems to have used other forms similar to the earliest polyphony in Western church music, such as the so-called free and melismatic types of *organum*.

There is no doubt that many of the folk dances of Europe were originally dances of medieval and later towns and courts. This is true of the square dances, which grew out of quadrilles; of the polka, a more stately dance; and of the waltz, which originated in part in the slower and more dignified minuet. Frequently, of course, a dance almost completely changed character when it moved from court to countryside or vice versa. Thus the sarabande, one of the slowest and most stately dances of seventeenth-century Western Europe, is thought to have been derived from a quick and violent Spanish folk dance which, in turn, had been brought from the Spanish-American colonies in the sixteenth century. More rarely, the music accompanying folk dances can also be traced to earlier forms of art music. In such cases we have musical instances of *gesunkenes Kulturgut*. Examples can be found in Sweden, where one of the important folk dances is the *polska*, which is a form of the polonaise. Anyone familiar with Chopin's polonaises or with those of late baroque composers such as G. Ph. Telemann or J. S. Bach will recognize the characteristic rhythm in Example 4-9, which is played by violins. Aside from rhythm, moreover, the melodic configurations are also definitely in a style reminiscent of baroque and pre-Classical music: Note the arpeggios and the triad-like figures in the second section, reminiscent of the Alberti bass. The form, in which each phrase is repeated with first and second endings, is common in Western European instrumental music and similar also to the earliest known examples of medieval instrumental music, the *estampie* or *stantipes*. (Only the melodic line—not the accompaniment—is given in Example 4-9.)

Tunes of various sorts, frequently more ornamented, are played in other Scandinavian countries on folk instruments such as the Norwegian *hardingfele*. This is a violin with four or five sympathetic strings under the fingerboard (which are not played but are caused to vibrate by the vibrations of other strings activated by the bow). The four main strings are tuned in various ways, for example , , or .

EXAMPLE 4-9. Swedish polska, played by two violins; melody only, transcribed by Bruno Nettl from recording issued by Sveriges Radio (Radio Sweden), RAEP 8. Collected in Halsingsland.

The *hardingfele* has attained the status of national folk instrument of Norway. But the normal fiddle has a tradition of comparable strength.

Another instrument prominent in Scandinavia is the dulcimer, which exists in a great many forms. The term *dulcimer* applies to a category of string instruments that lie flat on a table or one's lap and are plucked or struck (or, in rarer instances, bowed); these may have anywhere from three to over a dozen strings, and usually one or more of them are fretted. Shapes vary from that of an oblong violin to rectangular and irregularly triangular. The *hummel*, once prominent in Sweden, had died out almost entirely by the end of the nineteenth century. For the Norwegian *langleik*, on the other hand, there has been a continuous playing tradition. The instrument is used mainly for solo performance, and the manner in which it is played results in complex rhythmic structures. The right hand plays the base rhythm with a plectrum, stroking in two directions and at the same time providing a drone, while the left hand plucks or strikes the strings to produce the melody. It seems likely that the American dulcimer was brought from Scandinavia or northern Germany, though similar instruments do exist elsewhere in Europe, particularly in Hungary, whose *cimbalom* (derived from the Persian *santour*) is something of a national instrument.

Throughout Europe, folk music enthusiasts are deploring the gradual disappearance of folk singing and knowledge of folk music on the part of the rural population. Attempts to reintroduce folk music through schools and festivals have been only moderately successful. Nevertheless, there

Swedish dulcimer, or *hummel*

still seem to be many people who know and can sing folk songs from their family or village traditions. For example, we have available in a case study, made over a period of time by the Danish musicologist Nils Schiørring,[9] all of the songs known by one woman, Selma Nielsen. Mrs. Nielsen, also a Dane, produced some 150 songs from memory, including material of every diverse origin—ballads from the Middle Ages, sea shanties, soldiers' songs, humorous ditties. It is possible to see throughout her repertory the close relationship between the development of folk and art music, for we find modal materials, jaunty songs in major and somewhat in the style of the lighter art songs of the pre-Classical period, and sentimental tunes obviously from nineteenth-century popular music. Scandinavia offers good illustrations of the interdependence of folk and art music in Europe.

GERMAN FOLK SONG

Nowhere is the interrelationship between art and folk music stronger than in the German-speaking nations. The influence of urban musicians on their rural counterparts has sometimes been so great there that the old practices of the German countryside seem to have disappeared and can be traced only through old documents or through the music of Germans whose ancestors emigrated from their homeland centuries ago. This is analogous to the study of British folk music through American folk song. The types of German folk song are similar, so far as text and function are concerned, to the British—medieval ballads, work songs, sailors' shanties, dances, year- and life-cycle songs, and so forth. In Germany proper, the vocal music seems to have developed much more vigorously than the instrumental. But in Switzerland and Austria, instruments as well as special forms of singing have flourished. In the period since World War II, the emigrants from German-speaking communities in Hungary, the Balkans, and parts of Russia who returned to West Germany after centuries of isolation have produced singing informants with a knowledge of many older songs thought to have disappeared from the tradition.

The influence of the church on German folk song is of early medieval origin. Many of the German ballads with medieval themes have words of partly or entirely religious character. There are folkloric descendants of mystery plays in the modern moralities and in children's religious pageants. Much of the music fits in with the system of church modes as well as with the rhythmic structure of the early Lutheran hymns. The singing style is more frequently tempo giusto than it is in the oldest British ballads.

---

[9] Nils Schiørring, *Selma Nielsens viser* (Copenhagen: Munksgaard, 1956).

German ballad texts remind us of the British ones, but the proportion of ballads with religious background is larger than in the British repertory. A greater dimension of tragedy seems to be present as well. Indeed, the historical and cultural differences between Germany and Britain can very well be illustrated by the differences in their ballad texts, although many of the story types used in these texts are identical in the two countries. For example, a German version of Child 95, "The Maid Freed from the Gallows," tells the story of a merchant who gambles away his son's life in a game of cards. The boy's sister is told by the judge that she can redeem him by running naked around the gallows square nine times, and she does this to save her brother. The dramatic impact of this detailed account is quite different from the formulaic recitation of the dialogue between the maid and her relatives in the British version, in which the listener never finds out how the maid came to be condemned in the first place, and in which ordinary payment of a fine, rather than humiliation of the sister, is the conclusion. German ballads contain more rape and seduction, more violence on the part of authorities than the British ones, and, generally, reflect the stormier and less isolated history of their country.

If the music of some of the old German ballads has medieval roots, the majority of extant German folk songs seem to stem from a later period, from the time—beginning in the seventeenth century—when the German countryside was dotted with minor courts, many of which had a sophisticated musical life, with court composers, orchestras, and opera. In this way even the smallest hamlets and the most remote farms began to have contact with art music, and the result seems to have been the assimilation of elements of the art styles into folklore. The folk music from that period, typically, is in major mode and has melodies making liberal use of triads with implied harmony. Tempi and meters are even and constant, and the singing style

EXAMPLE 4-10. German children's song, "Laterne, Laterne," from pamphlet accompanying the recording *Deutsche Volkslieder, eine Dokumentation des deutschen Musikrates,* ed. Deutsches Volksliedarchiv, Freiburg (Wolfenbüttel: Moseler Verlag, 1961), p. 19.

is definitely tempo giusto. There is also a later layer of song, that of the German broadside ballads, mainly from the nineteenth century. Here the style is that of nineteenth-century popular music, with some chromaticism, modulation, instrumental accompaniment, and what we today feel is a sentimental quality.

A children's song still widely heard is shown in Example 4-10. It is sung in autumn by children while walking in pairs or small groups, carrying lanterns. The structure, which consists essentially of one line repeated with variations, is typical of children's songs throughout Europe and may, historically, represent an archaic layer of style that preceded the various national folk styles, which are evidently mainly of medieval origin. Especially typical

EXAMPLE 4-11. German woodsmen's song, from pamphlet accompanying the recording *Deutsche Volkslieder, eine Dokumentation des deutschen Musikrates,* ed. Deutsches Volksliedarchiv, Freiburg (Wolfenbüttel: Moseler Verlag, 1961), p. 11.

is the scale, which is tetratonic, but which emphasizes the tones, E, G, and A. The added C may be interpreted as a result of the importance of the triad in German folk song style.

In contrast to Britain and Scandinavia, polyphonic singing is common in Germany, Austria, and Switzerland. Canons are, to be sure, found throughout Europe, but a form of polyphony characteristic of Germany is parallelism, particularly parallel thirds. Whether this came about through the influence of art music or whether it originated as a folk practice cannot be said. Most likely it was once exclusively a folk practice that was reinforced by similar forms in art music. Much of the part-singing (which is concentrated in southern Germany and the Alpine region) is definitely in the category of chordal harmony. This is surely the case in Example 4-11, a woodcutters' song from Bavaria. But at one point it leaves the widely accepted art music tradition: Line 4 has several parallel fifths, which are performed consistently stanza after stanza. This song also, of course, indicates the importance in German folk song of triads in both harmony and melody.

GERMAN FOLK MUSIC IN THE ALPS AND EASTERN EUROPE

The Alpine region of south Germany, Austria, and Switzerland has developed a regional body of folklore and folk music, including certain unique practices that contrast with those of Germany proper. It is sometimes thought that the extreme isolation of the mountain dwellers as well as their exceptional physical environment are responsible for this regional peculiarity, and some scholars have tried to draw parallels between Alpine folklore and that of other mountain regions in the belief that geography plays an important role in determining the nature of a people's traditions. Two characteristic aspects of the Alpine musical heritage are the *alphorn* and yodeling.

The *alphorn* is a Swiss instrument, a wooden trumpet from four to twelve feet long, used to call cattle and to signal across valleys; it is played also at sunset rites. Similar instruments are found in other countries, including Estonia, Poland, and Romania. Its repertory is mostly short calls, but there are also a few traditional tunes. Because its sound can be heard for miles, especially with the help of echoes, its presence in the Alps can be explained, at least partly, by the geographic environment. The fact that the player uses the higher partials has caused its music to make use of a peculiar scale—C-D-E-F sharp-G (transposed, of course, to various pitches when the instrument varies in size)—which has also been used as the basis of some Swiss folk songs.

Yodeling, the rapid alternation between chest and head voice while singing nonlexical syllables, is also a practice due partly to the possibility of communicating over long distance from one mountainside to another. Although we do find the use of falsetto in various continents, true yodeling is rare outside the Alpine region. Yodeling usually appears in the refrains of songs, although there are also some songs which consist entirely of yodeling. There is in the Alps also some polyphonic yodeling with parallel thirds or triads, for polyphonic singing of the type described for Germany is particularly strong in the Alps. The practice of yodeling has led to the emergence of a class of semiprofessional musicians in the Alpine region, for certain individuals achieve fame as yodelers and give paid performances. Yodeling and *alphorn* performances, aimed at tourists and local townspeople and supported by numerous organizations in the Alpine countries, have played an important role in the folkloristic movement.

Brief mention of European Jewish folk music is suitable here. The Yiddish folksongs are related to German folklore, for Yiddish is essentially a German dialect of the late Middle Ages that has been penetrated by words borrowed from Hebrew, Polish, Russian, and other languages. During the late Middle Ages, the Jews were driven out of Germany and sought refuge in Eastern Europe, keeping their special brand of German folk culture. Thus the songs of the Yiddish-speaking Jews have retained some of the German medieval character. But to a greater degree their songs partake of the styles of the nations to which they moved—Russia, Poland, Romania, and elsewhere. And there are also traces of Hebrew liturgical music in their folk songs. Thus the styles of Yiddish folk song have great variety, and the whole corpus of Yiddish folk music is not a homogeneous one. A similar development, incidentally, occurred among the Sephardic Jews who, during the Middle Ages, lived in Spain but were driven out in 1492 and carried with them a Spanish-derived language, Ladino, and songs partially Spanish in style. (For a discussion of Israeli folk music, see William P. Malm's book in this series, *Music Cultures of the Pacific, the Near East, and Asia*.)

There are—or there were, before World War II—many enclaves of German population in various parts of Eastern Europe (Russia, Hungary, Yugoslavia, Romania), in South America (particularly Brazil and Argentina), and in the United States and Canada. These consist largely of descendants of individuals who left Germany in quest of religious freedom between the sixteenth and the nineteenth centuries. Their folk music has occasionally been collected. As we might expect, it has sometimes been influenced by their new surroundings; German-Americans have, for instance, incorporated British tunes into their repertory. But, more important, these groups have tended to keep intact some of the styles and many of the songs that were evidently once current in Germany proper, but that have disappeared in the original center of their distribution.

There is much variety in the music of the Germanic-speaking peoples of Europe, but their styles stand together when compared with those of the Slavic and Finno-Ugric speaking peoples of Eastern Europe, or with those of Italy, France, and the Iberian peninsula. No doubt peoples that speak related languages very frequently share other aspects of culture such as music, but it is not always so. And although we can perhaps speak of a Germanic style of folk music, we must also be aware of the interchange of materials and styles between these and neighboring peoples—the impact of German and Austrian music in Czechoslovakia and Poland, the similarity between Dutch and Belgian songs and styles, the impact of Italy on Austria, and the relationship between Scandinavian and Russian music.

BIBLIOGRAPHICAL AND DISCOGRAPHICAL NOTES

Cecil J. Sharp is the author of a number of fundamental works on British folk music; one of the important ones is *English Folk Song, Some Conclusions,* 4th ed. (London: Mercury Books, 1965). Maud Karpeles, *An Introduction to English Folk Song* (London: Oxford University Press, 1973), is a good survey for the general reader. A readable discussion of the British ballad is Evelyn Wells, *The Ballad Tree* (New York: Ronald Press, 1950); a very useful introduction to both texts and tunes is Roger D. Abrahams and George Foss's *Anglo-American Folksong Style* (Englewood Cliffs, NJ: Prentice-Hall, 1968). Bertrand H. Bronson's article "About the Commonest British Ballads," *J-IFMC,* IX (1957), 22–27, is important reading. A number of his studies of texts and tunes are reprinted in *The Ballad as Song* (Berkeley: University of California Press, 1969). Other studies of ballads concentrating on texts are collected in *The Ballad Image: Essays to Bertrand H. Bronson,* ed. James Porter (Los Angeles: University of California Press, 1983). The most comprehensive collection of British ballad tunes, reprinting tunes from many important collections, is Bronson's *The Traditional Tunes of the Child Ballads* (Princeton, NJ: Princeton University Press, 1958–72). Also worthy of note are *Cecil Sharp's Collection of English Folk Songs,* 2 vols., ed. Maud Karpeles (London: Oxford University Press, 1974), which presents about half of the items that Sharp collected in Britain in the first quarter of the twentieth century; and Peter Kennedy, *Folksongs of Britain and Ireland* (London: Cassel, 1975), an anthology of English, Gaelic, and other materials. The concept of tune families is examined in Samuel P. Bayard, "Prologomena to a Study of the Principal Melodic Families of British-American Folk Songs," *Journal of American Folklore,* LXIII (1950), 1–44; Anne Dhu Shapiro, "The Tune-Family Concept in British-American Folk-Song Scholarship" (Ph.D. diss., Harvard University,

1975); James R. Cowdery, "A Fresh Look at the Concept of Tune Family," *Ethnomusicology*, XXVIII (1984), 495–504; and John M. Ward, "The Morris Tune," *Journal of the American Musicological Society*, XXXIX (1986), 294–331. The tunes of one well-known ballad are discussed in Charles Seeger, "Versions and Variants of the Tunes of 'Barbara Allen,'" UCLA *Selected Reports in Ethnomusicology*, I (1966), 120–67.

Irish folk song and instrumental music are surveyed in Tomás Ó Canainn, *Traditional Music in Ireland* (London: Routledge & Kegan Paul, 1978). A number of good collections are available, among them Donal J. O'Sullivan, *Songs of the Irish* (New York: Crown, 1960); Brendán Breathnach, *Folk Music and Dances of Ireland* (Dublin: Mercier Press, 1977), illustrated by a cassette tape sold separately; and a new combined edition of songs and tunes first published by F. O'Neill in the early twentieth century, Miles Krassen, *O'Neill's Music of Ireland* (New York: Oak Publications, 1976). The traditions of a small parish in Northern Ireland are documented in Hugh Shields, *Shamrock, Rose and Thistle: Folk Singing in North Derry* (Belfast: Blackstaff Press, 1981); this work is supplemented by a disc (Leader Records LED 20270, published 1976) and two cassettes, all bearing the same title (cassettes published in 1982 by European Ethnic Oral Traditions, Language and Communication Centre, Trinity College, Dublin 2, Ireland).

Authoritative studies of Scottish folk music include Francis Collinson, *The Traditional and National Music of Scotland* (Nashville: Vanderbilt University Press, 1966), and *The Bagpipe: The History of a Musical Instrument* (London: Routledge & Kegan Paul, 1975); and George S. Emmerson, *Rantin' Pipe and Tremblin' String: A History of Scottish Dance Music* (London: Dent, 1971). Donald A. Fergusson, Aonaghus Iain MacDhomhnuill, and Jean F. Gillespie, *From the Farthest Hebrides* (Toronto: Macmillan Press, 1978), contains songs in Gaelic and English, mainly from North Uist. Also recommended is John L. Campbell and Francis Collinson, *Hebridean Folksongs*, 2 vols. (Oxford: Oxford University Press, 1969 and 1977). *The Grieg-Duncan Folk Song Collection*, Vol. I, ed. Patrick Shuldham-Shaw and Emily B. Lyle (Aberdeen: Aberdeen University Press, 1981), is the first of a projected series of eight volumes devoted to the publication of an enormous collection compiled in the northeast of Scotland in the early twentieth century.

Several works on the traditional music of Wales have been published by W. S. Gwynn Williams, among them *Welsh National Music and Dance*, 4th ed. (Llangollen: Gwynn, 1971), and a collection titled *Caneuon traddodiadol y Cymry* (Traditional Songs of the Welsh), 2 vols. (Llangollen: Gwynn, 1961–63). D. Roy Saer, *Caneuon Llafar Gwlad* (Songs from Oral Tradition) (Wales: National Museum of Wales, 1974), is a small collection designed for both singer and scholar. *The Traditional Music of Britain and Ireland: A Select Bibliography and Research Guide* by James Porter (New York: Garland) is in preparation. Printed sources and recordings of American folk song and instrumental music are included in the bibliographical and discographical notes for Chapter 11.

A set of volumes covering the *hardingfele* repertory (approximately two thousand tunes) has been published as *Norwegian Folk Music*, 7 vols. (Oslo: Universitetsforlaget, 1958–81), Vols. I–V ed. Olav Gurvin, Vols. VI–VII edited by Jan Petter Blom, Sven Nyhus, and Reidar Sevåg (U.S. distributor: Columbia University Press). Vol. VII contains a pioneering study by Blom of the rhythm of *hardingfele* music. This instrument and its traditions are also treated in Pandora Hopkins, *Aural Thinking in Norway: Performance and Communication with the Hardingfele* (New York: Human Sciences Press, Inc., 1986). Other studies of individual traditions or instruments include Daniel Sundstedt Beal, "Two Springar Dance Traditions from Western Norway," *Ethnomusicology*, XXVIII (1984), 237–51; Sven Nyhus, *Pols i Rørostraktom* (Oslo: Universitetsforlaget, 1973) (concerning a genre for normal fiddle); Reidar Sevåg, "Neutral Tones and the Problems of Mode in Norwegian Folk Music," in *Studia instrumentorum musicae popularis III: Festschrift to Ernst Emsheimer*, ed. Gustav Hilleström (Stockholm: Nordiska Musikförlaget, 1974), pp. 207–13; and Ola Kai Ledang, "Instrument-Player-Music: On the Norwegian *Langleik*," in *Festschrift to Ernst Emsheimer*, pp. 107–18, and "Revival and Innovation: The Case of the Norwegian Seljefløyte," *Yearbook for Traditional Music*, XVIII (1986), 145–56. A classic collection of folk songs and instrumental music that inspired Edvard Grieg—Ludvig M. Lindeman's *Æeldre og nyere norske fjeldmelodier* (Christiana: P. T. Malling, 1853–67)—is available in a reprint edition (Oslo: Universitetsforlaget, 1963).

Several early Swedish folk music collections are available in reprint editions, among them A. A. Afzelius and O. Åhlström, *Traditioner af swenska folkdansar* (Stockholm, 1814–15; reprint 1972), and Nils Andersson and Olof Andersson, *Svenska låtar*, Vols. VIII–IX (Halsingland, Gästrikland, 1928–29; reprint n.p.: Bok och Bild, 1973). *Jojk* (Yoik) (Stockholm: Sveriges Radios Förlag, 1969) is a collection of Lapp songs, together with seven discs. In the field of musical instruments, Stig Walin, *Die schwedische Hummel* (Stockholm: Nordiska Museet, 1952), is an excellent, profusely illustrated study of the Swedish dulcimer. A discussion of the keyed fiddle, or *nyckelharpa*, appears as Jan Ling, *Nyckelharpan: studier i ett folkligt musikinstrument* (Stockholm: Norstedts, 1967) (with English summary; see also p. 114). The folk music revival of the 1970s in Sweden is the subject of Birgit Kjellström and others, *Folkmusikvågen* (The Folk Music Vogue) (Stockholm: Rikskonserter, 1985), with an abridged English translation and accompanying cassette. *Folkmusik boken*, ed. Jan Ling, Gunnar Ternhag, and Märta Ramsten (Stockholm: Prisma, 1980), is a collection of essays dealing with various aspects of Swedish folk music.

A series devoted to the traditional instrumental music of the Finlanders, the Swedish-speaking inhabitants of Finland, has been published under the title *Finlands svenska folkdiktning*, 6 vols. (Turku (Åbo), Finland: Ab Sydvästkusten, 1963–75). Also of interest is *Suomen Antropologi*, IV (special issue on Finnish ethnomusicology), ed. Erikki Pekkilä (Helsinki: University of Helsinki, 1983). Svend Nielson, *Stability in Musical Improvisation: A Repertoire of Icelandic Epic Songs* (Copenhagen: Forlaget Kragen, 1982), is an examination of the repertory and style of a single performer.

An interesting collection of Danish folk music collected from one informant is Nils Schiørring, *Selma Nielsens viser* (Copenhagen: Munksgaard, 1956). A monumental collection of medieval Danish ballads has been published under the title, *Danmarks gamle folkeviser*, Vols. I–X (containing texts only), edited by Svend Grundtvig and others (1853–1965; new edition published Copenhagen: Universitets-Jubilæets Danske Samfund, 1966–67), Vols. XI and XII, coordinated by Erik Dal and containing tunes, essays, and reference materials (Copenhagen, 1976). A. Knudsen and T. Knudsen, *Folkemusikhus* (Hogager, 1974–), presents folk music from the collection of the Folklore Archives at Hogager in Jutland.

A short survey of Dutch folk music, with examples, is Jaap Kunst, "On Dutch Folk Dances and Dance Tunes," *Studies in Ethnomusicology*, I (1961), 29–37. Many collections of German folk music are available. A classic is Ludwig Erk and Franz Magnus Boehme, *Deutscher Liederhort* (Leipzig, 1893–94; reprint Olms: Hildesheim, 1962). A more recent publication is *Deutsche Volkslieder mit ihren Melodien* ed. John Meier and others (Freiburg: Deutsches Volksliedarchiv, 1935–). Many publications by German scholars on German folk song are worth reading; those by Walter Wiora and Erich Stockmann are particularly to be noted. An impressive study of Swiss folk music instruments is Brigitte Bachmann-Geiser, *Die Volksmusikinstrumente der Schweiz*, Handbuch der europäischen Volksmusikinstrumente Series 1, Vol. IV (Leipzig: VEB Deutscher Verlag für Musik, 1981). The *alphorn* tradition is treated in Geiser, *Das Alphorn in der Schweiz* (Berne: Paul Haupt, 1976), with summaries in French and English. M. P. Baumann, *Musikfolklore und Musikfolklorismus: eine ethnomusikologische Untersuchung zum Funktionswandel des Jodels* (Winterthur: Amadeus, 1976), is a history of yodeling in Switzerland. Tilman Seebass and others, *The Music of Lombok: A First Survey* (Bern: Francke Verlag, 1976), is a regional study. Ruth Rubin, *Voices of a People: The Story of Yiddish Folksong* (1960; reprint Philadelphia: Jewish Publication Society of America, 1979), is a pioneering work on Yiddish traditional song in Eastern Europe.

The number of recordings of British folk song, both field collections and artistic interpretations, is enormous. To be mentioned especially is a set of Child ballads produced by the British traditional singers A. L. Lloyd and Ewan MacColl for classroom and other educational use: *English and Scottish Popular Ballads*, Washington Records 715–723. Two other series of note are *The Folk Songs of Britain*, 10 vols., ed. Peter Kennedy and Alan Lomax, Caedmon TC 1142–46, 1162–64, 1224–25, and the Scottish Tradition Series of cassettes and discs issued by the School of Scottish Studies at the University of Edinburgh, on the Tangent label. Among the many fine recordings in this series are *Music from the Western Isles*, Tangent TNGM 110, featuring a wide range of music in Gaelic; *Waulking Songs from Barra*, Tangent TNGM 111, which corresponds to material in Campbell and Collinson, *Hebridean Folksongs*, Vol. II; and *Pibroch: George Moss*, Tangent TGMMC 506 (a 60-minute cassette), which presents tunes in older Gaelic styles and more popular competition styles, with full transcriptions and notes by Peter Cooke. Also worth hearing are *Sussex Folk Songs and Ballads*, ed. Kenneth Goldstein,

Folkways FG 3515; *Songs and Pipes of the Hebrides*, Folkways P 430; *The Streets of Glasgow: Ballads and Songs, Tunes and Squibs from Clydeside*, Topic 12 TS 226; *The Art of the Bagpipe* (with elaborate annotations), Folk-Lyric Records FL 112; and *John Burgess: The Art of the Highland Bagpipe*, Vol. III, Topic 12 TS 393. Child ballads as sung by American informants are available on many recordings published by the Library of Congress. See particularly *Child Ballads Traditional in the U.S.* (AAFS 57–58).

Songs and Dances of Holland, Folkways 3576, and *Songs and Dances of Norway*, Folkways FE 4008, are both educational and entertaining selections. *Norsk folkemusikk*, a series of rereleases of material from the archives of the Norwegian Broadcasting Corporation, is available on the RCA Victor label. Among these excellent recordings are *Religiøse Folketonar* (FLP 21) and *Johannes Dahle, Gunnar Dahle: Hardingfele* (FLP 10). *Folk Music of Norway*, Topic 12 TS 351, with notes by L. Y. Daliot, is a collection of songs, hymns, and tunes featuring the *hardingfele* and the *langleik*. An unusual collection of singing games collected in Norwegian schoolyards by Egil Bakka, Ola Kai Ledang, and Berit Østberg is *"-og vil du være kjæresten min:" Barnesangleik i Arendal, Moss, Trondheim, Tromsø, Ålesund*, Arctic Records ARC 8652, with notes and transcriptions of all the songs. A fine series of Swedish folk music has been issued on the Caprice label by the Swedish Center for Folksong and Folk Music Research together with the Institute for National Concerts (with notes in Swedish and English). Approximately half the discs are devoted to fiddle music, among them *Riksspelmän i Närke och Västmanland* (CAP 1146), which highlights well-known players of the older generation; *Spelmän i Jämtland och Härjedalen* (CAP 1098), featuring fiddle and other instruments; and *Unga Spelmän från Södra Sverige* (CAP 1099) and *Unga Spelmän från Värmland* (CAP 1122), both of which present instrumentalists of the postwar generation. *Spelmans Musik i Stockholm* (CAP 1249) documents a variety of fiddling styles in Stockholm (recorded 1981). *Visor i Skillingtryck* (CAP 1097) is a collection of broadside ballads. A survey of musical traditions of the *kantele* (see p. 96) is presented on *Kantele*, Suomalaisen Kirjallisuuden Seura SKSLP 3 (available on disc or cassette from the Finnish Literature Society, Hallituskatu 1, 00170 Helsinki 17 Finland; a descriptive pamphlet in Finnish and English is sold separately). *Viljo Karvonen: Kantele*, Kansanmusiikki-instituuti KILP 10, is a collection of contemporary field recordings made by Heikki Laitinen of a traditional *kantele* player from Halsua.

For German folk song, a set produced by the famous Freiburg archive is recommended: *Deutsche Volkslieder*, Deutsche Grammophongesellschaft 004–157 to 004–160 (2 discs), with a pamphlet giving texts, notes, and complete transcriptions. Several discs, each devoted to the music of one or more Swiss instruments, are available (with notes by Brigitte Bachmann-Geiser) on the Claves and Ex Libris labels. *Yodel of Appenzell, Switzerland*, Philips 6586 044, and *"Yüüzli:" Yodel of the Muotatal, Switzerland*, Le Chant du Monde LDX 74716, both with commentary by Hugo Zemp, are illuminating documents of yodeling in traditional settings.

FIVE

EASTERN EUROPE

The area east of Italy, Austria, Germany, and Scandinavia has on the whole been much less under the influence of art music than has the western half of Europe. This may partially account for the great variety of folk music traditions found in Eastern Europe. Yet peoples as diverse as the Greeks, the Russians, and the Hungarians can hardly be expected to share one style of folk music. For many centuries, parts of Eastern Europe have repeatedly been conquered and reconquered by several peoples from the outside—Mongols, Turks, Romans, Germans. Its culture has many roots, among them Hellenistic, Islamic, Oriental, and north Asian, and it is inhabited by peoples speaking languages of several distinct families and groups: Slavic, the largest group; Finno-Ugric (Finnish, Hungarian, Estonian, and several minority languages in Russia); Turkic (the Turks, the Chuvash of the Russian interior, and others); Romance (Romanian); Albanian; and Caucasian. Musical influences have come from sources as diverse as the music of the Byzantine Church, the pentatonic tunes of Mongolia, and the complex rhythms of the Arabic and Hindu spheres. And certainly there are important links between Eastern and Western Europe: tunes found in both areas and identical uses and functions of music in the culture.

In view of this great diversity, this chapter makes no attempt to discuss the individual nations one by one; in fact some are entirely omitted. Instead, we discuss certain techniques of composition and types of music which are found in several of the cultures. But let us bear in mind that each of the Eastern European countries, from gigantic Russia to tiny Albania, has a rich folk music heritage; each has enough music to fill a multivolume anthology and a musical culture of sufficient wealth to keep scholars busy for several lifetimes. It is also important to bear in mind that although there is a common flavor to East European folk music, there is probably more variety of practices and styles in each of its nations than there is in the typical Western European country.

MELODIC SEQUENCE: HUNGARIANS, CZECHS, CHEREMIS

East European scholars have studied intensively their native musical traditions, and nowhere has this been more true than in Hungary. For much of the nineteenth century it was thought that the folk music of Hungary was the music of the gypsies who supplied ethnic entertainment in the cities, but in the twentieth century the great wealth of true Hungarian peasant music (which has little in common with the gypsy tunes) was discovered, largely by Béla Bartók and Zoltán Kodály. Because the Hungarians are linguistically related to the Finns, it was thought that the styles of these two peoples would have something in common. This is only partially the case, but other Finno-Ugric speaking peoples living for centuries in isolation from the Hungarians, inside Russia, do have music somewhat similar to that of Hungary. The most important of these groups is the Cheremis, who live in a semiautonomous republic of the Soviet Union some five hundred miles east of Moscow.

The musics of these peoples have elements in common that are also found far to the east, among the Mongolians, and even to some extent farther on, in American Indian music. This strengthens our belief that the essential features of the oldest Hungarian folk music are very old, and that they were brought by the Finno-Ugric tribes when they moved westward in the early Middle Ages. The most striking of these features is the practice of transposing a bit of melody, once or even several times, to create the essence of a song. Many Hungarian songs have the form $A^1A^2A^1$(a fifth lower)A^2(a fifth lower), for example. Transposition is usually up or down a

EXAMPLE 5-1. Cheremis song, from Bruno Nettl, *Cheremis Musical Styles* (Blooming-ton: Indiana University Press, 1960), p. 37.

fifth, perhaps because this interval is an important one in the series of overtones, or perhaps because this practice may have originated long ago, in the Far East, where fifths are also significant, or for any of several other possible reasons. In Hungarian folk music, and even more in that of the Cheremis, pentatonic scales composed of major seconds and minor thirds predominate. Such scales have sometimes been called "gapped scales" on the assumption that they are simply diatonic scales with certain tones left out. Of course there is no real justification for such a label, for there is nothing any more natural about a scale made up of seconds (of two sizes) than there is about one made up of seconds and thirds, or, for that matter, one made up of quarter tones or augmented fourths. To demonstrate the integrity of the kind of pentatonic scale we have mentioned, let us examine a Cheremis song that makes use of the principle of transposition (Example 5-1).

The song consists of three lines, the last two of which are identical except for the fact that the final E is held. The first consists of two halves, the second of which is derived from the first (and is therefore designated as B_a). The first half of the second line is a downward transposition of the first half of the first line, by a fifth (and is therefore designated as A_5). But there are further ramifications of this notion of transposition, as our analysis will indicate.

First we assign to each of the notes in the scale a number: beginning with the lowest tone, B—1, C sharp—2, E—3, F sharp—4, G sharp—5, B—6, C sharp—7, E—8. Then we compare the section labeled A with that labeled A^5. Obviously their melodic contours are similar, but at some of the points at which A has a minor third, A^5 has a major second, and A^5 begins a minor sixth below A but ends on a perfect fifth below A. Now, if we translate the tones into the numbers we have assigned, and compare musical lines A and A^5, we have the following sequences:

Line A⁵   5 5 4 5 4 3 2 3 3 2 3 2 1
Line A   8 8 7 8 7 6 5 6 6 5 6 5 4

The relationship between the number sequences is constant because the principle involved in this transposition is not a constant relationship of the frequencies (which would occur if the method of transposition were an exact one), but that of tonal transposition. Presumably the scale used in this song existed, in an unconscious sense, in the mind of the composer when making up the song, and when transposing began it was done within the framework of the scale, which is made up of both thirds and seconds.

To some degree, the use of transposition as a structuring device is found in a great many cultures throughout the world, and certainly everywhere in Europe. It takes on special significance in parts of Eastern Europe because of its greater frequency there. The practice of transposing as an integral part of the composition process seems to have radiated from Hungary to its neighbor countries. The Slovaks and, to a small extent, the Czechs make use of it also. The Slovaks transpose sections largely in the manner of the Hungarians (up or down a fifth), the Czechs more frequently up or down a third or second. Perhaps the difference between the Czech and Hungarian practice is due to the greater frequency of diatonic, especially major, scales among the Czechs. Or the influence of neighbor nations may be at work, for the Czechs have lived in an area surrounded by Germans and they participated, more than their neighbors to the east, in the development of art music. Thus their songs sound more like Western art music, and they have variants of many tunes found also in Germany. Example 5-2 is a Czech song using transposition.

EXAMPLE 5-2. Czech folk song. "Vrt sa devca," learned by Bruno Nettl from oral tradition.

WORDS, MUSIC, AND RHYTHM:
THE BALKANS AND CZECHOSLOVAKIA

It is natural to look to the characteristics of a language to explain the characteristics of the songs sung by its speakers. Indeed, the structure of folk songs is frequently determined by the form of their texts, and the rhythmic, even the melodic, quality of a musical repertory may be substantially influenced by the stress, length, and patterns of the words to which it is sung. Of course we could not claim that the rhythmic structure of a folk music style automatically comes from the language, and we could easily find examples in which the rhythm of folk songs contravenes that of their language. However, there is no doubt that the nature of a language has much to do with shaping the style of the folk songs for which it is used.

It is interesting, in this light, to compare the rhythmic structure of Czech and German folk songs. That of the Czech songs frequently is more accented, whereas the German flows more smoothly. The German songs more frequently have an *anacrusis*—a pickup or upbeat, as it is popularly called—and the Czech ones rarely do. These distinctions may come from one of the major phonological differences between the two languages. Czech speakers tend to accent their stressed syllables heavily, and the Czech language automatically places an accent on the first syllable of each word. Also, Czech has no articles such as *a* or *the* that would be unstressed. As a result, Czech utterances begin with accents, and so do Czech songs and instrumental folk compositions. German, with its accents coming on any syllable, and with its unstressed articles preceding nouns, has given rise to a musical structure in which an unstressed beat in the music often precedes the first measure.

The rhythm of Czech and Slovak songs is relatively simple, with the meter typically an isometric duple or triple. Hungarian folk songs are frequently in similarly simple meter, but there are also many Hungarian songs with irregular metric patterns, and some that move steadily in 5/4 or 7/4 meter. One of the common features of Hungarian rhythm is the use of dotted figures—♩. ♪ or, even more typically, ♪♩. —with heavy stress on the first note. Perhaps, again, the rhythmic structure of the language is evident here, for in Hungarian, as in Czech, there are no articles, and the first syllable is automatically accented. Also common in Hungarian and some other Eastern European folk styles is the use of *isorhythmic* structure. This means that a given rhythmic pattern is repeated for each line. The meters may vary and the measures may have irregular numbers of beats, but the sequence of note values remains the same from line to line in this type of song. The following rhythmic patterns appear in some of the Hungarian as well as the Romanian folk songs with isorhythmic structure:

① ♫♫♩♩   ② ♫ ♪   ♫♪

③ ♫♪♫♪♪♪   ④ ♪♪│♪♪│♪♪│♪♪ │

The reason for the frequency of this kind of structure in some Eastern European styles may lie, again, in the structure of the poetry. In Western Europe, it is the number of metric feet (iambic, trochaic, dactylic, anapestic) which is constant. Each foot corresponds to one or to a half measure of music. The actual number of syllables per line may vary, because a line consisting of iambic feet may suddenly be broken by a foot of anapest:

"Thĕre wás ă yoúth aňd ă jól-l̆y youth" ("aňd ă jól-" is the anapest foot).

But in most Eastern European styles of poetry it is not the number of accented syllables that is constant, but the number of syllables in toto. Thus an isorhythmic arrangement, even if each phrase has several measures of different lengths, is better for accommodating the kind of line sequence that makes up the poetry.

On the whole, the Balkan countries have in common an unusual degree of rhythmic complexity. It appears in three forms: (1) freely declaimed melodies, which can only with difficulty be classified as to meter, and which are performed with extremes of the parlando-rubato technique; (2) tunes with few different note values, but with frequently changing meter; and (3) tunes with a single dominant meter which, however, is based on a prime number of beats—5, 7, 11, 13, and so on. The first type is well

EXAMPLE 5-3. Examples of metric patterns found in Bulgarian folk songs.

exemplified in the Yugoslav epic, which is discussed later in this chapter. The second and third types are especially common in the Romanian and Bulgarian traditions, so much so that songs in 11/8 or 7/8 have been called tunes "in Bulgarian rhythm" among Balkan folk song scholars. Example 5-3 gives some of the rhythms found in these songs.

Example 5-4 is a Romanian Christmas carol with a meter of 10/16 kept consistently throughout the song. Actually it might be possible to divide the song into measures of different lengths, but in spite of the rather complicated relationship between such note values as eighths and dotted eighths, or sixteenths and dotted sixteenths, there is a steady rhythmic pulse which is followed throughout: ♪ ♪. ♪. ♪ . The curious thing is that the pulse is not regular. It alternates between eighths and dotted eighths. Perhaps this is the key to the rhythmic complexity of some Balkan songs as, for instance, the one given in Example 5-4. The transcription by Béla Bartók gives the way in which the first stanza was sung, and then, by means of numbered references, indicates the way in which subsequent stanzas differ from the first. There is a meter—10/16 in this case—but the denominator of the fraction does not indicate the length of the beat, as it would in most Western European music, because the length of the beat varies, depending on its position in the measure. It would seem almost

that ♪♪. ♪. ♪ is another version of ♪♪♪♪ and that 𝅘𝅥𝅮𝅘𝅥𝅮.𝅘𝅥𝅮𝅘𝅥𝅮 is simply an

elongation of a simpler figure, 𝅘𝅥𝅮𝅘𝅥𝅮𝅘𝅥𝅮𝅘𝅥𝅮 . We should point out, incidentally,

that there is a vast body of Christmas carols in the Romanian folk repertory. Bartók collected several hundred tunes, and they seem to be particularly archaic, being short, with forms that do not correspond to the simple line organization of Western European, Czech, or Hungarian songs and are

EXAMPLE 5-4 Romanian Christmas Carol, from Béla Bartók, *Rumanian Folk Music. Vol. IV: Carols and Christmas Songs (Colinde)*, ed. Benjamin Suchoff (The Hague: Martinus Nijhoff, 1975), 102 (melody no. 81f). Used by permission of Kluwer Academic Publishers, Dordrecht, Holland.

irregular not only in the structure of the measures but also in the number of measures and phrases per song.

One might expect the dances of the Balkan countries to be based on simple metric schemes; after all, people have two legs and two arms, to which movement in duple meter lends itself; no one has seven feet. Nevertheless, among the five most important folk dances of the Bulgarians, only one is in duple meter. The Bulgarians have (1) the *Pravo Horo,* a simple round dance, in 2/4 meter; (2) the *Paiduška,* in quintuple meter, with two beats— ♩ ♩. ; (3) the *Povărnato Horo,* a back-and-forth round dance, in 9/16, with four beats— ♪♪♪♪. ; (4) *Račenica,* danced by couples in 7/8 meter, with three beats— ♩ ♩ ♩. ; and (5) *Eleno mome* ("My Helen"), a more recent introduction, also in 7/8, with four beats— ♩ ♩ ♪ ♩ . The metric structure of these dances, once established, is quite consistent.

The tunes with frequently changing meter are illustrated by Example 5-5, a simple Romanian Christmas carol with the range of a sixth, with alternation of 3/8, 4/8, and 5/8. The simple yet irregular rhythmic structure of many Balkan songs is illustrated by the fact that the rhythm of the first three measures reappears in the last three.

We are not able, in this short book, to discuss the words of folk songs to any significant extent, especially their content. In general, however, it must be pointed out that there are broad but recognizable differences between Eastern and Western European folk song texts. For example, the widespread importance of the ballad in Western Europe, particularly in the Germanic-speaking countries, is balanced by the greater importance in Eastern Europe of lyrical songs, particularly of songs involving activities of and feelings about tilling the land. Both types of songs are found throughout Europe, but it is in Eastern Europe that songs truly reflective of a peasant economy are found in large number. Possibly, this is a result of the earlier and greater urbanization of the Western part of the continent. As samples of Eastern European lyrical songs, we present here a few Czech

EXAMPLE 5-5 From Béla Bartók, *Rumanian Folk Music. Vol. IV: Carols and Christmas Songs (Colinde),* ed. Benjamin Suchoff (The Hague: Martinus Nijhoff, 1975), 138 (melody no. 62o). Used by permission of Kluwer Academic Publishers, Dordrecht, Holland.

folk song texts, in English translation,[1] from the many that deal with agricultural life and are among the most popular. They are usually not real work songs, but lyrical poems sung after work.

> Around Trebon, around Trebon
> Horses are grazing on the lord's field.
> Give the horses, I'm telling you,
> Give the horses oats.
> When they have had their fill
> They will carry me home.

Often the songs concern love among young peasants. For example:

> Come, young man, to our house in the morning.
> You shall see what I do.
> I get up in the morning, I water the cows,
> And I drive the sheep to pasture.

The fruits of agriculture may be used as special symbols in the text:

> Under the oak, behind the oak
> She had one or two
> Red apples; she gave one to me.
> She did not want to give me both,
> She began to make excuses,
> That she hasn't, that she won't give, that there are too few.

Many of the Czech lyrical songs deal with or mention music, such as this—

> In the master's meadow I found a ducat.
> Who will change it for me? My sweetheart is not at home.
> If she won't change it I'll give it to the cimbal [dulcimer] player.
> The music will play until dawn.

FORM IN BALKAN FOLK SONGS

The forms of Balkan songs exhibit similarities to those of Western Europe, but there are also considerable differences. In Western Europe we are overwhelmed by a large number of four-line stanzas, in which there is either progressive development (ABCD, each line a new melody with

---

[1] Czech folk song texts quoted from Bruno Nettl and Ivo Moravcik, "Czech and Slovak Folk Songs Collected in Detroit," *Midwest Folklore*, V (1955), 40–48.

no repetition) or some recurrence of the first line. As we have seen, AABA is very common in German folk music, in British broadside ballads, and in modern popular and popular-derived songs. ABBA is common also in the older British ballads, especially those exhibiting a curved melodic contour. The reverting forms—AABA and ABBA—are common also in the western part of Eastern Europe, in Czech, Polish, and Hungarian song. AABA especially is found in Czech and Polish music, perhaps because of strong German influence. ABBA is found in Hungarian and other Finno-Ugric groups, but more common is a variant of this form, A A(5) A(5) A, indicating transposition of the first section up or down a fifth for the second and third sections. The use of three sections, such as ABA, with the middle section longer or shorter, and sometimes at a tempo different from the first, is sometimes found in the Balkans and sometimes among the Czechs. (Example 5-5 has a shorter middle section, for instance.) Songs with two, five, and six or more lines are found throughout the Balkans and in the Baltic area. Often these can be subdivided into asymmetrical units (like the measures in Bulgarian rhythm). Simple general principles may govern the development of greatly varied groups of forms. Many Romanian Christmas songs can be divided into two parts, the first longer than the second, with both having common material. The second part is often a condensation of the first (e.g., ABC-AC; A^1A^2B-A^1B).

An area of the world as rich in both folk tunes and folk song scholars as the Balkans was perhaps bound to produce pioneer work in the classification of musical forms. Bartók devised a system which he used for his collections of Hungarian, Slovak, Romanian and Serbo-Croatian songs. In his Slovak collection, the songs are first divided according to the number of melodic lines (normally two, three, or four) without counting repetitions of material. Thus a tune with the form ABBA has two different melodic lines, but the form ABCD has four. Each class is then subdivided according to the position of the final tones of the lines in relationship to the last tone of the song. For example, a song in which all lines end on the same pitch is in one class, one in which the sequence of final tones of lines is GAAG would be in another, and so on. Beyond this, each of the categories is then divided according to rhythm—dotted rhythms are separated from even rhythms. Finally, each of these groups is subdivided according to the number of syllables per line, distinguishing the songs that have the same number of syllables in each line from those in which the number varies from line to line. Bartók's scheme of classifying melodies differs greatly from that used by most students of British folk music, such as Cecil Sharp, who classified tunes according to mode. The reason for this difference is probably related to the fact that there is in the British (and other Western European) styles less formal variety than there is in East European folk music, because the former, being based on poetry with metric feet, relies on more or less constant meter and length of line.

Folk music scholars in Eastern and Central Europe, particularly in Hungary and Czechoslovakia, have followed Bartók's lead and continue to work with great energy to find more adequate methods of classifying folk tunes, now frequently using computers to process the vast amounts of data at their disposal as a result of the wealth of collected tune material. The purposes of classification are (1) to make it possible to find tunes by the musical characteristics; (2) to show that tunes are related genetically, that is, that they are members of one tune family; and (3) to provide a basis for broad analytical and descriptive surveys of the style of a folk music repertory. The folk music scholars who are most involved in questions of classification have made great strides, but their methods still do not easily and automatically provide solutions for these problems.

EPIC SONG: YUGOSLAVIA, FINLAND, RUSSIA

Traditions of epic poetry are important in a number of European folk cultures, but especially in those of Eastern Europe. An *epic* is a narrative poem, distinctly longer than the ballad, usually sung, with a main character who is usually a national hero and has many adventures in war and love. Its basic unit of organization is usually the individual line of poetry rather than a stanza consisting of several lines. In the Middle Ages the epic was fairly widespread in Western Europe; the French *chansons de geste* and such famous works as the "Song of Roland" are examples. In Western Europe, the epic tradition was evidently one in which folk and art traditions shared and mixed, for it was presumably carried by professional minstrels who at least occasionally used written texts. In Eastern Europe the epic tradition is today much more alive and much more closely associated with the genuine folk culture. We find epic material in the Slavic world, in Albania, and also in Finland, where the main body of folk epics, the *Kalevala*, consists of songs dealing with the Finnish mythical culture hero, Väinemöinen. The *Kalevala* is structured in couplets, and the songs were performed by pairs of bards who would alternate, which is probably responsible for the peculiarly repetitive form of the text, as shown in this excerpt:[2]

> O thou wisest Väinemöinen,
> O thou oldest of magicians,
> Speak thy words of magic backwards,
> And reverse thy songs of magic.
> Loose me from this place of terror
> And release me from my torment.

[2] From the book *Kalevala: or, The Land of Heroes*. Trans. from the Finnish by W. F. Kirby. Everyman's Library Edition. Published by J. M. Dent & Sons Ltd. Used by permission.

You may recognize the style as that also used in Longfellow's "Song of Hiawatha." The influence of the *Kalevala* on nineteenth-century poets was considerable. The Finnish bards sang to the accompaniment of the *kantele*, a psaltery with 20 to 30 strings.

The Russian tradition of epic poetry is typically unaccompanied. The Russian poems are called *byliny* (or *bïlinï*); they are slow-moving, unrhymed, and performed in a rhythmically free style. Their stories—in contrast to the mythical past of the Finnish *Kalevala* cycle—deal with historical or semihistorical events of eleventh-century Russia and of the wars against the Tartars which took place over the next two hundred years. They employ some literary motifs that are found in many nations: for instance, the poor and neglected prince who becomes a hero, found in all European folklore but perhaps without historical foundation. The practice of singing *byliny* seems to have reached a peak of artistic perfection in the seventeenth century, when like the epic tradition of Western Europe in the Middle Ages it was penetrated by professional minstrels. The Ukrainian version of the epic is the *duma*, which deals largely with the struggles of the Ukrainians against the Tartars and Poles in the late Middle Ages.

One of the most interesting folk song types of the Greeks is the *Klephtic song*. The Klephts (meaning bandits in Turkish) were the men who fought against the Turks from the fifteenth to the nineteenth centuries for Greek independence. Klephtic songs deal with these fighters, who have become folk heroes, in a way somewhat similar to that of the Yugoslav epics. The songs are performed in a rubato manner, with much ornamentation and complex metric arrangements. They do have a strophic structure, but the melodic and poetic forms do not coincide; in fact, the musical line ordinarily covers one-and-a-half textual lines. Thus, in a sense the modern Greeks share in the epic traditions of Eastern Europe.

The most accessible body of epic singing today, however, is that of the Yugoslavs (mainly the Serbs, but also the Croatians and Montenegrans whose style is also found in Bulgaria and Albania). Their songs deal mainly with the struggles against the Turks from the thirteenth to the seventeenth centuries. Some of the epics are told from the Christian point of view, others from the Muslim. The songs deal mainly with the rulers and the leaders in war. That the tradition is still alive is attested to by the mention of modern devices such as the telephone, and by the existence of an epic about the shooting of Archduke Ferdinand at Sarajevo at the beginning of World War I. That it is also ancient is proved by the songs' musical structure. There have been attempts to link the Yugoslav tradition to that of the Greek Homeric epics, and certainly we can learn a great deal about the possible genesis of the *Iliad* and *Odyssey* and about the way in which these great epics must have been performed from the structure and cultural context of the Yugoslav epics.

The Yugoslav epics take from less than one to perhaps ten hours to perform; they are performed by semiprofessional minstrels in cafes, and they are sung only by men. They are accompanied on the *gusle* (which the singer himself plays), a simple fiddle with one string made of a strand of horsehair, a belly of stretched skin, and a crude bow. The *gusle* usually plays a more ornamented version of the singer's melody, or it performs a drone and plays ornaments between the singer's lines.

It would be surprising if songs of such length were sung exactly the same way by any two singers, or even twice alike by the same one. To a considerable extent they are improvised, recreated each time. Thus the process of creation and performance are to a degree united.

There are points where adherence to a norm is required, of course; a particular epic has certain themes, certain motifs, and certain formulas— similar to the conceits of the British ballads—which recur. In the structure, one of the typical arrangements is the ten-syllable line, which remains constant throughout the hours required to complete the poem. That singers who are partly improvising can consistently and undeviatingly produce lines of exactly ten syllables is one of the wonders of this ancient tradition. They must learn to sing in accordance with certain patterns, mastering first the stories and the formulas, then singing single episodes, and only later being permitted to sing complete songs. Even more exacting than the overall structure is the requirement of a "word boundary" after the fourth syllable in some of the Yugoslav styles; that is, the fourth syllable always ends a word, and no word occupies both fourth and fifth syllables. Here is a sample of this kind of poetry:[3]

> Beg sad priđe| đamu đo penđera,
> Pa dofati| knjige i hartije,
> Kaljem drvo| što se knjiga gradi,
> A mastila| što se knjiga piše,
> Pa načinje| knjigu šarovitu,
> Sprema knjigu| ljićkom Mustajbcgu.

(Translation): Now the bey went to the window
And he took letter paper,
A quill with which letters are made,
And ink with which letters are written,
And he prepared a well-writ letter;
He directed the letter to Mustajbey of the Lika.

---

[3] Albert B. Lord, *The Singer of Tales* (Cambridge, MA: Harvard University Press, 1960), p. 84.

Example 5-6 gives a short sample of the music, showing its very ornamental style of singing and playing, and its use of some small intervals. The scale could not be notated without the use of additional marks; arrows indicate slight raising or lowering. The notes played by the *gusle* include, consistently, a tone between C-flat and C, and one between G and G-sharp. Several possible reasons for this use of microtones have been advanced: the influence of Turkish and Arabic music; the ancient Greek tradition, with its enharmonic genus; and the use of the *gusle*, which, when fingered by the human hand in natural position of tension, produces such intervals.

The rhythm of Yugoslav epics is also worthy of discussion. If the many vocal ornaments were disregarded, we would find two main types of line:

But near the beginning of a song or an episode (usually preceded by introductions played on the *gusle*) the rhythm varies more, the first note of each

EXAMPLE 5-6. Sample of Yugoslav epic song (transcribed by Béla Bartók), from Milman Parry and Albert B. Lord, *Serbo Croatian Heroic Songs* (Cambridge, MA: Harvard University Press, 1954), I, 440. Reprinted by permission.

line is elongated, and the singing has an even more dramatic character than it does in the remainder of the song.

Finally, we should point out that regional and individual styles of singing are very highly developed in Yugoslav epic poetry. Two singers will sing the same song with many points of difference. Albert Lord narrates an incident of great interest which affords unusual insight into the relationship of tradition and individual creativity:

> When [the epic collector and scholar Milman] Parry was working with the most talented Yugoslav singer in our experience, Avdo Mededović in Bijelo Polje, he tried the following experiment. Avdo had been singing and dictating for weeks; he had shown his worth and was aware that we valued him highly. Another singer came to us, Mumin Vlahovljak from Plevlje. He seemed to be a good singer and he had in his repertory a song that Parry discovered was not known to Avdo; Avdo said he had never heard it before. Without telling Avdo that he would be asked to sing the song himself when Mumin had finished it, Parry set Mumin to singing, but he made sure that Avdo was in the room and listening. When the song came to an end, Avdo was asked his opinion of it and whether he could now sing it himself. He replied that it was a good song and that Mumin had sung it well, but that he thought he might sing it better. The song was a long one of several thousand lines. Avdo began and as he sang, the song lengthened, the ornamentation and richness accumulated, and the human touches of character, touches that distinguished Avdo from other singers, imparted a depth of feeling that had been missing in Mumin's version.[4]

SCALES AND INTERVALS: BULGARIA, GREECE, POLAND

If we measured the intonation of genuine folk singers anywhere we would probably find that their intervals do not coincide as well with those in Western music theory as our notations indicate. Especially in Eastern Europe, and perhaps more in the Balkans than elsewhere, we would find intervals smaller than the minor second, thirds which are neither major nor minor, and the like. The Balkans have for centuries been under the cultural influence—now strong, now weaker—of the Near East, where small intervals are common. But they have also conformed to a degree with the diatonic system found in Western folk and art music, and with the widespread pentatonic modes which use minor thirds and major seconds and can be derived from the circle of fifths. Thus we find a great deal of variety in the melodic material used in Balkan folk music.

[4] Lord, *The Singer of Tales*, p. 78.

The use of small intervals—some microtones, but more frequently minor seconds—is an important feature of some Balkan styles outside the epic tradition. The importance of ornamentation seems to have contributed to this predilection, for vocal ornaments as well as instrumental ones seem especially made for the use of small intervals. Thus a Macedonian song uses a scale with the tones E-flat, D, C, B, and A-sharp. The fact that the ranges of Balkan songs are typically small may also be a contributing factor. According to Kremenliev,[5] Bulgarian songs rarely exceed an octave in range, and a great many of them are within the compass of a fifth. Occasionally one even finds two-tone melodies with only a minor second between the tones. Ornaments in Bulgarian folk song are improvised; they vary from stanza to stanza and, in any single song, from singer to singer. Their purpose may be that of pleasing the audience through vocal virtuosity, of calling attention to the song or to particular words (this is evidently the purpose of melismatic passages preceding a song, a practice common also in the Yugoslav epics), or of imitating instrumental passages.

Greek folk music, like that of some other Balkan countries, seems to be a combination of archaic and more recent melodies and contains a great diversity of styles. It is possible to find traces of the ancient Greek modes, and many Greek songs fit perfectly into the system of the diatonic modes. Many other songs, however, are more chromatic. Perhaps the combination of these two concepts—diatonic modes with small chromatic steps—is responsible for the existence of heptatonic scales that have four minor seconds, such as the so-called gypsy scale: C-D-E flat-F sharp-G-A flat-B. In most ways, however, Greek folk music seems to show the influences of centuries of Turkish and Muslim occupation. What remains of the ancient Greek traits seems best preserved in Asia Minor and the islands of the Aegean.

Polish folk music is different from that of the Balkans and is quite distinctive, but in some ways it is close to that of Russia, and in others it is obviously related to the music of Western neighbors, the Czechs and the Germans. It is also similar to the folk style of two Slavic-speaking peoples, the Wends and the Sorbs, who lived in eastern Germany, first as a numerous group and, by the nineteenth century, as a small minority, eventually becoming completely absorbed by the Germans. The folk songs of these peoples were collected in the middle of the nineteenth century; they form something of a link between the German and Polish styles.

The oldest layer of Polish songs is pentatonic, but the majority make use of seven-tone scales, which can be classed as church modes. Those modes similar to the modern minor mode, with lowered sixth and seventh

---

[5] Boris Kremenliev, *Bulgarian-Macedonian Folk Music* (Berkeley and Los Angeles: University of California Press, 1952), p. 78.

or lowered third, are the most common; that is true also of Russian folk music. But both Poland and Russia also have many songs in major. In contrast to Russia, Poland has little polyphonic folk music and what part-singing there is seems to be of recent origin and emphasizes parallel thirds. The ranges of the songs are relatively small. A peculiarity of the singing style—typical perhaps of many and varied peculiarities of singing through Europe that never seem to appear in the printed collections of folk songs—is the practice of holding the final note of a song for several seconds, or of trailing off with a downward *glissando* (slide).

MUSICAL INSTRUMENTS

Perhaps the most characteristic feature of East European folk music is its wealth of instruments and instrumental music. There are far too many instrument types to enumerate or describe, so again we must be content with a sampling. Instruments may serve as clues to the musical past of a nation or region. For example, the association between ancient Greek and modern Near Eastern and Slavic cultures is evident in their use of similar instruments. The ancient Greek *aulos* was a reed instrument with two tubes; similar instruments are found today among the Persians, Arabs, Turks, and southern Slavs, and in India and central Asia. In Yugoslavia, an instrument of this type is the *dvojnice* which is, in effect, a double recorder or plugged flute. The right-hand tube has, typically, four or five finger holes and is used for playing simple, embellished melodies; the left-hand side has three or four holes and is normally used to play an accompanying drone. Sometimes the two pipes are played in unison.

The Czechs, Slovaks, and Hungarians all have a large number of instruments. One of the most widely used is the bagpipe, which (perhaps to the surprise of some) is by no means limited to the British Isles; on the contrary, it is found throughout Europe and parts of Asia, and evidently was brought to Scotland from the East. The kinds of bagpipes found in different countries vary from the very simple kinds found among the semi-literate tribes in Russia (such as the Cheremis) to the beautifully fashioned and sonorous instruments with three and four pipes found in Western Europe. In Scottish and Irish piping, the tunes are most frequently unrelated to the vocal music, and complex compositional types, such as *pibroch*—a kind of theme with variations—make up the repertory. In Eastern Europe, however, much of the bagpipe music consists of the same tunes used in vocal music; some Hungarian folk songs, for instance, appear—with richer ornamentation—in the bagpipe repertory.

In Czechoslovakia and Hungary we also find many instruments related

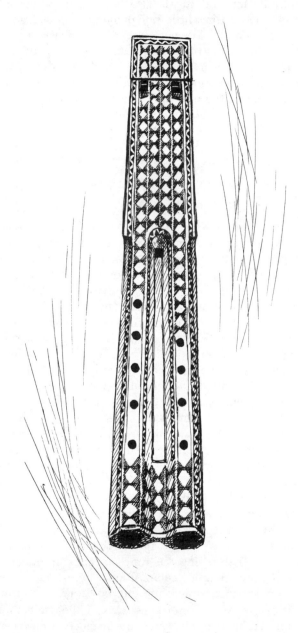

Yugoslav double recorder, or *dvojnice*

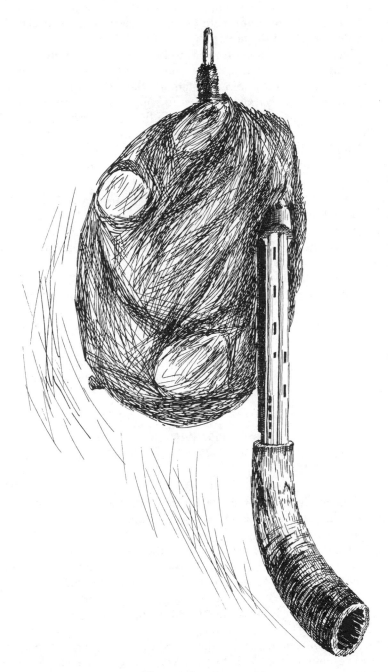

Cheremis bagpipe

to those of other areas; for example, the Hungarian *cimbalom*, a large hammered dulcimer; many kinds of flutes; the ordinary violin, especially prominent in Bohemia; and the accordion.

Folk music instruments seem to be especially numerous in Poland. Many forms of several basic types—flutes, fiddles, bagpipes—exist, each with regional variants. For example, among the stringed instruments, there is a one-stringed *diabelskie skrzypce* (devil's fiddle); a musical bow with three strings; several types of *gensle* (fiddles in various shapes with four and five strings, some held on the knee, some under the chin); the *mazanki*, a small fiddle with three strings tuned in fifths; and the *maryna*, a very large three-stringed fiddle, a form of the medieval Western European *tromba marina*.

Perhaps because of the proliferation of instruments, Polish folk music is dominated by instrumental tunes, most of them used for dancing. There is an immense number of dance types, each with regional origins. Some of these have been taken over into art music by Chopin and other composers—the polonaise, the mazurka, the polka, the krakowiak. Typically, the Polish dances are quick, and the majority use triple meter.

Although many Eastern European peoples have instruments derived from art music, or closely related to it, one finds pockets in which the instruments closely resemble some of those in the world's simpler cultures. This is the case among the Cheremis of Eastern European Russia, who use long wooden trumpets without finger holes, simple bagpipes and flutes, horns made of bark, a one-string fiddle, a simple drum, and whistles made of fired clay.

POLYPHONY:
THE SLAVIC COUNTRIES AND THE CAUCASUS

Polyphony is one type of music that characterizes all of Eastern Europe. Although it seems to exist everywhere except among the Finno-Ugric and Turkic peoples, its development has been greatest in Russia and the Caucasus. The existence among the Georgians of polyphonic songs similar to the *organa* of medieval Europe has long tantalized the historian of Western art music, who can hardly assume that the Caucasus could have had an influence on Western European practices and who finds the East too remote to have received stimuli of such a specific nature from the medieval West, but who also believes that the two forms are too similar to have been invented independently twice. This is one of the riddles of historical ethnomusicology that may never be solved. The existence of *orga-*

num-like folk music in Iceland and of other polyphonic types in Spain, Italy, and elsewhere (sporadically) indicates a possible solution: Polyphonic singing was once widespread in folk practice but receded to the marginal areas of Europe. Example 5-7 is a song of the Gurians, a tribe in the Caucasus, in three voices. The solo phrase at the beginning is typical also of Russian and Ukrainian polyphony. The first part of the song makes liberal, though not consistent, use of parallel triads. The second part also uses the principle of the drone, above which parallel thirds appear.

The role of Eastern (Orthodox) Church music in the development of this kind of polyphony may have been considerable. Polyphony was officially adopted by the Eastern Church in the seventeenth century, and its

EXAMPLE 5-7. Gurian polyphonic folk song, from Robert Lach, *Gesänge russischer Kriegsgesangener* Band 3, 1. Abt. (Vienna: Wiener Akademie der Wissenschaften, 55. Mitteilung der Phonogrammarchivs Kommission, 1928), p. 108.

style was strongly influenced by Western European polyphony, with its absence of parallel fifths and triads. Russian folk polyphony must have felt the impact of this polyphonic singing in the churches, for although there are occasional parallel fifths and fourths, the tendency is to have four voices which sing harmony largely in the Western tradition. In Russia and the Ukraine, the practice of polyphonic singing is extremely important. Singing is typically a group activity, except in the case of narrative poetry; there are reports from the 1950s of young people in Russian cities walking in groups and singing informally. The polyphonic songs are traditional, but some improvisation in the lower parts seems to be acceptable. In the Russian songs, the upper voice is definitely the melody, but in the Ukrainian ones, the two or three voices seem to be roughly equal in importance.

Since World War I, the Soviet government has attempted to preserve the folk heritage not only of the Russians but also of some of the many minority populations in the Soviet Union, at the same time making their songs servants of the communist ideology. The result is a large body of folk song in the traditional musical styles—although the traits of Russian songs per se have to an extent penetrated the domain of some of the minority groups—with words of recent origin, often mentioning the leaders of the Soviet Union and the communist ideology.

The Cossacks of the Don River basin (who have produced the famous professional Don Cossack choruses) have developed the art of polyphonic singing to especially great heights; evidently even the epic *byliny* were sometimes sung by them in chorus. Another area of Russia in which polyphony flourishes is the North, especially the area around the monastery of Pečory. The Ukrainians also have a polyphonic style of great interest; Example 5-8 is typical of those Ukrainian songs which make use of parallel fifths. The polyphony of the eastern Slavs, although essentially relying on parallel movement, does not follow this principle throughout. There is occasional oblique and contrary motion, use of the drone and even of imitation. Nor does the interval between the voices remain constant in one song. Example 5-8 contains parallel thirds as well as parallel fifths, with an occa-

EXAMPLE 5-8. Ukrainian polyphonic song from Poltava, collected by Ossyp and Roman Rosdolsky, transcribed by Bruno Nettl.

sional fourth and seventh. The beginning by a soloist is typical, and the choral parts may be doubled at the octave when both men and women sing. Tonality, in the case of the parallel fifths, may be difficult to identify, for each voice retains its own distinct tonality in order to preserve strict parallelism. But a common closing formula that establishes the final tonality proceeds from a third or triad built on the second degree of the scale to an octave on the tonic.

As we move westward, polyphony decreases in prominence, and the vertical intervals become smaller. Poles, Czechs, and Slovaks use parallel thirds (and occasionally sixths), perhaps under the influence of the Alpine style with its emphasis on triadic harmony and melody. In the Balkans we also find vertical seconds and, occasionally, parallel seconds.

In Yugoslavia, there are also various types of polyphony, the most distinctive emphasizing major and minor seconds not only as passing intervals but as the main supports of polyphonic structure. For example, there are vertical and even parallel seconds in the type of singing called *ojkanie*, whose melodies are sometimes similar to the melodic lines of the epics. The members of the Balkan folk cultures evidently do not consider the parallel seconds complex or difficult to perform, for in Bulgaria even children's songs may contain them.

Although polyphony is not common in the Baltic area, it does occur in some interesting forms also using vertical seconds. Example 5-9 is a Lithuanian round, sung by three groups, in which only two tones are sung simultaneously. The reason is that one of the three groups is always resting. Thus, the tune, consisting of phrases A and B and the rest, X, has the following form when sung as a round:

Voice 1	A	B	X	A	B	X
Voice 2		A	B	X	A	B
Voice 3			A	B	X	A

Our examples have shown that Eastern Europe possesses one of the richest traditions of folk music. Variety and regional diversity are tremendous, but if we had to divide the area into geographic subdivisions with some stylistic homogeneity, it would have to be into four groups: (1) the western Slavs—Czechs, Slovaks, Poles—who tend to show Western European characteristics and the influences of Western art music; (2) the Russians, Ukrainians, and Caucasians, who have highly developed polyphony; (3) the Balkan peoples, with music of small intervals and strong influence of the Near East; and (4) the Hungarians and other Finno-Ugric peoples who, in spite of their isolation from each other, have retained some elements of their common heritage, such as the prominence of the pentatonic scale

EXAMPLE 5-9. Lithuanian round in three parts, from pamphlet accompanying the recording *Lithuanian Folk Song in the United States* (New York: Folkways Records FE 4009), p. 2.

without half tones and the practice of transposing phrases as an essential part of song structure.

BIBLIOGRAPHICAL AND DISCOGRAPHICAL NOTES

The *New Grove* articles on Eastern European countries include surveys of folk music traditions and scholarship that are particularly valuable, given the small number of authoritative works on these subjects in English. The folk music of some of the Western nations in Eastern Europe is a field that was thoroughly studied by Béla Bartók and Zoltán Kodály, and their publications are to be recommended, among them the following. Bartók's *Slovenské l'udovné piesne* (Bratislava: Slovakian Academy of Sciences, 1959–70) is a monumental collection of Slovak folk song which also shows Bartók's method of classifying the songs. Zoltán Kodály, *Folk Music of Hungary*, 2nd ed., trans. Ronald Tempest and Cynthia Jolly (Budapest: Corvina, 1971), is an important discussion. Bartók's *Melodien der rumänischen Colinde* (Vienna: Universal Edition, 1935) includes the melodies of hundreds of Romanian Christmas carols; an English edition has appeared as *Rumanian Folk Music. Vol. IV: Carols and Christmas Songs (Colinde)*, ed. Benjamin Suchoff, text translations by E. C. Teodorescu (The Hague: Martinus Nijhoff, 1975). Hungarian folk music is also treated in Lajos Vargyas, *A Magyarság Népzenéje* (Budapest: Zeneműkiadó, 1981). Folk instruments of Hungary and Czechoslovakia are treated in Bálint Sárosi, *Die Volksmusikinstrumente Ungarns*, Handbuch der europäischen Volksmusikinstrumente Series 1, Vol. I, ed. Ernst Emsheimer and Erich Stockmann (Leipzig: VEB Deutscher Verlag für Musik, 1966); and in Ludvik Kunz, *Die Volksmusikinstrumente der Tchechoslowakai*, Handbuch der europäischen Volksmusikinstrumente Series 1, Vol. II (Leipzig, 1974). Sárosi has discussed the interaction of Hungarian music and gypsy music in "Gypsy Musicians and Hungarian Peasant Music," *Y-IFMC*, II (1970), 8–27, and in *Gypsy Music* (Búdapest: Corvina Press, 1978). An English translation of Tiberiu Alexandru's authoritative study, *Muzica populara românească* (Bucharest: Editora Muzicala, 1975), has appeared as *Romanian Folk Music*, trans. Constantin Stihi-Boos, translation revised by A. L. Lloyd (Bucharest, 1980). George Marcu, *Folclor muzical aromân* (Bucharest: Editura Muzicala, 1977), is a substantial collection of songs and tunes of the Aromunian people, who speak a Romanian dialect and span the Balkan area. *Treasured Polish Songs with English Translations*, published by Polanie Club, selected by Josepha K. Contoski (Minneapolis: Polanie, 1953), is a collection for practical use.

Among the many good readings on Yugoslav folk music, we suggest Bartók and Albert B. Lord, *Serbo-Croatian Folk Songs* (New York: Columbia University Press, 1951), also published as Vol. I of *Yugoslav Folk Music*, ed. Benjamin Suchoff (New York: State University of New York Press, 1978); Albert B. Lord, "Yugoslav Epic Folk Poetry," *J-IFMC*, III (1951), 57–61, and *The Singer of Tales* (Cambridge, MA: Harvard University Press, 1960); George Herzog, "The Music of Yugoslav Heroic Epic Folk Poetry," *J-IFMC*, III (1951), 62–64; and Barbara Krader, "Slavic Folk Music: Forms of Singing and Self-Identity," *Ethnomusicology*, XXXI (1987), 9–17. Svetozar Koljević, *The Epic in the Making* (New York: Oxford University Press, 1980), is a historical study of the Serbo-Croatian oral epic. The first two volumes of a critical edition of Slovenian folk songs (from Slovenia and elsewhere) have appeared as *Slovenske ljudske pesmi* (Ljubljana: Slovenska matica, 1970 and 1981). Birthe Trærup, *East Macedonian Folk Songs* (Copenhagen: Akademisk Forlag, 1970), contains songs (with tunes) collected among the Slavs on both sides of the Yugoslavia-Bulgarian border. Bulgarian folk music is treated in Vemelin Krustev, *Bulgarian Music* (Sofia: Sofia Press, 1978), and in *The Folk Arts of Bulgaria* (Pittsburgh: Duquesne University Tamburitzans Institute of Folk Arts, 1976). Timothy Rice, "Aspects of Bulgarian Musical Thought," *Y-IFMC*, XII (1980), 43–66, is also recommended. A detailed discussion of one Balkan style is Boris Kremenliev, *Bulgarian-Macedonian Folk Music* (Berkeley: University of California Press, 1952). Nicolai Kaufmann, *Narodni pesni ot yugozapadna Bulgaria, Pirinski krai* (Sofia: Bulgarian Academy of Sciences, 1967), is a collection of folk songs from the Pirin region of northern Bulgaria; Kaufman and Todor Todorov, *Narodni pesni ot Rhodopskia krai* (Sofia: Bulgarian Academy of Sciences, 1970), contains songs from the Rhodope region. Two important discussions of Greek folk music are Solon Michaelides, *The Neohellenic Folk-Music* (Limassol, Cyprus: Nicosia, 1948), and Rodney Gallop, "Folksongs of Modern Greece," *Musical Quarterly*, XXI (1935), 89–98. Among the collections available are Ellen Frye, *The Marble Threshing Floor: A Collection of Greek Folksongs* (Austin: University of Texas Press, 1973), and Samuel Baud-Bovy, *Chansons populaires de Crète occidentale* (Geneva: J. Minkoff, 1972); the latter includes a disc containing six songs. Lucy Duran, "Greek Folk Music: A Selected and Annotated Discography," in *Bulletin of Modern Greek Studies*, VI (May 1975), 9–23, is a guide to recordings.

Rose Rubin and Michael Stillman, *A Russian Song Book* (New York: Random House, 1962), is a collection for practical use. Polyphonic Russian songs are collected in A. Listopadov, *Pesni donskikh kazakov* (Moscow: Musgys, 1949–53). Six of a projected ten volumes of Ukrainian folk melodies have appeared as *Ukrajins'ki narodni melodiji* (New York: M. Kots, 1964–71), compiled by Zinovij Lys'ko. Aspects of Caucasian folk music are discussed in Victor Belaiev, "Folk Music of Georgia," *Musical Quarterly*, XIX (1933), 417–33. The music of one ethnic group in the USSR is presented in László Vikár and Gábor Bereczki, *Cheremis Folksongs* (Budapest: Akadémiai Kiadó, 1971), and in Bruno Nettl, *Cheremis Musical Styles* (Bloomington: Indiana University Press, 1960).

Recordings documenting the various branches of Hungarian folk music traditions are being issued on the Hungaroton and Qualiton labels, with full notes in Hungarian and English (available from Qualiton Records, 6537 Austin St., Rego Park, NY 11374). Among discs now available we mention the following: *Magyar hangszeres népzene* (Hungarian Instrumental Folk Music), Hungaroton

LPX 18045–47 (3 discs), ed. Bálint Sárosi; *Magyar népzene* (Hungarian Folk Music), Qualiton LPX 10095–98 and Hungaroton LPX 18001–4 (8 discs), ed. Benjamin Rajeczky; and *Magyarországi cigány népdalok* (Gypsy Folk Songs from Hungary), Hungaroton SLPX 18028–29 (2 discs), collected and ed. Rudolf Vig. *Folk Music of Hungary*, Folkways P 1000, and *Hungarian Folk Songs*, Folkways FM 4000, both presenting material collected by Béla Bartók, are also to be recommended. A valuable series of at least fifteen recordings of Greek traditional music has appeared from the Society for the Dissemination of National Music (Ersis 9 and Pulcherias, Athens, Greece), with notes in Greek and English. The following recordings give samplings of Eastern European folk music: *Czech, Slovak and Moravian Folk Songs*, Monitor MF 389; *Czech Songs and Dances*, Apon 2473; *Slovak Instrumental Folk Music Anthology*, Opus Stereo 9117 1021–3; *Folk Music of Yugoslavia*, Folkways 4434; *Were You of Silver, Were You of Gold: Original Music Folklore of Croatia*, Jugoton LPX-V-739, recorded by Ivan Ivančan and Jerko Bezić; *Traditional Songs and Dances from the Soko Banja Area* (in eastern Serbia), Selo LP-1, recordings and commentary by Robert Henry Leibman (available from Festival Records, 161 Turk St., San Francisco, CA 94102); *Music from the Island of Krk, Yugoslavia*, Folkways FE 4060, recorded by Wolfgang and Dagmar Laade; *Folk Music of Rumania*, collected by Bartók, Folkways 4419; *Rumania: Traditional Folk Music*, EMI Odeon C 064–18120; *Folk Dances of Greece*, Folkways FE 4467; *Folk Music of Greece*, Folkways FE 4454; *Polish Folk Songs and Dances*, Folkways FW 6848; and *Grajcie Dudy Grajcie Basy: Polish Folk Music*, Polskie Nagranie Muza SX 1125–26. *Greek-Jewish Musical Traditions*, Folkways FE 4205, recorded and annotated by Amnon Shiloah, is a more specialized collection. *Liptov: Panoráma l'udovej piesňovej a hudobnej kultúry*, Opus Stereo 9117 1211–14, recorded by S. Straćina and others, is an intensive investigation of the folk music of one valley region in Slovakia.

SIX

FRANCE, ITALY,
AND THE IBERIAN PENINSULA

The area comprising France, Italy, Spain, and Portugal is distinguished by its particularly long and close association with art music. This is especially true of France and Italy, the nations which, since the Middle Ages, have perhaps more consistently than any others had a tradition of urban civilization, of learned courts and monasteries, and of the trappings of art music such as notation and written theory. It has often been thought that these countries, as a result, now have little folk music except for a residue of earlier art music which has somehow trickled down to the rural communities. Indeed, certain song and dance types now part of folklore did originate in the art music tradition of the Middle Ages; for that matter, this art music tradition (for example, that of the troubadours and trouvères) certainly had more in common with folk traditions than did later art music traditions in Europe, such as the symphony orchestras of the nineteenth century and their music. Some of the forms of contemporary folk music, such as that of the French *branle* in Example 6-1, are pointedly similar to

EXAMPLE 6-1. Excerpt from "Branle carré," French instrumental piece, played on the hurdy-gurdy. Transcribed by Bruno Nettl from the recording *Folk Music of France*, edited by Paul Arma, with introduction and notes on the recordings by Paul Arma (New York: Ethnic Folkways Library FE 4414, 1951), Side A, Band 1.

forms found in medieval instrumental music—in this case the *stantipes*, which also consists of a series of repeated musical lines with first and second endings. Whether this form originated in folk or art music, it is obviously an example of the close relationship between the two traditions. But folklorists have also uncovered enclaves in which folk music seems to have developed with much less influence from the cities, and styles which appear to have grown with an amazing degree of independence.

FRENCH FOLK MUSIC AND ITS TIES TO ART MUSIC OF THE PAST

In France, the main areas preserving old traditions are in the South, near the Pyrenees, and in Brittany—relatively isolated regions, as one might expect. On the whole, the French folk songs have the same kinds of functions and uses as those in England, Germany, and the Low Countries. Ballads are not quite so numerous, nor are songs involving religion, and lyrical love songs, humorous songs, and dance music are among the most prominent types.

A large number of dances—whether they were used in the peasant culture, in the towns, or at the courts we don't always know—are described in Thoinot Arbeau's *Orchésographie* (1589); and a number of these dances are still alive in folklore today. Notable among them is the previously mentioned *branle*, performed either as a round dance or by two lines of dancers facing each other, in moderately quick duple meter.

Example 6-1 is a *branle* performed on a hurdy-gurdy. The tune exhibits some interesting characteristics. It is in straight duple meter. (Most French folk music is in duple or triple meter, with little evidence of the parlando-rubato style in either instrumental or vocal music.) The tune is heptatonic and, if it made use of the note A, could be considered as alternating between the major and Lydian modes. It contains a tritonic tetrachord (e.g., C-D-E-F#), which is also common in several styles of instrumental folk music, particularly in the Alps, and which composers of art music have sometimes consciously introduced to impart a folk flavor. The form of this piece is related not only to Western European medieval forms, but also to instumental folk music forms found throughout Europe, even as far away as the Cheremis in interior Russia.

The hurdy-gurdy performing Example 6-1 is a string instrument, and is not to be confused with the barrel organ also known by that name. It has a number of strings, all but one of which are used only as drones. Instead of fingering the instrument, the player uses a kind of keyboard with mechanical stops which shorten the melody string. And instead of a bow, a rosined wheel is cranked; this touches all of the strings and automatically produces a melody with drone accompaniment. The unbroken character of the music gives it a bagpipe-like effect. The hurdy-gurdy is known in France as the *vielle*, but this should not be confused with the simple medieval fiddle also known by that name. Indeed, known by a Latin name, *organistrum*, the hurdy-gurdy was important in the Middle Ages, and was evidently used (probably in a somewhat larger form, played by two men) in churches. It was evidently once much more widespread in Europe, and variants of it appear in corners of the continent, for example, in Sweden, whose *nyckelharpa* is almost identical with the French hurdy-gurdy except that it is played with a bow instead of a wheel.

The importance of melodies accompanied by drones is remarkable in European folk music, perhaps sufficiently so to make this one of the special characteristics of Europe. However, the drone is of great importance in Middle and Near Eastern music as well. A number of otherwise unrelated instruments seem fashioned especially for use as drones. Besides the hurdy-gurdy there is, of course, the bagpipe (which, known as *cornemuse*, is common in France and has evidently been popular there for centuries, as is attested to by the many pieces entitled "Musette" in seventeenth- and eighteenth-century art music). The double flutes or clarinets of the Balkans, such as the Yugoslav *dvojnice*, use one pipe for melody, the other for drone. The dulcimer is frequently used in similar fashion. But even in the music of instruments that because of their structure are not especially suited to drones, the drone principle is often present. Thus Anglo-American fiddle

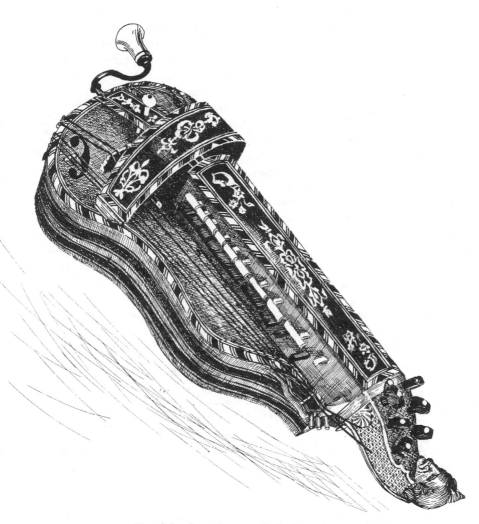

French hurdy-gurdy, or *vielle* (eighteenth century)

players and the performers on the Norwegian *hardingfele* often strike open strings in addition to the melody tones, producing a kind of interrupted drone effect. And the chordal accompaniment on instruments such as the banjo and the guitar frequently revolves around a single chord, which gives an effect related to the drone.

In spite of regional diversity and even though archaic styles of French music exist in isolated pockets, the predominant style of French folk music shows the powerful impact that art music through the centuries must have had. The typical tunes are isometric, they have major or (much less commonly) melodic minor tonality, they are monophonic or accompanied by chords or drones, and they move briskly in strophic forms. Singing is with relaxed voice and with little ornamentation. The fact that some of the French forms can be related, whether through the etymology of their names or through their structure, to some of the genres of music (such as the dances) of the Renaissance and Middle Ages should prove to us the close contact that exists between art and folk music. In the last three or four centuries, this relationship can also be shown in the diffusion of the quadrille and its relative, the square dance. This type of dance evidently originated in France some time before the eighteenth century and was a sort of transition between round and couple dances. It became a dance popular in the cities and at the courts, had a period of being stately and dignified, and then its tempo was again accelerated. In the nineteenth century it gradually declined as an urban dance but found its way again into rural folk culture, eventually becoming the typical folk dance of the English-speaking world. Similarly, remnants of medieval forms of troubadour song seem to have found their way into contemporary folk culture. For example, Carlos Vega[1] claimed to have found variants of medieval troubadour melodies from Provence in Argentine folk tradition.

ITALIAN FOLK MUSIC—THE ANCIENT AND THE MODERN

Earlier in this century it was widely believed that Italy had no folk music and that the country had been in the grip of musical sophisticates for so long that no folk heritage with its characteristic traits—oral tradition, communal recreation, and the like—still remained. In the 1950s, however, through the collecting efforts of several scholars including Diego Carpitella and Alan Lomax, a great treasure of folk music quite different from art music and exhibiting great variety of style and forms was uncovered. Carpitella[2] maintained the existence of a rather sharp division between an

---

[1] Carlos Vega, in a paper read at the First Inter-American Conference on Musicology, Washington, DC, May 1963.

[2] Diego Carpitella, "Folk Music: Italy," *Grove's Dictionary of Music and Musicians*, 5th ed. (New York: St. Martin's Press, 1960), X, 137.

ancient style, found largely in lullabies, work songs, and funeral laments, and a modern style, found largely in lyrical songs. The ancient style is characterized by the church modes and, occasionally, by scales with five and fewer tones. The later style (which evidently really did come about through the growth of art music) is characterized by the use of major and of harmonic and melodic minor scales, as well as by the use of harmonic accompaniment and of melodies constructed on a latent harmonic background. The ancient style is found mainly in those regions of Italy which have remained relatively undeveloped and unmodernized, and which, even after 1950, had a noticeably lower standard of living than did the rest of the nation; these regions are the mountains of south and central Italy, and the islands of Sicily and Sardinia.

Among the most interesting finds of the recent upsurge in ethnomusicological research in Italy is a rich tradition of polyphony. Among the simpler instances is Example 6-2, a kind of duet recitative. A beginning by a soloist who is joined by a second voice is typical of this style, though not found in this example (see Example 5-8 for a Ukranian example of this feature which is found in many European countries and in Africa). In Example 6-2, the movement is largely in parallel thirds, which is a feature also common in Italian popular and light classical music. Of special interest is the divergence of the two voices from unison to fifth in the second half of the first line, the parallel fifths in the middle of the song, and the ending on a unison: These are reminiscent of medieval *organum*.

A characteristic of some of the more complex Italian polyphony is the alternation of melodic movement among the voices. While one voice sings a bit of melody, the other one is sustained; in the next phrase, the previously sustained voice becomes the carrier of the melody, and so on in alternation. The use of different kinds of rhythmic structure in each voice is also typical; one voice may carry the main tune, another may sing sustained notes supplying harmony, while a third may sing a rapid rhythmic figure with nonlexical syllables on one tone perhaps imitating a drumbeat. Polyphonic singing is found in various kinds of Italian song—shepherds'

EXAMPLE 6-2. Italian polyphonic folk song, from Alberto Favara, *Corpus di musiche siciliane* (Palermo: Accademia de Scienze, Lettere e Arti, 1957), I, 225.

Mas - sa - ru Ma - ri - a - nu, mi vog - ghiu spi - a - ghè,

Se suo ch'a vi 'na fig - ghia, se'a vu - li — ma - ri - è.

songs and songs of dock workers and sailors. Some of the polyphony makes use of instruments as well as of voices; in such cases the singers are often accompanied by instruments that can produce a drone, bagpipes, a small organ, or the *launeddas* (see following section).

The influence of cultures outside Italy on Italian polyphony may explain some of the regional differences. The North of Italy, which is dominated by the more modern style of folk song and by singing in parallel thirds and sixths, has had close contact with the Alpine musical cultures with their love of triadic structures. The South has had less contact with Europe and has preserved older forms. Influences from Africa and the Near East can perhaps also be felt in the South. According to Carpitella,[3] a type of song sung in the tunny-fishery areas near North Africa is characterized by the kind of call-and-response patterns common also in sub-Saharan African music and found sometimes in North Africa as well. If he is correct in his belief that this song type actually came from Africa, he has come upon an interesting early example of the kind of influence on Western music that African music has come to exercise so strongly in the last two centuries, for it is precisely this call-and-response pattern which has been one of the cornerstones of the various Afro-American styles in folk and popular music.

The instruments most evident in Italian folk music are those which have been taken over from the cultivated tradition: violin, guitar, mandolin, clarinet, and accordion. But there are also much older instruments, some of which seem to have remained relatively unchanged since classical times, in the more isolated parts of the nation: various percussion instruments (clappers, rattles), conch trumpets, the Jew's harp, panpipes, simple bagpipes with up to three drone pipes, recorder-like plugged flutes, reed pipes, and ocarinas made of fired clay. One of the most intriguing, found mainly in Sardinia, is the *launeddas*, which consists of three reed pipes. The longest and medium-sized of these are fastened together and held in the left hand (these are called *tumbu* and *mancosa* respectively); the smallest one, *mancosedda*, is held in the right hand. The *launeddas* is used for polyphonic music of the drone type, similar to that played on the Yugoslav *dvojnice*, and often accompanies dances or songs. One of the problems faced by the player is the need to keep blowing without pausing for breath; it is solved by a technique of blowing air out of the mouth while inhaling with the nose called circular breathing, also found in distant parts of the world such as Australia, whose aboriginal *didjeridu* players use the same technique. A boy learning to play the *launeddas* learns circular breathing, as have Mediterranean musicians since Egyptian antiquity, by blowing through a straw into a pail of water. The teacher can see whether the pupil is succeeding by observing the bubbles in the water.

[3] Carpitella, "Folk Music: Italy," p. 140.

The close relationship between Italian folk and art music during the past few centuries is also illustrated by the sources of the words of some of the songs. In central Italy, a type of song (or perhaps a sequence of songs) known as *maggio* is sung during May. Its words are frequently taken from the works of famous poets—Ariosto, Tasso, Dante, even classical poets such as Virgil and Ovid. Its structure is evidently related to some of the earliest manifestations of opera around 1600. The form of the *maggio* consists of a choral or instrumental introduction, recitatives, and instrumental or choral interludes which recur, functioning rather like refrains or *ritornellos* (instrumental refrain-like pieces in early opera). In thematic content the various parts of a *maggio* are not necessarily related; the recitative may be in the modal style of ancient Italian folk music, the choral section may have some features found in the part-songs of Renaissance Italian art music, and the instrumental sections may be popular dances such as polkas or tarantellas.

THE BASQUES—EUROPE'S OLDEST FOLK CULTURE?

Legend has it that the Basques are the oldest people in Europe, but they seem to have retained little of their ancient heritage of folklore. On the contrary, they seem to have partaken of the traditions of northern Spain and southwestern France, and their culture is a repository of archaic forms of that region, both French and Spanish. For example, young Basque men have a custom, also found in other parts of Europe, of going from house to house on the last Saturday of January, wishing the inhabitants good health and a good life, and singing songs to them. Elsewhere, this may be done before Christmas and even at Easter, and the singers may be young boys and girls. Another custom shared by the Basques with some other areas of Europe is the singing of "rough music" around the house of people who have engaged in some presumably immoral act.[4] An adulterous couple, an old man who marries a young girl, or a wife who beats her husband may be visited by a group who use pots, pans, and cowbells as rhythmic accompaniment to improvised, insulting songs. In Germany and other countries, similar music is performed on a wedding night or on the night before a wedding.

We know very little about the ways in which European folk songs were composed. This applies to words as well as music, although we realize that some of the material was composed by sophisticated song writers and then passed into oral tradition. Among the Basques, improvisation has been particularly important; it is even thought that most of the Basque folk songs originated on the spur of the moment. Evidently the Basque language (which

[4] Rodney Gallop, "Basque Songs from Soule," *Musical Quarterly*, XXII (1936), 461.

is said to be so difficult that not even the devil can learn it) lends itself easily to improvisatory rhyming. Many improvised poems of the Basques have a humorous or satirical character and deal with events of village interest, politics, and the church. Many are anticlerical in sentiment. Evidently the improvised text was sung to a traditional tune, and most Basque men participated in the practice of improvising words. A few of them gained preeminence, and some of their songs still carry their names after years and decades. This is one of the few examples in a folk culture of a composer's being recognized and associated with works years after he composed them. The most famous Basque improviser, or *kolaris*, was known as Etchahoun and was born in the valley of Soule in 1786.

Like a large proportion of the Spanish and French songs, Basque songs are frequently in 6/8 meter and make use of the church modes; the latter is true of the ballad in Example 6-3, which is Dorian. More complex meters, such as 5/8, are also common, as are songs without ascertainable metric structure. The most famous illustration of quintuple meter in Basque folk music is the *zortziko*, a type of melody used mainly for dance tunes. The forms of Basque songs consist of from four to six phrases, interrelated in various ways. Lullabies frequently consist of varied repetitions of a single

EXAMPLE 6-3. French singing game, "Yan petit," from Violet Alford, "Dance and Song in Two Pyrenean Valleys," *Musical Quarterly*, XVII (1931), 253.

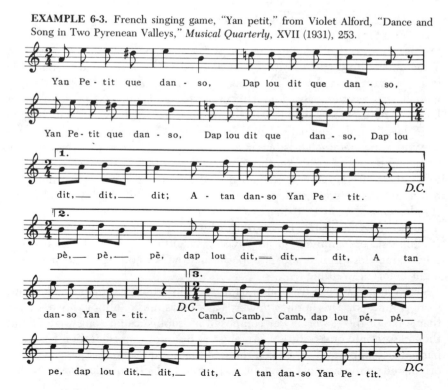

musical line (A^1 A^2 A^3 . . .), and love songs and dance songs have forms such as ABCC, ABCB, AABCD, AABB, and AABCDC.

Instrumental folk music among the Basques features a three-holed flute (*chirula* or *txirula*) and the *ttunttun*, an instrument with six strings, similar to the dulcimer but held in the arm. The same player uses both instruments, accompanying the tunes of the *chirula* with a drone on the *ttunttun*. Instrumental music is used in dances and for *mascaradas*, processions accompanied by dances performed at carnival time. This custom is one found throughout Europe, but it is preserved in very elaborate form in the Basque country. Ceremonial dances are performed by certain stock characters—the hobby horse, which is surely a remnant of the tournaments of the Middle Ages, the fool, the sweeper, and the lord and the lady. Similar practices are found in the Afro-Uruguayan *candombe*, which, interestingly enough, features a broommaker analogous to our "sweeper" (see Chapter 10). Among the Basques there is a sword dance which, like those of France, Spain, and England, was probably originally a representation of the century-long struggle between Christians and Moors. There is also an acrobatic dance in which dancers leap and turn in complicated steps around and over a tumbler of wine without upsetting it. Basque instrumental music is similar in style to the songs, but the song tunes themselves do not normally seem to be used by the instrumentalists.

The Basques have also retained a form of the medieval mystery play, called *pastorales*. These folk plays make use of interpolated songs which appear at particularly important points in the plot. The themes of the *pastorales* are biblical or legendary and frequently hark back to the battles of Christians against Moors in the Iberian peninsula. No matter what the plot, the characters are divided into Moors or Turks dressed in red costumes, and Christians, in blue. The battles for national or cultural survival in Spain and France have evidently had just as great an impact on the development of folklore as have the struggles against the Turks in Yugoslavia, with its epic tradition, or as did the fights between Christian and Tartar in Russia.

SPAIN AND PORTUGAL—A REGION OF GREAT DIVERSITY

There is great variety in the folk music of the Iberian peninsula. Particularly, there is a great difference between the North, which is closely related to France and Italy, and the South, which bears much resemblance to North Africa and the Middle East, and, thus, also to the Balkan peninsula (due to the importance of Arabic influences on Spanish culture throughout the Middle Ages and to a smaller degree ever since). Beyond this major difference, each area has its own folk music repertory and styles. Nevertheless, there is also considerable unity: Few listeners would fail, after some experience, to recognize a Spanish folk melody. Of course, the many kinds of folk songs have also spread to Latin America, where together with Afro-American and, to a smaller degree, American Indian elements, they form the basis of a huge wealth of folklore.

It is difficult to identify and separate those traits which make Spanish or Portuguese folk music distinctive. Triple meter abounds: Slow triple meter, usually noted as 3/4, and quicker, compound meters such as 6/8 and 9/8 are very common. But songs in duple meter are also found, as are some in quintuple. There is also a great deal of recitative-like singing, without metric structure, and with considerable ornamentation, similar to types of song found in the eastern Mediterranean. Scales tend to be diatonic and the tonality major, natural minor, or characterized by the use of augmented and minor seconds, thus:

Intervals are small, and large leaps are rare. The forms of the songs are often strophic, like those of Italy and France, but the length of the lines is often less regular. But other kinds of formal organization, less tight and less standardized, are also found. There is a good deal of polyphonic singing, mainly in parallel thirds or sixths or with the accompaniment of a drone.

The influence of Arabic music on Spanish folk song seems to have been considerable, which is not surprising when we remember the long period of Arab rule over the peninsula (ninth through fifteenth centuries). Specific tunes from the Arabic tradition do not seem to have remained in any large numbers, however. The scales with augmented seconds may have been introduced by the Arabs, or they may have developed as a result of Arabic influence; such intervals are a typical feature of much Arab music. The great amount of ornamentation found in some of the melodies that have no metric structure may also ultimately be of Near Eastern origin, for singing of a related sort is found in some Arab music of today. Example 6-4 is such a melody from Santander.

Perhaps a more important feature common to both Spanish and Arab music is the manner of singing, which is rather tense, nasal, and harsh-sounding. Again, similarities to the Balkan styles of singing may be noted. Ornaments of a modest sort are found in many songs; the mordent and the turn are particularly common. The tempo of Spanish songs may be rapid, vigorous, and downright driving, or, on the other hand, slow and stately.

Among the many kinds of song in Spain and Portugal we should mention the *copla*, which is a short, lyrical type, often improvised and usually with only one stanza. Ballads are also found in Spain; they deal, frequently, with the heroism of medieval warriors such as Charlemagne and El Cid, and their content has more in common with the epics of Eastern Europe than with the old tragic ballads of Britain, impersonal as the latter usually are. The arrangement of a group of ballads around a hero is rather

EXAMPLE 6-4. Spanish folk song, from Kurt Schindler, *Folk Music and Poetry of Spain and Portugal* (New York: Hispanic Institute in the United States, 1941), song no. 530.

Vi - va la Mon - - - ta ña! vi - -

- - - - - - - - - - va! ijuji!

Vi - va la Mon - - - ta - ña!

vi - - - - - - - va!

Vi - va el hom - bre - - - - -

mon - ta - nes! - - - - - ijuji!

Vi - va el hom - bre mon - ta -

ñes!

Que si la Mon - ta - ña mue - - re

Es - pa - ña per - - - - -

di - da es a!

like the clustering of epic tales around a leader such as the Serbian Kraljevic Marko (Prince Marko), and it has something in common with the cycle of Robin Hood ballads, which were once sung throughout Great Britain. Some of the themes of Spanish balladry are of wide origins, however; the same stories have been found, on occasion, in French and Scandinavian songs.

When one thinks of Spanish folk music one perhaps thinks automatically of dancing, and, of course, there are many Spanish folk dance types: the *jota*, the *gitana*, the *seguidillas*, the *bolero*, the *fandango*, the *murciana*, and others too numerous to mention. Each district has its own version of the dance types of national provenience. The *jota*, a combination of song and dance, is one of the most interesting. In rapid triple meter, it is danced by a couple—originally it was probably a dance of courtship—whose complicated footwork and tricky castanet rhythms are especially fascinating.

The *flamenco* tradition of Andalusia in southern Spain is perhaps the most widely known aspect of Spanish folk music. It is not typically Spanish, for it is particularly the music of the Spanish gypsies (although it probably did not originate with them but was simply taken over by them). The gypsies, who inhabit many countries of Southern and Eastern Europe, have a tradition of entertaining and, evidently, a talent for emphasizing and exaggerating the most characteristic elements of the folk music in each country in which they live (in addition to continuing their native tradition). Thus, for example, the Russian gypsies have developed a style out of the Russian folk tradition, and the Spanish gypsies have fashioned the *flamenco* style out of elements already present in Spain.

One type of *flamenco* music is the *cante hondo*, which means "deep" or "profound song." The words are frequently tragic, sometimes verses of complaint against injustices. The range of these songs rarely exceeds a sixth, and the structure is not strophic but consists of irregular repetitions and alternations of two or more phrases with variations. The singing is highly ornamented and contains occasional microtones; a hoarse, nasal vocal quality is a distinctive feature of *flamenco*. The *cante hondo* is often accompanied by the guitar, which performs simple repetitive chord sequences dominated by figures such as ♩ ♫♫ , and may also contribute more melodic passagework and interludes. The words of *flamenco* proper are usually erotic, and the dance is performed by a soloist or a couple, with the audience participating with encouraging shouts of "olé."

In order to give a somewhat more intimate insight into one aspect of Spanish folk music culture, let us consider briefly the performers on the *dulzaina* (*dulzaineros*) in the province of Léon, in northwestern Spain.[5] The *dulzaina* is an oboe-like instrument that has evidently been widely used in the area for centuries, but is not necessarily known in all of its

---

[5] The material here on the *dulzaina* is based on field research carried out by Martha E. Davis, when a graduate student in anthropology at the University of Illinois.

villages. In earlier times, the *dulzaina* was used by shepherds in order to help pass the time. It was also played in various social situations—dances, serenades, and spontaneous gatherings, such as feasts held after a hunt. Furthermore, it was used on semireligious occasions, such as the dances performed on Epiphany or certain saints' days, and it was even used as part of the liturgy, playing processionals and recessionals in church, and even parts of the mass. There was usually one *dulzainero* per village, and, clearly, he occupied an important role in village life. These musicians seem to have been professionals who performed without pay in their own villages, but were paid when asked to perform elsewhere. The *dulzainero* was frequently accompanied by singing (sometimes his function was to stimulate people to join in and sing), and by a drummer (who was the junior partner of a rather stable combination), and sometimes by tambourines and castanets. Today, the instrument is used far less. Most of the *dulzaineros* are elderly men, some of them reluctant to play because their music is regarded as backward by more modern-minded villagers, and they restrict their music to their own homes and to the late evenings. One reaction to the dwindling of *dulzaina* playing and the modernizing trend has been the establishment of *dulzaina* competitions with prizes. Shepherds no longer play the instrument, and in social gatherings it has been replaced by accordion and saxophone. Priests have forbidden its use in certain churches. But the instrument has not disappeared, having been adapted to new repertories such as urban popular songs, and having been changed to resemble, in appearance and sound, the modern clarinet.

Throughout these discussions of European folk music, we have pointed out the close relationship of this body of music with musics elsewhere. Despite the fact that European folk music forms a rather homogeneous unit, contrasting markedly with the musics of other cultures such as China, India, Africa, and aboriginal America, those parts of Europe which are near other continents exhibit influences that testify to the mobility of music. Spanish folk music is perhaps the best example of this kind of mobility. The music of Spain has received much of its character from Asia, by way of North Africa; it has, in turn, passed on this material to the Americas, where it combined with elements of yet other cultures, to form new and characteristic styles. At the same time, the musics of Spain and Portugal partake of the general character of European folk music through their similarity to the musics of France and Italy, the nations to whom they are historically and linguistically most closely related.

BIBLIOGRAPHICAL AND DISCOGRAPHICAL NOTES

A large collection of French folk song is Émile Barbillat and Laurian Touraine, *Chansons populaires dans le Bas-Berri*, 5 vols. (Paris: Gargaillou, 1930–31). The best discussion in English of French folk music is by Claude Marcel-

Dubois in *The New Grove Dictionary of Music and Musicians*, VI, 756–64. Rodney Gallop, "Basque Songs from Soule," *Musical Quarterly*, XXII (1936), 458–69, and Violet Alford, "Dance and Songs in Two Pyrenean Valleys," *Musical Quarterly*, XVII (1931), 248–58, are interesting readings on the area common to France and Spain; Jean-Michel Guilcher, *La tradition de danse en Béarn et pays basque français* (Paris: Maison des Sciences de l'Homme, 1984), explores dance traditions in the Basque provinces of France and in the adjoining province of Béarn.

Kurt Schindler, *Folk Music and Poetry of Spain and Portugal* (New York: Hispanic Institute, 1941) is a large and comprehensive collection of Spanish and Portuguese music. Josep Crivillé i Bargalló, *El folklore musical* (Madrid: Alianza Editorial, 1983), is an authoritative study of Spanish folk music. Israel J. Katz, "The Traditional Folk Music of Spain: Explorations and Perspectives," *Y-IFMC*, VI (1974), 64–85, presents an overview of Spanish folk music scholarship and collections. An illuminating study of the *flamenco* tradition, written by a participant in the tradition, is Paul Hecht, *The Wind Cried* (New York: Dial Press, 1968). Israel J. Katz's article, "Flamenco," in *The New Grove Dictionary*, VI, 625–30, surveys its history and musical characteristics.

The best discussions in English of Italian folk music are by Diego Carpitella, in *Grove's Dictionary of Music and Musicians*, 5th ed., the supplement volume (1960); and Roberto Leydi, in *The New Grove Dictionary*, IX, 382–92. Ralph Carriuolo, *Materials for the Study of Italian Folk Music* (Ann Arbor: University Microfilms, 1974), is a comprehensive English-language bibliography. Among folk song collections we mention Roberto Leydi, *I canti popolari italiani* (Milan: Armando Mondadori, 1973), and Alberto Favara, *Corpus di musiche popolari siciliane*, 2 vols. (Palermo: Accademia di Scienze, Lettere e Arti, 1957). Discussion of one song type appears in Wolfgang Laade, "The Corsican Tribbiera, A Kind of Work Song," *Ethnomusicology*, VI (1962), 181–85. The interaction of folk and popular traditions in Trent is examined by Marcello Sorce Keller in "Life of a Traditional Ballad in Oral Tradition and Choral Practice: 'Sul castel di Mirabel,'" *Ethnomusicology*, XXX (1986), 449–69. A comprehensive treatment of one important instrument is Andreas Fridolin Weis Bentzon, *The Launeddas: A Sardinian Folk-Music Instrument*, 2 vols. (Copenhagen: Akademisk Forlag, 1969).

For selections of French, Hispanic, and Italian folk music, the appropriate discs from the *Columbia World Library of Folk and Primitive Music* are very useful. *Folk Music of France*, Folkways 4414, and *Anthologie de la musique traditionnelle française*, Le Chant du Monde LDX 74516, 74635 (2 discs), Vol. I recorded by Jean-Loup Baly and others, Vol. II by Alain Ribardière, are also to be recommended. The hurdy-gurdy is featured on *Sonneurs de vielles traditionnels en Bretagne*, Le Chasse-Marée SCM 005 (2 discs). Portuguese folk music is collected on *Music of Portugal*, Folkways FE 4538 (2 discs), *Chants et danses du Portugal*, Le Chant du Monde LDY 4150, 4190 (2 discs), and *Portugal*, EMI-Odeon C 064–17843. Good collections from Spain are *Songs and Dances of Spain*, Westminster WF 12001–5, with notes by Alan Lomax, and *Flamenco Music of Andalusia*, Folkways 4437. *Early Cante Flamenco*, Folklyric 9001, is a set of rereleases of *flamenco* performances recorded in the 1930s.

The volumes of the *Columbia World Library of Folk and Primitive Music* devoted to Italian folk music, recorded by Alan Lomax and Diego Carpitella in the 1950s, are important documents. Samplings of Italian folk music may be found on *Folk Music from Italy*, Folkways F 4220; and *Music and Songs of Italy*, Tradition TLP 1030, with notes by Lomax and Carpitella. Of the many recordings issued more recently, two ongoing series of discs based on field recordings are particularly worthy of note. A six-volume series from Folkways presents the folk music of various regions of Italy, complete with extensive notes by Lomax, Carpitella, and others. Among volumes released to date are *Piedmont, Emilia, Lombardy* (Vol. I), FE 4261, and *Naples, Campania* (Vol. V), FE 4265. Recordings of Italian folk music are also being produced by the Vedette Company of Milan as part of the series *Documenti originali del folklore musicale europeo*, on the Albatros label (with notes by Roberto Leydi). *La canzone narrative lo spettacolo popolare*, Albatros VPA 8088, presents urban and rural material from several areas of Italy; *La zampogna in Italia e le launeddas*, Albatros VPA 8149, highlights two folk instruments.

SEVEN

MUSIC OF SUB-SAHARAN AFRICA

The music of sub-Saharan Africa has been regarded as an essentially homogeneous mass, despite the many inhabitants and the large number of distinct cultures, and despite the many contacts that Africa has had, over the centuries, with peoples of other continents. It is true that hearing a few records of African music will probably give the listener a fairly good overview of the mainstream of the African styles. But it has become increasingly clear that the total picture of African music is a very complex one, that there is a large variety of substyles, and that cultures vary greatly in the nature of their music, in its quantity and significance, and in the attitudes that people hold toward it. As in other chapters, we must here confine ourselves to a few examples of the kinds of things that are found, realizing that generalizations about African music can be made only with great caution.

We are considering the music of Africa, south of the Sahara only, in this volume. The area north of the Sahara and the Sahara itself have music which is very closely related to that of the Middle East and is thus discussed in another volume in this series, William P. Malm's *Music Cultures of the Pacific, the Near East, and Asia.* But there has, of course, been a great deal of exchange between the North Africans and the inhabitants of the rest of the continent. Instruments, such as harps and drums, have evidently been carried from one area to the other; similar formal types and certain techniques, such as responsorial singing, are held in common. There are some peoples, at the boundary between the two areas, who have music in both the distinctly sub-Saharan African and the North African styles. On the other hand, whereas North African music has ties with the Middle East, the music of sub-Saharan Africa has had, in the past two or three centuries, an enormous impact on the musical development of Europe and the Americas.

The part of Africa discussed here—and, for the sake of brevity, we will call it simply "Africa" from now on—is composed of (or was, before parts of it became thoroughly modernized) four culture areas, each of which has considerable homogeneity, and each of which contrasts in some rather specific ways with its neighbors. The western part of the very tip of southern Africa is called the Khoi-San area; it is inhabited by the Bushmen and Hottentots. The Bushmen are a somewhat different group, racially, from Negroes, shorter and lighter skinned; the Hottentots are evidently the result of a racial mixture between Bushmen and Negroes. The Khoi-San area has a simple culture dependent mainly on nomadic gathering of food.

The eastern part of our Africa, from Ethiopia southward, is called the Eastern Cattle Area. Its cultures are complex and revolve about cattle, one of the main sustaining forces of life and also the symbol of wealth. Some of the tribes are warlike; some, such as the Masai and Watusi, are very tall and rule over neighboring tribes of smaller stature, living near them and maintaining a caste-like relationship.

The southern coast of the western extension of the continent, which includes Ghana, Nigeria, Ivory Coast, and Liberia, is known as the Guinea Coast. This area lacks cattle and is characterized by elaborate political organization which, before the imposition of European rule, gave rise to powerful kingdoms. Carved masks of great beauty are also typical here. The Congo area, north of the Khoi-San area and centered in the Congo republics, has to some extent a combination of Eastern Cattle and Guinea Coast traits. It includes a number of Pygmy and Negrito tribes who live in relative isolation in the jungle. The Congo area probably has the most highly developed visual art tradition in Africa.

A fifth area that properly belongs to sub-Saharan Africa consists of a strip immediately north of the Guinea Coast, and includes the northern sections of such nations as Ghana and Nigeria. Its cultures are related to those of the Guinea Coast and the Congo, but many of the peoples who inhabit it are Muslims.

There are several characteristics, found in a majority of African musical cultures, that give African music its distinctiveness. Several of them are discussed in some detail further on, but here is a brief listing: (1) Instruments are numerous; they are used individually, as accompaniment to singing, and in small ensembles. (2) There is a tendency to have at least two things going on at a time. Thus polyphony is widespread; polyrhythms performed by percussion ensembles are common; and even the players of simple instruments, such as the musical bow or the flute, may find ways, by manipulating the overtones produced by the bow, or by humming along with blowing, for example, to have two musical entities produced simultaneously. (3) The percussive sound is evidently an ideal; percussion instruments such as drums, xylophones, and rattles are important, but even in the use of wind instruments that are played in groups, with each producing only one tone, the percussive principle seems to be present, and plucked string instruments greatly outnumber those played with a bow. (4) Variation of and improvisation upon short melodic motifs dominate melodic structure. (5) There is a close relationship between language and music. (6) Melodies are built of major seconds and minor thirds. (7) Even more than elsewhere, music is associated with dance. (8) Perhaps most significant, there is a tendency toward dualism: thus melodies often consist of two phrases; performance is often by a leader and a chorus; polyphony is usually structured so that there are two parts or two groups of vocalists or instruments; and in various other obvious or subtle ways, one can detect the essentially binary nature of this music.

However, almost the opposite of these characteristics is found in the northernmost part of sub-Saharan Africa, where Middle Eastern influences are strong. Thus solo performances, monophony, nonpercussive instruments, such as fiddles and oboes, and smaller intervals, such as minor seconds, are more prominent. Some peoples, such as the Hausa of northern Nigeria, have music in both the typical African and the Middle East-influenced styles.

THE USES OF MUSIC IN AFRICA

In Africa, music has many uses. It serves as accompaniment to all sorts of activities, but also as entertainment. Some of the general characteristics usually given for music in nonliterate societies do not appear strongly in Africa. For example, the idea that participation in music in a primitive society is quite general and that all persons participate equally cannot be accepted. In contrast to many peoples elsewhere, there are professional musicians who actually make their living from music, or who are regarded as trained specialists. There are so many instruments that it would be ridiculous to think that all members of a society could perform on all of them and know all the society's music. But it cannot be denied that Africans, on the whole, do participate in musical life much more—and more actively, in singing, playing, composing, dancing—than do Westerners.

In at least some of the African cultures, elaborate classification of types of musicians exists. According to Merriam,[1] the Basongye of the Congo have five classes of male musicians: (1) the *ngomba*, the professional instrumentalist; (2) the performer of slit drums; (3) the player of rattles and double-bells; (4) the song leader; and (5) the member of a singing group. These are listed here in the order of their prestige; only the first is a full-time musician, the second and third also receive some pay, and the lowest two classes are never paid. Despite this evidence of concern with the relative status of various kinds of musicians, the Basongye generally do not regard musicians highly, and in this they reflect a tendency found in the majority of the world's cultures. Rather, they regard musicians as being of low status. Musicians are said to be heavy drinkers, debtors, unreliable, impotent, adulterers, poor marriage risks, and they are the butt of many jokes. People do not want their children to become musicians, but the musicians are nevertheless tolerated because they are essential to the life of the whole group. The picture presented by Merriam appears to be roughly similar to that of some other African cultures.

Obviously, also, Africans think about music a good deal. For example, some groups recognize many different types of songs and have elaborate terms for them. Thus, according to Merriam, the Bahutu of Ruanda-Burundi have at least twenty-four different types of social songs, including "those played by professional musicians for entertainment, songs for beer drinking, war homage to a chief, hunting, harvesting, and general work; songs sung at the birth of a child or to admonish erring members of the society, to recount a successful elephant hunt, to deride Europeans; songs of death, vulgar songs, and others."[2] These categories are separate from the other large group of ceremonial or religious songs. Some of these types are again subdivided by the Bahutu, who, for example, distinguish among different kinds of songs associated with canoes: different songs are used when paddling against a strong current, when paddling with the current, and so forth.

Also of Ruanda-Burundi, the Watusi, whose lives center about their cattle, have many song types involving them: "songs in praise of cows, songs to indicate the importance of having cows, songs for taking cattle home in the evening . . . for drawing water for the cattle,"[3] and the like.

[1] Alan P. Merriam, *The Anthropology of Music* (Evanston, IL: Northwestern University Press, 1969), pp. 129–30.

[2] Merriam, "African Music," in *Continuity and Change in African Cultures*, ed. William Bascom and Melville J. Herskovits (Chicago: University of Chicago Press, 1959), p. 50.

[3] Merriam, "African Music," p. 53.

There are special children's cattle songs, songs to praise the royal cattle, and songs that recount historical events in which cattle have played a part. There are two points to remember here: (1) This classification of songs is one developed by the Africans themselves, and (2) The music is a part of those activities which are most fundamental in the culture. In this sense, perhaps, music in African life can be said to have a greater or more important role than it does in the West.

It would be useless to attempt to catalogue all the uses of African music. In many ways they parallel those of European folk music. Religious and ceremonial music is an ever-present category whose importance evidently increases as we move from complex to simpler cultures. The large amount of music for entertainment, such as the playing of xylophones at markets, is remarkable. Social songs, such as those mentioned earlier, are a larger category than in most folk and nonliterate societies. Examples of the association of music with political strata and with the ruling individuals or classes abound. Among the Hausa of Nigeria, elaborate fanfares are played for ruling chiefs. The "royal drums" of the Watusi signal the appearance of the ruler in public. And among the Venda of South Africa we find an elaborate system (by no means unique in its general character but similar to systems found elsewhere in Africa) of classifying musical types in accordance with the level of political leadership permitted to sponsor it. Evidently in some of the African cultures it is easier to indicate discontent with employers or with the government if the discontent is couched in song. We therefore find many songs expressing criticism of authority, but also songs composed especially to praise chiefs and wealthy men. Songs are used also to spread information on current events of interest and gossip, and to perpetuate knowledge, much in the way that broadside ballads functioned as newspapers in eighteenth-century England and America. Work songs—songs not only dealing with labor but also accompanying rhythmic work by groups and making it easier—are prominent in Africa. In the Western Congo, song-like passages appear in the litigations of clans and individuals who may argue about ownership of territory, wives, or honorific titles.

INSTRUMENTS OF AFRICA

One of the characteristics of Africa is its enormous variety of musical instruments. Far from being a land only of drums, as it was pictured by some early sources, it is an area in which varied instruments and instrumental music play a role equal to that of the voice and vocal music. There is in all areas a great deal of music for solo instruments, and there are instrumental ensemble groups consisting of unrelated instruments, or of several instruments of the same type. Also, accompanied singing is widespread.

The importance of rhythm in African music can be seen in the percussive quality of much of the instrumental sound. As we have noted, percussion instruments—drums, rattles, and melodic percussion instruments such as the xylophone—occupy a major role. Among the wind instruments, those in which each pipe performs only one note (in a group of flutes or horns, or on a single instrument such as the panpipes) are important. Among string instruments, those that are plucked are more prominent than the bowed ones. The percussive nature of much of the instrumental sound as well as the absence of the possibility of *legato* in the playing of most of the instruments is probably caused by the desire for strong rhythmic articulation.

It is impossible to describe or even to name all African instruments; some of the most important ones are discussed briefly in the next few paragraphs. Among the idiophones, the xylophone is one of the most widespread. Consisting of anywhere from seven to twenty-five slabs of wood, it varies greatly in size. The largest ones lie on the ground, supported by small tree trunks; the smallest hang around the player's neck. In Central Africa, xylophones are frequently built with calabashes, gourds, or other hollow vessels attached to the slabs in order to add to the resonance. They are frequently played in groups; in parts of Central Africa, three players will entertain at a market together. In the eastern part of southern Africa, among the Chopi, orchestras of six and more xylophones of various sizes are used. This point is of great interest, because there is some evidence for the belief that xylophones were brought to Africa from Indonesia, perhaps a thousand years ago. The people of Madagascar speak Malayo-Polynesian languages which must have originated near Indonesia. And for centuries the Indonesians have had a very complex musical culture with instruments made of metal, of the xylophone type. It seems possible that the xylophone was brought to Africa, or that the musical culture of Indonesia influenced the particular direction in which xylophones and xylophone playing developed in Africa. Xylophones of the simplest type—one or two slabs of wood which are struck—are found throughout the world, including indigenous Latin America; this has evidently given rise to an erroneous belief that the xylophone (or rather, its form with resonators, the marimba) came from Central America and was brought thence to Africa.

One instrument that apparently originated in Africa, and which is related to the xylophone, is the *mbira* or *sansa*, which is sometimes also called the "thumb piano." Its provenance is largely East and Central Africa, and, except for some Afro-American cultures, it is not found outside Africa. It consists of a small board or wooden box on which is nailed a bridge.

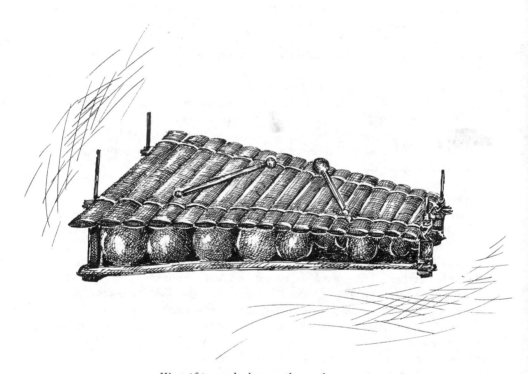

West African xylophone with gourd resonators

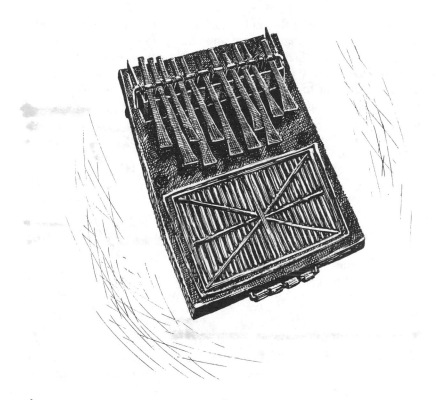

Mbira or sansa

Tied to this bridge are a number of keys, made usually of iron pieces pounded flat, but occasionally of reeds. These are gently plucked by the thumb or the fingers to produce a soft, tinkling sound. The number of keys varies from eight to about thirty. Frequently a calabash resonator is attached to the instrument; sometimes beads, which produce a rattling percussive accompaniment, are also attached. The *mbira* is played as a solo instrument or in groups. It is frequently used to accompany singing, and in some African music of recent origin it provides an ostinato accompaniment not too different from the piano accompaniments of certain Western popular songs. The tuning of the *mbira* varies, but in general the keys are positioned in such a way that desired melodic patterns can be divided conveniently between the hands. The keys of the *mbira* may be tuned by moving them forward or backward in relationship to the bridge, or by adding some pitch or tar to them in order to increase their weight.

Other idiophones include rattles, bells, and the misnamed log drums. There are many types of rattles—pebbles enclosed in small woven containers (West Africa) and in antelope ears (the Hottentots); rattles made of fruits, nuts, reeds, or cocoons strung together (South Africa); and so on. Sometimes they are tied to the ankles of dancers. One characteristic of these instruments is the importance evidently placed on distinctions in pitch. Rattles and bells (there are both metal and wooden bells) often appear in pairs, with one smaller than the other so that two pitches can be distinguished. This is also characteristic in the playing of the log drum, a hollowed log with one or two slits, which is most frequently used for signaling. Thus, although the rhythmic element seems to be pronounced in the melodic aspects of music and its instruments, we may also say that the melodic aspects of music are developed in that music and those instruments whose main function is rhythm.

There are several types of true drums, that is, drums with skin heads. The most common kinds have one head and are relatively tall; they are usually closed at the bottom. Two-headed drums and drums with an open end are also found. The drums are beaten with sticks, or with the hands, or both. Hand beating is characteristic, however, and the complex rhythms are often the results of intricate manipulation and alternation of fingers, thumb, and heel of the hand. Techniques somewhat similar to those of Africa are found in India, and there is a possibility that the rhythmic intricacies of Indian and African musics have a common origin. Typically drums are played in groups of three or more. They may stand on the ground, hang from a strap around the player's shoulder, be held in the player's arm or between the legs, or be sat upon when they are played.

The types of drums and of drumming may be intimately associated with different activities. Among the Yoruba of Nigeria, different types of drums are used for the various cults associated with the numerous gods in the Yoruba pantheon. For example, the *igbin* drums are upright drums with a single head, open-ended, with small wooden legs; *dundun* are hour-glass drums; *bata* drums are long truncated cones with two heads, one head being appreciably smaller than the other and producing a higher pitch; and there are several other types. Each type is used for one or several deities, and each deity has its distinctive rhythms, a practice carried over into parts of the Americas such as Haiti. Thus, as Bascom notes,[4] the *igbin* drums are sacred to *Orishanla* ("the great deity") and are played by members of his cult, among whom are albinos, hunchbacks, and cripples. *Bata* and *dundun* drums are played by professional drummers. *Dundun* are used for signaling—they are the "talking drums"—and are also used by the cult of *Egungun*, younger brother of the powerful *Shango* (the thunder god). *Bata* are sacred to the god *Shango* and his wife *Oya*, but may be played for other deities as well.

Several types of *aerophones* (wind instruments) are of great interest. Horns are common in various parts of Africa. They are made of natural horn, wood, or ivory, and are used for music as well as signaling. They usually have no finger holes or valve mechanism, and only the open or natural tones can be played. In recent times, however, finger holes seem to have been introduced. One characteristic of African horns is the position of the mouthpiece or hole used for blowing, which is frequently on the side of the instrument rather than at the small end as is common in European horns. One use of horns that produce only one pitch is in the *hocket* technique, in which each horn plays only when its note is supposed to appear in the melody.

Flutes are also frequently without finger holes; they are sometimes used for performance in the *hocket* technique in a fashion similar to horns. This is done particularly by Negro tribes of South Africa. Ensembles of flutes with finger holes are also found, as among the Mbuti pygmies of the Congo, who use as many as six flutes, each of which varies its own short ostinato figure. The flutes are most commonly true flutes rather than the plugged flutes like the recorder. Both end-blown and transverse flutes are found, the former being held vertically. Panpipes are also present in most of sub-Saharan Africa, but little is known of the music that they produce.

Many instruments have very specific and restricted uses. Thus the *epudi*, a kind of ocarina used by the Basongye of Kasai, is associated with hunting. It accompanies hunters' songs before and after the hunt, and it is used as a signaling device during the hunt. It has one finger hole and produces two tones, about a major second apart. Its principal use in signaling

[4] William Bascom, notes accompanying the recording *Drums of the Yoruba of Nigeria*, Folkways FE 4441.

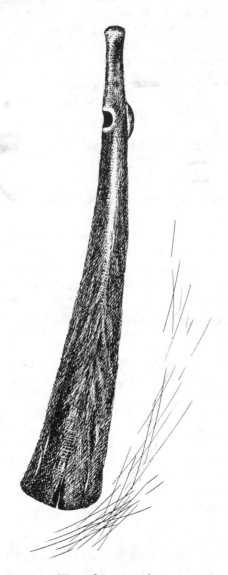

West African ivory horn

is for reproduction of the tones of the language in ways similar to drum and horn signaling techniques.[5]

Africa has developed a large number of *chordophones*, or string instruments. The simplest is the musical bow, which normally has only one string but sometimes produces fairly complex music. It is found throughout sub-Saharan Africa, but evidently has more forms in southeast Africa than elsewhere. It is shaped essentially like a hunting bow whose string is plucked or struck with a stick, and its sound is soft. Thus a resonator is almost always required. This may be attached to the end of the bow or to its middle. In the latter case, the string is usually stopped at the point at which the resonator is attached, so that in effect two strings, with contrasting pitch, are used. If the resonator is not attached, the bow may be held against an inverted pot. A third way of producing resonance is by holding the end of the bow in the mouth, which then acts as the resonator. If the configuration of the mouth is changed, different overtones will be produced. The bow is used as a solo instrument as well as an accompaniment to song.

There has evidently been a development from the musical bow, through single-string fiddles and lutes, to more complex string instruments; the most important ones among African peoples are zithers (with several strings stretched across a block of hollowed board); harps (usually with four to eight strings); and fiddles (with one to five strings). The shapes, arrangements, and tunings of these are almost innumerable. For example, the Ganda of Uganda tune their harps into five roughly equal intervals, each of about 240 cents (100 cents equal a tempered semitone) or five quarter tones. The *lulanga* of the Bashi (Congo), a trough zither in which eight strings are stretched along a concave block of wood between two and three feet long, has a tuning using mainly major and minor seconds. Frequently the tunings and thus the music produced seem to have little relationship to the intervals and scales of vocal music. The harps of East Africa bear a close resemblance to those of ancient Egypt.

Instrumental ensembles in Africa exhibit enormous variety. Ensemble playing on a single instrument is found, as in the zither playing of the Bashi, in which one man plays the strings and another, opposite him, raps rhythmically on the instrument with his knuckles, or in the playing of large xylophones by two men next to each other or opposite each other, in West Africa and the Congo. At the other extreme are the xylophone orchestras of the Chopi of South Africa; these consist of some thirty men who play in a heterophonic style, with a conductor. Between these extremes there are ensembles of many sorts. Some consist of several instruments of the same

[5] Alan P. Merriam, "The Epudi, a Basongye Ocarina," *Ethnomusicology*, VI (1962), 175–77.

Central African musical bow, played using the mouth as a resonator

type, such as xylophones, *mbiras*, or drums. Others are heterogeneous, consisting, for example, of drums, rattles, and bells (West Africa) or *mbira*, zither, and rattle (Congo), and a great many other combinations.

The distribution of instrument types in Africa is broad. Many instruments are found in almost all parts of the continent south of the Sahara. Drums, xylophones, and the *mbira* are practically universal. Musical bows are widespread. Nevertheless, there seems to be a great variation in the specific instruments, and in their number, used in individual groups, and even neighboring peoples sometimes exhibit substantial differences. Thus the Ganda of Uganda have an enormous store of instruments: many kinds of idiophones, from the simple percussion beam to rattles, bells, and xylophones; several types of musical bows, lyres, a tube fiddle and a harp; flutes, animal horns, gourd trumpets; and many kinds of drums. On the other hand, the Bashi of the Congo area have only a few instruments: two types of zithers, two types of *mbiras* or *sansas*, a flute, and one kind of drum.

MUSIC AND LANGUAGE IN AFRICA

All over the world, music and language interact, but in Africa, this interaction appears to be more intense than elsewhere. In addition to music in the usual sense of the word, the use of musical sounds for signaling purposes is common in Africa. The relaying of drum signals over a long distance is legendary; horns are also used for this purpose, and also, as a way of communicating over short distances. In some societies, signaling takes on the character of Morse code, that is, arbitrary signals are used to indicate words or concepts. More frequently, however, the system of signaling is tied to the pitch structure of the language.

The languages spoken in sub-Saharan Africa belong mainly to three families: Khoi-San, characterized by clicks in the throat and mouth, which is spoken by the Bushmen and Hottentots; Niger-Congo (including the Bantu group), which occupies most of the area through the Congo region and the Guinea Coast, and which is a closely knit group of languages clearly related to each other; and Sudanic, which is spoken in the northeastern region of our Africa. Most of the Bantu and many of the Sudanic languages are tone languages; that is, the relative pitch at which a syllable is spoken helps determine the meaning of the word. Thus, in Jabo, a language spoken in Liberia, there are four "tones"; that is, four different relative pitch levels of speech are distinguished for purposes of meaning, which we can number from 1 to 4, highest to lowest. In Jabo, the word *ba* may mean four different things, depending on the pitch. *Ba* (1) means namesake, *ba* (2) means "to

be broad," *ba* (3) means "tail," and *ba* (4) is a particle expressing command.[6]
In signaling, the pitches of the words—or rather their internal relationship,
for of course the language tones are not fixed pitches but are relative to
the pitch of the surrounding syllables and the speaker's voice range—are
transferred to the drum. Jabo signaling is done with two drums made of
hollowed logs with slits, one large, the other smaller. (They are not true
drums, of course, but idiophones.) The pitch of each drum varies according
to the place at which it is struck. And, interestingly, the two lower tones
of the language are combined into one tone on the large drum. The fact
that many words or sentences have the same sequence of tones, and that
in the drum language tones 3 and 4 are indistinguishable, would seem to
make deciphering of messages difficult. Only a few men are qualified to
signal, and only certain things may be said in signal language. Understanding
must come from knowledge of the kinds of messages likely to be signaled,
and evidently the Jabo restrict themselves to expressing urgent thoughts,
such as, "Our neighbors are on the warpath," or, more appropriately today,
"Hide! The tax collector is coming!"

Just what happens when words in a tone language are set to music
for the purpose of creating song? Does the melody slavishly follow the
pitch movement of the words? Or is there free melodic movement which
violates and to some extent obscures the meaning of the words by ignoring
the linguistic tones? Not too much is known about this intricate relationship
between music and speech, but it is obvious that no simple rule describes
it. And it may well be that each African culture has evolved its own accommodation between language and music in song. It is evident, however, that
melody does not slavishly follow speech, but that the tones of the words
do have an influence on shaping the melody.

The Ibo in Nigeria, according to one kind of analysis, use two tones,
high and low. If it were possible to formulate a rule for the Ibo on the
basis of a small sampling of songs, we would have to say that the musical
pitch sometimes moves up and down together with the pitch in speech,
and that it sometimes remains the same while the speech tones change,
but that pitch movement in the music is hardly ever contrary to that of
the language. On the other hand, an example from the Chewa in Central
East Africa, where the language also has two tones (marked in Example 7-1
by acute and grave accents, respectively), indicates very close correspondence. These samples are intended only to show some of the kinds of
things that may be found; they should not be used to draw conclusions
regarding the way tone languages are set to music throughout Africa.

Another example of the close relationship among music, language,

---

[6] George Herzog, "Speech-Melody and Primitive Music," *Musical Quarterly*, XX (1934),
453.

EXAMPLE 7-1. Chewa song, from George Herzog, "Speech-Melody and Primitive Music," *Musical Quarterly*, XX (1934), 457.

and other activities appears in some of the xylophone music of the Jabo in Liberia. According to Herzog, one form of evening entertainment is the repeated playing of short phrases on large xylophones which consist of big slabs laid across banana tree trunks.[7] These phrases are ordinary music to most listeners, but to a few who have inside knowledge they are musical versions of the tone patterns of sentences commenting on current events or mocking a member of the group. The person being mocked may not realize it, and the audience may burst into laughter when a piece that makes fun of an oblivious bystander is played. Sometimes this music is performed by two players sitting on opposite sides of the xylophone. They may perform a single melody together, they may play a canon, or they may repeat a tiny contrapuntal piece based on the speech tones of two sentences or phrases.

GENERAL CHARACTERISTICS OF AFRICAN FORMS

The most striking thing about the forms of African music is their dependence on short units, and in many cases on antiphonal or responsorial techniques. Most African compositions do not have units as long as the stanzas of typical European folk songs. They consist of short phrases that are repeated systematically, or alternated, or on which are based longer melodies in which a motif reappears repeatedly in different forms. Typical of the brevity of the phrases is Example 7-1, which in actual performance was probably repeated many times.

In instrumental music, short forms of this type are also found distributed over a large part of Africa. Example 7-2, recorded in Johannesburg and performed on the musical bow, consists of a systematic repetition of a rhythmic phrase that uses only two fundamental pitches. The upper voice in Example 7-2 is produced by overtones, and it, of course, is varied, but the piece consists of the manifold repetitions of this phrase.

---

[7] George Herzog, "Canon in West African Xylophone Melodies," *Journal of the American Musicological Society*, II (1949), 196–97.

EXAMPLE 7-2. South African musical bow melody, from Charles M. Camp and Bruno Nettl, "The Musical Bow in South Africa," *Anthropos*, L (1955), 75.

　　　Solo performance is common enough in Africa, but the most character-istic African music is performed by groups with alternating performance techniques of various kinds. We say "characteristic" because this kind of performance is more developed in Africa than elsewhere, and because it is this element which, more perhaps than any other, has been retained in the Afro-American cultures. The simplest of these alternating techniques is responsorial singing, the alternation between a leader and a group which is sometimes also called the call-and-response technique. Example 7-3, from the Republic of the Congo (Brazzaville), shows what may frequently happen in such a form. Drums and an iron bell provide a constant rhythmic back-ground whose general outline and meter remain the same, but whose accent patterns and specific note values vary somewhat. A female soloist sings a two-measure phrase alternating with a two-measure phrase sung in unison by a group of women. The two phrases are different in content, but are similar at the cadence.

　　　Improvisation is an important feature in many African styles. Evi-dently there is some improvisation in the narrowest sense of the term— that is, the creation of music without the use of preexisting models as the basis—but this seems to be rare. More common is improvisation in which a tune is varied as it is being performed. Forms consisting of short phrases that are repeated many times lend themselves especially well to this kind of improvisation, because it is possible for a singer to begin with the standard version of a tune and then to create variations that depart increasingly from the standard. This is what happens in the successive repetitions of the soloist's phrase in Example 7-3. The members of the chorus also improvise variations, but they do not depart as much from the original.

　　　A further result of improvisation, presumably, is the creation of poly-phonic forms. Harmony and polyphony in African music are discussed later in this chapter. Here it is relevant to point out that improvisation in choral and ensemble performance adds to the number of pitches heard at one time. The fact that improvisation and variation are encouraged in some African cultures seems to have influenced the degree to which polyphony is accepted. Actually, variation by improvisation seems to be considered

EXAMPLE 7-3. Kuyu (Congo) women's dance, from Rose Brandel, *The Music of Central Africa* (The Hague: Martinus Nijhoff, 1962), p. 197.

the mark of good musicianship in some African cultures. We should mention also a feature found in some African music that is related to both form and polyphony, namely the tendency in some pieces, for a number of things to be going on at the same time. Some of this is due to the development of complex rhythmic polyphony, the simultaneous presentation of several rhythms which may seem, to the Western listener, to have little in common. It is hard to say whether the African listener feels all of these rhythms to be part of one overall rhythmic structure (as a Westerner can conceive of all of the voices in a Bach fugue as independent yet united), or whether the African conceives of music as consisting of the simultaneous presentation of unrelated phenomena. Whatever the case, it is possible, in such a piece, to have phrases and other units of varying lengths appearing in different voices or instruments.

The performances are at least in some cases intricately structured, despite the fact that they may consist only of repetitions and variations upon a short theme. In the music performed on the *mbira*, or *sansa*, in southern Africa, the repetitions and variations on a basic theme are grouped into nine steps or stages.[8] The *mbira* player begins by playing the basic chords of the underlying harmony; then, in the second section, these are varied slightly; in the third step, the player takes the basic chords and creates an accompanying melody out of them, playing their tones in alternation rather than together. This third step is considered the basic pattern which dominates the piece. In the fourth step, we find more and faster separation of the notes, rhythmic changes, and the addition of the singing voice. There is a climax at the end of this section, which is followed by variations on the vocal melody in the fifth and sixth steps. In the fifth, the singer introduces a yodel-like technique. Steps 7, 8, and 9 are more or less identical with the first three steps, presented in reverse order. Each of these stages has a name. The details of the sections, their length and specific content, may be improvised, but the form of the performance is essentially set.

Thus forms rivaling in sophistication those of European art music and the Far East are found in Africa, and they are built upon the basic formal principles of brevity, repetition and variation, binary structure, and improvisation. The amount of repetition and variation may be determined by the performer's interaction with the audience or by the needs of the activity which the music accompanies. Composite forms, consisting of series of pieces, are particularly common in ceremonial situations, where a large group of pieces, which may take a day or longer, must be performed in correct order. Perhaps the most complex forms are the suites performed by the xylophone orchestras of the Chopi, for here we find structures of six to eight related movements, each of which is cast in a mold similar to that of the *mbira* pieces described earlier.

MELODY

So far as the melodic elements of music are concerned, African music seems generally rather intelligible to the Western listener; it does not really have the exotic sound that some Oriental and some American Indian music has at first hearing. The conclusion we may tentatively draw from this fact

[8] These are illustrated and described in detail by Abraham Dumisani Maraire on the recording, *Mbira Music of Rhodesia*, University of Washington Press 1001.

is that African music, on the whole, fits more or less into the diatonic scheme that is also the basis of most Western art and folk music.

There have been attempts to identify a truly "African" scale. Ballanta-Taylor, an early West African scholar, believed that the basic scale of West African music has sixteen tones per octave, and statements regarding the importance of pentatonic scales in Africa have been made. But the consensus of scholars is that there is no single system, but that exact measurement of intervals would produce—at least in vocal music—a clustering about the intervals found also in diatonic scales, and that in many ways the kind of melodic structure in Africa corresponds to that of European folk music. As in Europe, so in Africa, we find songs with few tones (ditonic and tritonic scales). There are pentatonic tunes with minor thirds and major seconds and pentachordal ones as well. There are heptatonic songs and occasional chromatic pieces. There are, moreover, intervals that do not fit into the diatonic scheme, such as neutral thirds (found also in Europe). There is, finally, a reported tendency in the heptatonic songs to use the intervals of minor third and minor seventh above the tonic. Our interest in this feature stems from certain phenomena of jazz (the lowered seventh is one "blue note"), but it seems doubtful that these intervals constitute a special feature common to all African music. The fact that glides and ornaments are common in some African singing techniques also adds to the difficulty of defining a specific scale structure.

Types of melodic movement also exhibit great variety. In one area, Central Africa, we find the following kinds described by Brandel:[9] melodies clustering around a nucleus of one or two tones; melodies based on the perfect fourth, either descending directly from one tone to another a fourth below it, or making use also of the intervening tones; melodies built on the tones of the triad, and others using a whole string of thirds with only occasional use of intervening tones; melodies built on the triad with an added sixth ( ); melodies with the augmented fourth predominating, sometimes made up of three major seconds in a row ( );

and melodies with the range of an octave or more, in which the lowest tone and its upper octave are the most important.

The melodic contours also have various types. Rather large ranges seem to be characteristic of Africa. Europe has many songs with a range of less than a fifth, relatively few (except for what appears to be recent material) with a range much larger than an octave. In African music the number of pieces with a large range seems to be somewhat greater. Melodies move predominantly in three ways: (1) in a mildly undulating fashion, beginning on a low tone, rising gradually to a somewhat higher level, and returning

[9] Rose Brandel, *The Music of Central Africa* (The Hague: Martinus Nijhoff, 1962).

EXAMPLE 7-4. Batwa Pygmy song (Ruanda), from Rose Brandel, *The Music of Central Africa* (The Hague: Martinus Nijhoff, 1962), p. 70.

to the low tone; (2) beginning on a high tone and descending; and (3) tracing a pendulum-like movement, swinging rapidly back and forth between high and low tones. Example 7-4 illustrates this pendulum-like movement; it also exemplifies the melodies made up largely of strings of thirds.

Tone systems in African music are sometimes very restricted. The music of the Xhosa, a large group of people living at the tip of South Africa, lies almost entirely within the framework of a pentatonic scale, with minor thirds and major seconds. The melodies are almost always rather sharply descending. The tunes very frequently consist of two phrases, which are similar, identical, or analogous, the second phrase centering about a tone a major second below the tonal center of the first phrase. The music of the Mbuti Pygmies of the Congo is largely built on a pentatonic scale consisting again of major seconds and minor thirds, but with the two thirds adjacent (e.g., ♪♪♪♪♪). On the other hand, in some other African cultures there appears to be a wide variety of scale types and a rather complex tone system. In instrumental music, melodic movement is more specialized, for each instrument invites certain kinds of movement, range, and interval. Thus melodies played on the musical bow are likely to have a small range and use a melodic type clustering about one or two notes that are close together; horn music is likely to use larger intervals, and pendulum-like melody is more easily suited to the xylophone. We should also mention in this connection the great variety of tone colors achieved by the human voice. Yodeling, growling, raucous tones, and tense as well as relaxed singing are found. The imitation of animal cries and sounds of nature are also a part of vocal music in Africa. In general, singing in sub-Saharan Africa is relaxed, open-throated, and full-bodied, very much in contrast to the tense and tighter-sounding Middle Eastern singing style found in the North. It is also usually unornamented and straightforward.

RHYTHM

The feature of African music that has been most widely discussed is rhythm, and it has indeed been more highly developed in Africa than have some other elements such as melody and form. To some extent we may say that African rhythm is also more highly developed than the rhythm of other cultures. The latter statement must be made with caution, of course, for certainly it would be possible for a composer in the Western tradition to put together a piece with a rhythmic structure much more complex than that of any African piece. It is, however, very difficult for a Western musician to reproduce or even to comprehend the more complex African rhythmic structures with the use of the ear alone. The level at which African music seems to be rhythmically more developed is that of listener and performer perception. It is doubtful whether a Western listener could, without special training, perceive and reproduce the most complex structures in Western music, especially without a score, simply from sound. With training he or she might, of course, learn to match the performance and perception of African musicians. But this sort of training is not present in our culture, whereas it is—though not always formally—a part of the musical training of African listeners and performers.

The rhythm of African music must be approached from two points of view. First, we are interested in the rhythmic structure (and its complexity) in a single melodic line. Here the rhythm and meter are usually not too difficult to understand. Metric structure with regular beats appears to be the rule. Once beats are established it is possible to identify the presence of *syncopation*, which results from the regular articulation of notes at points other than the beginnings of beats. A distinctive feature of West African music that seems to have been carried over to Afro-American musics is the ability of musicians to keep the same tempo for minutes and even hours. Richard Waterman referred to this ability (which no doubt is learned, not inherited) as the "metronome sense." We will never know, of course, whether such strict adherence to tempo has ever been practiced in Western music. That it is not usual in Western art music in the twentieth century can easily be demonstrated by playing a symphony recording and keeping time with a metronome. Rigid adherence to tempo may have made possible the considerable variety of rhythmic motifs and patterns in African music, for the musician who has a steady beat in mind, and who does not deviate from it, can perhaps more easily elaborate the details of the rhythm. The compelling nature of rhythm is recognized in West African terminology, where the term "hot," applied to rhythmic drumming, evidently originated.[10] Hot rhythm in West Africa is particularly important in ceremonial music, and the more exciting the rhythm, the hotter the music is said to be.

The more spectacular rhythmic complexity of African music appears, however, in the rhythmic polyphony, the superimposition of several rhythmic structures. Its most obvious manifestation is found in drumming, but of course it is also present in the combination of several voices or, more fre-

---

[10] Richard A. Waterman, " 'Hot' Rhythm in Negro Music," *Journal of the American Musicological Society*, I (1948), 25–26.

quently, of instruments with voices. There is a great deal of drumming, but in other ways also the music seems to be dominated by a percussive quality. Individual tones in singing are attacked strongly without a semblance of *legato*. There are few instruments on which one can slur notes together, and generally the music is vigorously accented. Thus the importance of drumming can perhaps be traced to the need for strong rhythmic articulation.

The perception of various simultaneous meters seems to be widespread among Africans. Rhythmic polyphony of a rather complex type can be performed by a single person who may sing in one meter and drum in another. The superimposition of duple and triple meters, one type of hemiola rhythm, is evidently a basic ingredient of much West and Central African rhythmic polyphony.

In music using three or more drums, the rhythmic polyphony is developed to its most complex level. Although such music can be mechanically notated in a single meter, the various drummers are actually performing with independent metrical schemes; one drum may use duple, one triple, a third quintuple meter. Moreover, if the several drums or other instruments use the same basic metric scheme (such as 3/8), the beginning of the unit or measure may not come at the same time in all of the drums; thus we may have the following combination: 3/8, 5/8, 7/8, as in Example 7-5, which is a sample of Yoruba drumming with the pitch variations of the individual drums omitted.

Percussion ensembles of various types are important in the Guinea Coast area of Africa. Typically, they consist of drums, rattles, and bells. Let us examine, as an example, the Abadja rhythm, used in social songs of the Ewe people of Ghana. Three drums of various pitches (each with one skin), several large gourd rattles, and two double-bells are used. The instruments enter in order, each playing its own rhythmic pattern without change, beginning with the bells, followed by the rattle, and finally by the drums. The last to enter is the master drum, which improvises against the consistent rhythmic background produced by the others, using motifs

EXAMPLE 7-5. Yoruba drumming in honor of Ogun (god of war). The top part is the smallest and highest drum, the lowest part, the largest and lowest drum. From Anthony King, "Employment of the 'Standard Pattern' in Yoruba Music," *African Music*, II, no. 3 (1960), 53.

from their patterns, combining and rearranging them. The first bell is regarded as having the fundamental rhythm. The rhythms could be reduced to a common 12/8 meter, but the Ghanaian listener is more interested in the interaction of the various rhythms and hears them as individual entities rather than as "rhythmic chords." Thus the various instruments begin their patterns at various points, not simultaneously, and there is tension between those which are essentially in 6/8 and those that appear to be in 3/4. Example 7-6 gives the patterns of all but the master drum (which does not confine itself to a single pattern).

The melodic element in drumming, as illustrated by the "royal drums" of the Watusi, which accompany the supreme chief whenever he emerges from his tent, is also important; drums used together always contrast in size and thus in pitch, and it is possible to follow each drum individually. In music using several melodic instruments, or voices and instruments, the structure of the rhythm is as complex as it is in the drumming, and the various voices often perform in different meters. To what extent the performers are listening to each other cannot always be ascertained, and to what degree an African listener perceives the total rhythmic structure is also unknown. An important feature of West African rhythmic polyphony, and perhaps a major key to its understanding, is the hemiola concept. The juxtaposition of three beats against two, and of more complex rhythms composed of these units, both simultaneously and in alternation, is the basis of a great deal of this music; it can be found, for instance, in Example 7-6, in which the *kidi* (low drum) performs a rhythm that can be reduced

EXAMPLE 7-6. Abadja rhythm, used in Ghana. After William K. Amoakn.

to 3/4, and the *kagan* (high drum) another in 6/8, while the rattle alternates these two meters in its short repeated phrase.

POLYPHONY

Closely related to rhythmic polyphony and to the problem of perception of a group of individual rhythmic lines as a unit is the field of polyphony at large, and the question again is whether in Africa several voices are perceived independently or as forming a single vertical harmonic structure.

Whether it is polyphony or really harmony, the phenomenon is very well developed in African music, and it appears in many media. One finds choral singing, usually in the responsorial form; instrumental music of an orchestral nature, with a number of instruments of the same type playing together; and something similar to chamber music—instruments of different types playing together, alone or along with singing. Drumming and other percussion may of course act as accompaniment. There is polyphony of many types, and it seems to be present throughout the sub-Saharan area, although concentrated in the Eastern Cattle Area and the Congo or Central Africa.

The fact that many kinds of polyphony are present in Africa, and that this also seems to be the case elsewhere in the world where polyphony is found, strengthens our belief that polyphony is a unified concept. When a culture discovers or learns to perform polyphony it seems to learn several different kinds. There are cultures with no polyphony at all, but there are few, if any, that use, for example, only parallel fifths and nothing else.

Most African polyphony can be categorized as one of two types: that in which all of the voices use the same melodic material, and that which comes about through the peculiarities of the instruments. In the former category we find parallelism. There are parallel thirds, fourths, fifths, and occasionally sixths, but other intervals seem to be rare. In the case of parallel thirds, alternation between major and minor thirds is usual, made necessary by the diatonic seven-tone scales which, as we have said, are common in Africa. Parallel fourths and fifths seem to be more common in East Africa, and thirds and sixths seem to dominate in the Congo and Guinea Coast areas. Parallelism is rarely completely exact, for the tendency to improvise seems to militate against slavish following of one voice by another.

Example 7-7 illustrates parallelism among the Thonga of South Africa. A chorus of men and women is led by a female soloist and accompanied by a musical bow, which also plays interludes between the stanzas. The player of the musical bow, which is evidently limited to the tones D, E,

EXAMPLE 7-7. South African choral song with musical bow, from Charles M. Camp and Bruno Nettl, "The Musical Bow in Southern Africa," *Anthropos*, L (1955), 80.

and F, plays the melody along with the soloist and continues by doubling the second part of the chorus, but switches to an approximation of the highest part of the chorus when this becomes possible.

African music also features rounds, which often seem to have come about through antiphonal or responsorial singing. For example, if leader and chorus use the same tune, the chorus may become overanxious and fail to wait for the leader to finish his or her turn, and a round of sorts is born. The fact that many African rounds do have the entrance of the second voice near the end of the first voice's rendition of a tune points to this matter of origin; so does the fact that most known African rounds have only two voices. Also resulting from the antiphonal technique is the kind of polyphony in which one voice sustains a tone, perhaps the final tone of its phrase, while the other voice performs a more rapidly moving melody, at the end of which it, in turn, holds a long note while the first voice performs a moving part. This gives rise to a sort of drone relationship between the voices.

In southern Africa, where polyphony appears to be most widespread, we find a type of harmonic organization that appears to operate in a way similar to the Western harmonic system in its eighteenth- and nineteenth-century manifestations. The compositions are in two sections, each consisting of a melody, sometimes of accompaniment as well, and sometimes of several intertwined melodies. In most cases, however, the material in each section revolves about one triad, and the relationship of the two triads is analogous to the relationship between a dominant and a tonic chord, although the roots of the two African chords are separated not by a fourth or a fifth but by a major second. The consistency of the harmonic movement, however, justifies the hypothesis that here we have a harmonic system that dominates the music much as the Western harmonic system dominates Western music.

There is also a relationship between the voices that could be called real counterpoint, but this seems to appear most frequently in instrumental music, where the structure of the instrument may in itself be conducive to certain melodic patterns and devices. Thus the accompaniment of singers on a harp, xylophone, or *mbira* may have nothing to do melodically with the tune of the singers. *Ostinato* patterns are common in both vocal and instrumental parts. In these, a short bit, perhaps a two-measure phrase, is repeated (with variations) by the instruments, while the singer or singers perform a longer melody which, however, is also repeated with improvised variations. This sort of structure is similar to that of much Western music, especially of popular and folk musics; and Africans in the cities, who have been influenced by Western popular music, have composed songs in which the African sort of accompaniment by an ostinato figure, with a very short stanza by the singer, is used. Indeed, it seems to be generally true that in musical styles combining Western and African elements, those features in African music which are highly developed but which have a Western counter-part are preserved.

REGIONAL VARIATION IN AFRICAN MUSIC

We have noted that each African group has its own songs and music, which may differ in style from those of its neighbors. On the other hand, we have also cited a number of characteristics present in sub-Saharan African music as a whole. The degree to which these characteristics are pronounced varies. Just as there are culture areas in Africa, there are also music areas, regions in which the musical style is more or less homogeneous, and which contrast with their neighboring areas in some specific way. The music areas coincide, on the whole, with the culture areas, and this is not surprising when we consider the essential roles of music in the culture as a whole. Merriam[11] recognized the following music areas: the Khoi-San area (Bushmen and Hottentots), East Africa, Central Africa (mainly the Congo region), and the West Coast (plus several areas in the northern part of the continent that are largely under the influence of Islamic musical culture). The four areas we have mentioned comprise the main body of African music south of the Sahara. To them should be added the music of the Pygmies, who live in various isolated parts of central Africa surrounded by Negro groups but whose music is a distinctive unit. The differences among these groups are expressed not in clear-cut dichotomies but rather in statistical terms. What may be found in one area is also present in another, but with a markedly different degree of frequency or complexity.

The main characteristics of the West Coast are the metronome sense and the accompanying concept of hot rhythm, the simultaneous use of several meters, and the responsorial form of singing with overlap between leader and chorus. The Central African area is distinguished by its great variety of instruments and musical styles and by the emphasis, in its polyphony, on the interval of the third. East Africa has, for centuries, been somewhat under Islamic influence, though by no means to as great an extent as the northern part of Africa. Vertical fifths are more prominent here, and rhythmic structure is not so complex, nor are percussion instruments so prominent. The development of a sense of harmony seems likely. The Khoi-San music area is evidently similar in style to East Africa, but has simpler forms and instruments. It contains a good deal of music performed with the *hocket* technique, as does the Pygmy subarea of Central Africa, which is also characterized by the presence of a vocal technique similar to yodeling.

We have been describing those aspects of African music which seem to have developed without influence from other cultures, or of which Africans have made a specialty. But outside influence is not just a recent phenomenon in African music. It shares some traits with European folk music, indicating perhaps a period of contact many centuries ago. Also, contact with Indonesian music seems likely, and the influence of the Near East and possibly of India is ancient and has increased greatly in the last few centuries. The impact of Western culture has also played a part for centuries and has increased especially in the last hundred years. Thus we find African music now—and it has probably always been this way to a degree—in a state of change. We find that some groups have almost completely changed to music in a Near Eastern style. Others have retained, in part, a repertory of "pure" African music but have added to it songs in an Arabic style; this is true of the Hausa, and of the Watusi, who have solo drumming of a kind unknown

[11] Alan P. Merriam, "African Music," p. 77.

in the Near East but also songs strongly reminiscent of Arabic music. We find North and Latin American popular songs known among peoples that otherwise perform aboriginal songs. And we find that because of the improvement of communication and transportation as well as through the growth of unified African nations, African peoples are learning more from one another, musically and otherwise, than they did before.

Like music everywhere, African music has changed rapidly in the twentieth century, particularly because of the increased contact with Western music and musical thought and with Western technology. Africans hear much of their music on recordings and on the radio, and the degree of general participation in musical activities appears to be declining. They hear musics of other African peoples and have created popular musical styles by combining their resources and mixing them with Western elements. Such popular style-complexes as high-life, Afro-beat, and, in francophone West Africa, Congo music, combine these elements in various ways. One popular music, *juju*, is a western Nigerian synthesis of Yoruban praise singing with several Ghanaian-derived guitar-band styles. *Juju* is performed both in urban bars and in connection with Yoruba life-cycle ceremonies (such as naming ceremonies, weddings, and funerals). The instruments employed in this style in recent years include electric guitars, the Afro-Cuban percussion section common to many neotraditional African musics (congos, maracas, banjos, claves), Yoruban "talking drums" (members of the family of *dundun* drums), and on occasion, accordions, trap set, synthesizer, and clavinet. Today's *juju* has absorbed influences from such diverse styles as other African neotraditional musics (notably Cuban-influenced music from Zäire), Indian film music, soul, reggae, American country music, and disco.[12]

Throughout Africa one can find music which is essentially Western, but which retains those elements of African music that are most developed and most prominent. There have also been attempts, sometimes resulting from the increasing nationalism of the various new nations of the continent and sometimes from an antiquarian attitude, to preserve old forms, and the interest in African music has been stimulated by institutions of recent origin, such as contests among xylophone orchestras among the Chopi of South Africa. Thus African music continues as a lively and ever-changing art, but its most important features seem to remain relatively constant even in the face of the onslaught of Westernization.

We should not leave a discussion of African music without emphasizing its enormous impact on much of the world's music in the last hundred years. Its chief characteristics have been brought to the Americas and form the basic elements of all types of Afro-American performance practice. It

---

[12] Christopher A. Waterman, "Juju," in Bruno Nettl, *The Western Impact on World Music: Change, Adaptation, and Survival* (New York: Schirmer, 1985), pp. 87–90.

is less well known that Africans who were brought to various parts of the Old World over the past several hundred years also brought with them much musical material. Thus, for example, the folk music of the Persian Gulf area has many African characteristics, and their origin is attested to by the presence of many individuals of African descent. Most important, however, the main distinguishing features of the popular musics of the Western world, and of jazz, are ultimately of African origin.

BIBLIOGRAPHICAL AND DISCOGRAPHICAL NOTES

Several publications by Alan P. Merriam discuss sub-Saharan African music as a unit: "African Music," in *Continuity and Change in African Cultures*, ed. William J. Bascom and Melville J. Herskovits (Chicago: University of Chicago Press, 1959), pp. 49–86; "Characteristics of African Music," *J-IFMC*, XI (1959), 13–19; "The African Idiom in Music," *Journal of American Folklore*, LXXV (1962), 120–30; and "Traditional Music of Black Africa," in *Africa*, ed. Phyllis M. Martin and Patrick O'Meara (Bloomington: Indiana University Press, 1977), pp. 243–58. The first and last of these are also included in Merriam's anthology of his writings, *African Music in Perspective* (New York and London: Garland, 1982). Two recent books on African music are J. H. Kwabena Nketia, *The Music of Africa* (New York: Norton, 1974), and Ashenafi Kebede, *Roots of Black Music: The Vocal, Instrumental and Dance Heritage of Africa and Black America* (Englewood Cliffs, NJ: Prentice-Hall, 1982). Among the few published collections of African folk music are Nketia, *Folk Songs of Ghana* (Legon: University of Ghana, 1963), and J. O. Ajibola, *Orin Yoruba* (Yoruba Songs) (Ile-Ife, Nigeria: University of Ife Press, 1974).

As samples of regional studies of African music we mention Nketia, *African Music in Ghana* (Evanston, IL: Northwestern University Press, 1963), and Rose Brandel, *The Music of Central Africa* (The Hague: Martinus Nijhoff, 1962). George Herzog, "Speech-Melody and Primitive Music," *Musical Quarterly*, XX (1934), 452–66, is an excellent discussion of tone languages and their relationship to music. Three essays dealing with African music and language, by Gerhard Kubik, Hans-Heinrich Wängler, and Herrmann Jungraithmayr, are included in *Musik in Afrika*, ed. Artur Simon (Berlin: Museum für Völkerkunde, 1983). Specialized studies appear regularly in *African Music*, the journal of the African Music Society. Other studies include Ruth M. Stone, *Let the Inside Be Sweet: The Interpretation of Music Event among the Kpelle of Liberia* (Bloomington: Indiana University Press, 1982); Robert Kauffman, "African Rhythm: A Reassessment," *Ethnomusicology*, XXIV (1980), 347–92; David Locke, "Principles of Offbeat Timing and Cross-Rhythm in Southern Eye Dance Drumming," *Ethnomusicology*, XXVI (1982), 217–46, which deals with the music of the Eye-speaking people of the Guinea Coast of West Africa; James Koetting, "Analysis and Notation of West African Drum

Ensemble Music," UCLA *Selected Reports in Ethnomusicology*, Vol. I, no. 3 (1970), 116–46; David W. Ames and Anthony V. King, *Glossary of Hausa Music and Its Social Contexts* (Evanston, IL: Northwestern University Press, 1971); John Miller Chernoff, *African Rhythm and African Sensibility: Aesthetics and Social Action in African Musical Idioms* (Chicago: University of Chicago Press, 1979); and Paul Berliner, *The Soul of Mbira: Music and Traditions of the Shona People of Zimbabwe* (Berkeley: University of California Press, 1978), illustrated by two Nonesuch discs, H-72054 and H-72077 (see further on in this list).

Volume V of the UCLA *Selected Reports in Ethnomusicology* (1984) is devoted to studies in African music. Several articles relating to the topic are included in *Essays for a Humanist: An Offering to Klaus Wachsmann* (New York: Town House Press, 1977). Folk music as it relates to contemporary African musics is discussed in John E. Kaemmer, "Changing Music in Contemporary Africa," in *Africa*, ed. Phyllis M. Martin and Patrick O'Meara (Bloomington: Indiana University Press, 1977), 367–77; Gerhard Kubik, *The Kachamba Brothers' Band: A Study of the Neo-Traditional Music in Malaŵi* (Lusaka: University of Zambia, 1974), with a disc of recorded examples; Christopher A. Waterman, "'I'm a Leader, Not a Boss:' Social Identity and Popular Music in Ibadan, Nigeria," *Ethnomusicology*, XXVI (1982), 59–71; and David B. Coplan, "Go to My Town, Cape Coast! The Social History of Ghanaian Highlife," in *Eight Urban Musical Cultures: Tradition and Change*, ed. Bruno Nettl (Urbana: University of Illinois Press, 1978), 96–114, and *In Township Tonight! South Africa's Black City Music and Theatre* (London and New York: Longman, 1985). Vol. VI of *African Urban Studies* (1980) is a special issue on African urban music; V. Kofi Agawu, "The Impact of Language on Musical Composition in Ghana: An Introduction to the Musical Style of Ephraim Amu," *Ethnomusicology*, XXVIII (1984), 37–73, examines the use of traditional materials by a leading composer of art music in Ghana.

Sir Percival Kirby, *The Musical Instruments of the Native Races of South Africa* (London: Oxford University Press, 1934), is a classic on the instruments in one area and their musical styles. A book profusely illustrated, dealing with instruments of another region is Bertil Söderberg, *Les instruments de musique au Bas-Congo et dans les régions avoisinantes* (Stockholm: Ethnographic Museum of Sweden, 1956). P. N. Kavyu, *Traditional Musical Instruments of Kenya* (Nairobi: Kenya Literature Bureau, 1980), is a short survey. Ulrich Wegner, *Afrikanische Saiteninstrumente* (Berlin: Museum für Völkerkunde, 1984), is a catalog and extensive discussion of the collection of African instruments of the Museum of Ethnography in Berlin; a cassette of recorded illustrations accompanies the book. The use of a Sudanic instrument in West Africa is documented in Jacqueline Cogdell Dje Dje, *Distribution of the One-String Fiddle in West Africa* (Los Angeles: University of California Program in Ethnomusicology, 1980).

Many excellent recordings of African music are available. A standard discography is Alan P. Merriam, *African Music on LP: An Annotated Discography*

(Evanston, IL: Northwestern University Press, 1970). Noncommercial recordings are inventoried in Ruth M. Stone and Frank J. Gillis, *African Music
and Oral Data: A Catalog of Field Recordings, 1902–1975* (Bloomington:
Indiana University Press, 1976). South, Central, and East Africa are represented on a constantly growing set of field recordings, already over two hundred
discs in number, published by the International Library of African Music,
Johannesburg: *The Sound of Africa*, collected by Hugh Tracey; see *Catalogue:
The Sound of Africa Series*, 2 vols. (Roodepoort, Transvaal, S. Africa: International Library of African Music, 1973). Other excellent field recordings of
African music are available from the Collection du Musée de l'Homme (Paris)
on the Vogue label, and also as part of the series *Musique traditionnelle de
l'Afrique Noire* (Paris: Radio-France Internationale, Centre de Documentation
Africaine). *Africa South of the Sahara*, ed. Harold Courlander, Folkways
FE 4503 (2 discs), is a survey.

The Central African area is well represented on *Voice of the Congo*, ed.
Alan P. Merriam, Riverside RLP 4002; *Music of Equatorial Africa*, Folkways
P 4402; *Folk Music of the Western Congo*, Folkways P 427; *Music of Zäire:
Peoples of the Ngiri River*, Folkways FE 4241–42; *Sanza and Guitar: Music
of the Bena Luluwa of Angola and Zäire*, Lyrichord LLST 7313; and the
excellent recordings issued by the Royal Museum of Central Africa, Tervuren.
West African drumming in its many varieties is illustrated in *Drums of the
Yoruba of Nigeria*, Folkways FE 4441; *Drums of West Africa: Ritual Music
of Ghana*, Lyrichord LLST 7307, recordings and notes by Richard Hill; and
Africa: Drum, Chant and Instrumental Music, Nonesuch H-72073, recorded
and with notes by Stephen Jay. Also recommended are *The Music of the
Dan* [Ivory Coast], UNESCO Collection BM 30 L 2301; *Music of the Kpelle
of Liberia*, Folkways FE 4385, compiled by R. M. and V. I. Stone; *Ghana:
Music of the Northern Tribes*, Lyrichord LLST 7321, and *Music of the Dagomba
from Ghana*, Folkways FE 4324, both recorded by Verna Gillis with David
Moises Perez Martinez; and *Music of the Ga People of Ghana: Adowa*,
Vol. I, Folkways FE 4291, recorded and annotated by Barbara L. Hampton.
Musique d'Afrique occidentale: musique malinké, musique baoulé, Vogue LDM
30 116 (Collection Musée de l'Homme), recordings and commentary by G.
Rouget, presents two very different West African musics. The music of Madagascar is illustrated on *Valiha, Madagascar*, Ocora OCR 18. *Traditional Music
of Botswana, Africa*, Folkways FE 4371, recordings and commentary by Eliza-
beth Nelbach Wood, presents a sample of vocal and instrumental pieces.
Mbira music of southern Africa is found in *Mbira Music of Rhodesia*, performed
by Abraham Dumisani Maraire, University of Washington Press 1001 (currently
out of print but available on cassette, with original accompanying booklet by
Maraire, from the University of Washington Press, Seattle, WA 98105); and
on two discs of field recordings made by Paul Berliner: *The Soul of Mbira:
Traditions of the Shona People of Rhodesia*, Nonesuch H-72054, and *Shona
Mbira Music*, Nonesuch H-72077. Among recordings of music from East
Africa are the sampler album *Africa: Ceremonial and Folk Music*, Nonesuch
H-72063, recorded and with notes by David Fanshawe; *Kenya: Musique de*

mariage a Lamu, SELAF/ORSTROM CETO 791, recordings and notes by Françoise Le Guemmec-Coppens, which documents an entire Swahili musical event; and a three-volume set of discs edited by Ashenafi Kebede and presenting music from Ethiopia, Tangent TGM 101–3. The area that combines sub-Saharan and North African elements is exemplified on *Ethiopia: Azmari Music of the Amharas*, Anthology Records AST 6000, and *Nigeria-Hausa Music I*, Unesco Records BM 30 L 2306. *Voice of the Congo* (Riverside RLP 4002) and *Black Music of Two Worlds* (Folkways FE 4602, 3 discs), the latter compiled by John Storm Roberts, include examples of modern African music that combine traditional and Western elements.

EIGHT

THE AMERICAN INDIANS

This and the following chapters discuss the folk and traditional musics of the Americas. The American continents possess a great wealth of traditional music. That of the American Indians has been in existence for a long time, though no doubt in constantly changing forms. Other repertories have been brought from other continents, mainly Europe, and preserved more or less intact. Still other musics of the Americas began as offshoots from these imported traditions, then developed into independent styles with their own character and internal dynamics; this is true particularly of the various Afro-American traditions. Some musical repertories in the Americas came about through interaction and fusion of older musics which were found here or brought from elsewhere. And finally, although it would be difficult to state unequivocally that there are traditions in the Americas that grew up entirely without influence from older Indian, African, or European musics, there are some styles that can be said to be in real essence American.

    It seems logical to discuss the music of the Americas in three categories: (1) the music of the Indians, which is a tradition relatively undisturbed by the influx of other music; (2) the Afro-American musics, whose main characteristic is the combination of styles which were originally widely separated and highly distinctive; and (3) the folk music of peoples of European origin—Spanish and Portuguese, English, French, German, and Eastern European—which is characterized by the retention of archaic forms no longer known in their original home as well as by the development of distinctive offshoots of the European models.

There is little doubt anymore that the American Indians came from Asia across the Bering Strait in several or many separate waves, beginning some 50,000 years ago; that they are Mongoloid in race; and that the simplest tribes were pushed to the edges of the area (Tierra del Fuego, for example) and into relatively undesirable spots such as the jungles of Brazil and Bolivia, the Great Basin area of Nevada and Utah, and the tundra of north Canada and the icy wastes of the Polar area. Although we realize that in 50,000 years there must have occurred a great deal of change in the styles and uses of Indian music, and although we know practically nothing about the music of East Asia of thousands of years ago, it is still possible to discover certain similarities between Indian and Oriental music, and especially between the musics of the Eskimos and of the Paleo-Siberian tribes living in easternmost Siberia. These similarities involve emphasis on melody rather than on polyphony, some use of relatively large intervals (thirds and fourths) in the melodies, and, possibly, a rather strained, tense-sounding vocal production.

On the other hand, there are many different styles and style areas in North and South America, and music of the simplest sort as well as musical cultures of great complexity are found. The latter had largely disappeared by the time ethnomusicologists became competent to deal with them, and they can be studied only by archeological techniques, but some of the simplest styles are still with us. The size of the Indian population seems always to have been small; north of Mexico there were probably never more than one or two million, and South and Middle American Indians apparently never exceeded about five million. That such a small number of people developed so varied and intensive a musical culture is a fact that should inspire a good deal of respect. Today there is a great difference between South and North American Indians as a whole: The South American tribes, for the most part, have been absorbed into the Iberian-American cultures, to which they have contributed greatly, and whose music they have to a large degree adopted; thus, for knowledge of their aboriginal music, we must depend on a few isolated peoples. The North American tribes have generally remained more separate from their white and Afro-American compatriots and seem to have preserved earlier musical styles to a much greater degree. The emphasis in this chapter is on the North

American Indians; the music of Latin American Indians is discussed further in Chapter 9.

THE SIMPLEST STYLES:
EXAMPLES FROM BOLIVIA AND CALIFORNIA

Among some Indian tribes we find music as simple as any in the world. Melodies with only two or three tones, and with a single phrase which is repeated imprecisely many times, can be found in several areas. The Sirionó of Bolivia are an interesting example,[1] for they contradict one of the truisms often repeated about the "earliest" music: rather than fulfilling ritual functions, it seems to be used mainly for entertainment. The Sirionó have no instruments and only a few simple tunes. They sing in the evening after dark, and in the morning, in their hammocks, before beginning the day's activities. The words of the songs are evidently improvised and deal with all kinds of events, past and present, assuming in a way the role of conversation. The songs usually have descending melodic contour and are sung with a *decrescendo* as the singer's breath runs out. Curiously, it seems that each member of the tribe has one tune that is the basis of all the songs he or she sings. New words may be made up, but one and the same tune is used, possibly throughout a person's life. Even in such a simple musical culture there are some individuals who are said to be superior singers and who teach the young people to sing. Example 8-1 illustrates a Sirionó song.

Similarly simple styles are found in the music of some tribes of Northern California. Detailed analysis of the songs in such a repertory may reveal, however, that within the severe limitations that the composers in a tribe place upon themselves there is a great deal of variety and sophistication. The last living member of the Yahi tribe, Ishi, who was discovered

EXAMPLE 8-1. Sirionó Indian song, from Mary Key, "Music of the Sirionó (Guaranian)," *Ethnomusicology*, VII (1963), 20.

repeats many times

[1] Mary Key, "Music of the Sirionó (Guaranian)," *Ethnomusicology*, VII (1963), 17–21.

EXAMPLE 8-2. Two Yahi Indian songs, sung by Ishi, from Bruno Nettl, "The Songs of Ishi," *The Musical Quarterly*, LI (1965), 473, 474.

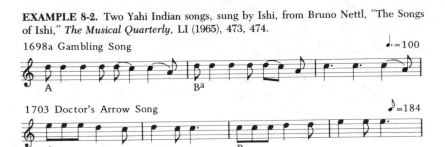

alone in 1911 and who sang all of the songs that he knew for anthropologists at the University of California Museum of Anthropology before he died in 1916, provides an interesting example. The songs of Ishi are all extremely short—five to ten seconds of music, repeated many times—and they use two, three, or four tones (in very rare cases, five) within a range of a fourth or fifth. Most of the songs consist of two or three short phrases, related to each other in various ways. The second phrase may be a variation of the first, an inversion, an extension, a condensation. A large number of different kinds of relationship between two or three short bits of music are exhibited; the composers had done everything possible, as it were, to provide musical variety and interest within the strict limitations that tradition had placed on them. Example 8-2 illustrates two of the songs of Ishi.

USES OF INDIAN MUSIC: AN EXAMPLE FROM THE PLAINS

In their traditional culture, Indian tribes with more complex musical cultures usually had several types of songs, each of which was associated with different activities. For example, the Arapaho Indians of the North American Plains had ceremonial and secular songs. Among the former, the most elaborate are the songs of the Sun Dance, a ceremony performed in the summer, when the various bands of the tribe came together after being separated all winter. The Sun Dance involves the search for a vision in which the individual warrior receives a guardian spirit. The vision is brought on by self-torture and by dancing around a pole while looking at the bright sun for hours. With the exception of the Ghost Dance and Peyote songs which are discussed later, all of the Arapaho songs are very much alike; they consist of two sections, each descending in a terrace-like contour; they have a range greater than an octave and scales of four, five, or six tones, and they are sung with great tension on the vocal chords and with rhythmic pulsations on the long notes. Even though they sound much alike, the various types of songs have certain individual characteristics. Thus the Sun Dance songs are a bit longer than the rest; have a slightly larger average range (about a twelfth); and their final phrase, in the last repetition at a performance of a song, is sung by the women alone. Songs learned in visions are another type, and songs belonging to the various age-grade societies, a third. (Each man was a member of one of seven age-grade societies, with elaborate initiations and with particular duties in war; as he aged he was promoted from one society to the next.) Among the secular songs, we may mention various types of social dance songs—the snake dance, turtle dance, round dance, and rabbit dance. Each has minor characteristics distinguishing it: The round dance songs are usually in rollicking triple meter; the rabbit dance—danced by couples and evidently introduced after contact with the whites—has songs that ordinarily begin with descending fourths. There are war songs intended to inspire warriors, and others used to recount events in recent battles. There are also songs said to be taught by the guardian spirit, which the recipient is to sing only when he is near death. There are also children's songs, lullabies, and love songs.

Finally we must mention two types of songs recognized as separate genres by the Arapaho and by other Plains tribes, the Ghost Dance and Peyote songs. The Ghost Dance is a religion that was introduced in the 1880s by tribes further west, in the Great Basin of Nevada; it was a cult, outlawed by the United States in 1891, which preached war and annihilation to the encroaching whites, a last-ditch stand against the inevitable. The Ghost Dance movement brought with it, from the Great Basin, a musical style different from that of the older Plains songs. Typically its songs had a smaller range and a form in which each phrase was repeated once, for instance, AABB or AABBCC. Among the Plains Indians, such as the Arapaho, these songs came to be associated with the Ghost Dance religion, and when the dance was outlawed, the songs continued to be sung. Their style was also associated with hand games and gambling games.

Another musical style was brought to the Arapaho and to many other tribes throughout the United States and particularly to the Northern Plains, by the Peyote religion. Peyote, a cactus indigenous in Mexico, has buttons which when chewed have a mild narcotic effect, producing euphoria and eventually pleasant hallucinations. The Aztecs already had a cult built around Peyote, but a religion of a different sort, preaching conciliation with the whites and including some superficial elements of Christianity, was based on this drug in North America. Peyote reached some of the Apache tribes after 1700 and spread from them to the majority of tribes in the United States during the nineteenth and early twentieth centuries. The style of Peyote music is essentially the same among all of the North American tribes that use the Peyote ceremonies, and it differs uniformly from the older musical styles of those tribes. Its form is similar to that of the older Plains songs, but its rhythm is characterized by the fact that it is rapid and composed mainly of only two note values which can be notated using quarter and eighth notes; also it is accompanied by rapid playing of the drum and rattle. Special kinds of nonlexical syllables and a particular closing or cadential formula are used. Peyote songs are definitely considered as a special type by the Arapaho.

The Arapaho culture did not have as many uses of music as did some other Indian tribes. For example, the Pueblo Indians had much more complex and numerous ceremonial songs. They also used music to accompany work, something unusual among Indians. The Navaho had elaborate curing rituals accompanied by several series of songs, and a large body of corn grinding songs. The Indians of the southeastern United States had many kinds of social dances. Throughout, music was associated with religion, and no description of a ceremony would be complete without a discussion of the songs. In most tribes, the most significant musical creations were those in the ceremonies. Among the Eskimos, some songs were used to settle disputes and to relieve the resulting tension.

MUSIC IN INDIAN THOUGHT

We have only little knowledge regarding the musical aesthetics of Native Americans. Ability to sing many songs, and to sing high, is the mark of a good singer on the Plains; the Pueblo Indians, on the other hand, prefer singers with low, growling voices. Songs are judged according to their "power" rather than their beauty. Various ideas regarding the origin of songs are found among the North American tribes. According to some, all songs were given to the tribe "in the beginning," and the idea that new songs can be made up is not accepted. Among the Yuman tribes of the extreme Southwest, songs are thought to be "dreamed," that is, made up or given to a person while he is asleep.[2] Yuman persons who are disturbed or emotionally maladjusted retire for a few weeks to a secluded hut, there to meditate and to "dream" songs, eventually to emerge much improved. Among the Pima of the Southwest, we find the idea that songs already exist, and that it is the job of the composer simply to "untangle" them. Among the Plains tribes, the idea that songs come in visions is prevalent; all songs do not come in this way, but those which are ceremonially most significant do. The possibility of learning songs from other tribes is accepted

---

[2] George Herzog, "Music in the Thinking of the American Indian," *Peabody Bulletin*, May 1933, pp. 1–6.

variously. Herzog found that the Pima, who sang songs with Yuma words, would not admit that these songs could have been imported. On the other hand, Plains tribes regularly label the songs borrowed from other tribes; thus the Cheyenne Indians have "Kiowa songs" and "Comanche songs."

The degree to which songs retain their form from year to year and from generation to generation also varies. Some tribes, such as those of the Northwest Coast, consider it important to keep a song intact. Change or error might invalidate its purpose in ritual or rob it of its power. Thus organized rehearsing was instituted and errors were punished. The attempt to retain the cultural heritage intact and the resistance to change in general is also felt, of course, in the musical culture. The Pueblo Indians, who have tended to resist change in all areas, have also kept their musical culture away from Western influence more than have some other tribes. The Plains Indians, who had a rather loose and informal political and ceremonial structure, evidently did not adhere to such standardized forms; one Arapaho informant, upon hearing a recording of one of his tribal songs, performed what he considered "the same song" by singing what seemed to the investigator a totally different melody.

MUSICAL INSTRUMENTS

The instruments of the North American Indians are relatively few in number, but the Middle and South American tribes had a considerable wealth of them. In North America, flutes and various sorts of percussion instruments constitute an overwhelming majority. Flutes are usually of the recorder type, with varying numbers of finger holes; the tunes they are used to perform are frequently those of songs that are also sung. True flutes, without the plug of the recorder, also appear. In some cases, ornamentation in the vocal line is faithfully reproduced on the flute; in others, the flute embellishes the tune. Flutes are most frequently used to play love songs, and they are played almost exclusively by men. Whistles of various sorts, made of bone, pottery, or wood, are used in conjunction with songs and ceremonies. Drums and rattles are the main percussion instruments of North America. The drums are usually beaten with sticks rather than the hand, and they (as well as the rattles) are used only to accompany song. Most Indian drums have a single drumhead; some are so large that they can be played by several players simultaneously. Some are held in one hand, the player grasping the leather thongs that hold the skin against the rim. Kettledrums, sometimes filled with water, are also used. The Peyote ceremony requires such a drum, its drumhead moistened to attain appropriate pitch. Typically, each drum is associated with one or several specific

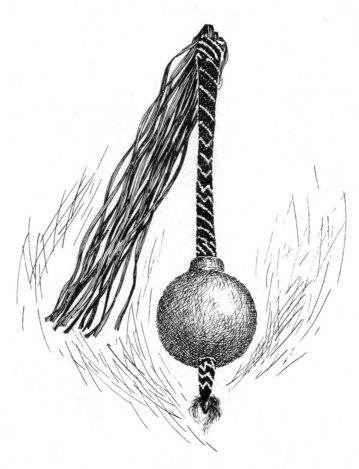

Plains Indian gourd rattle

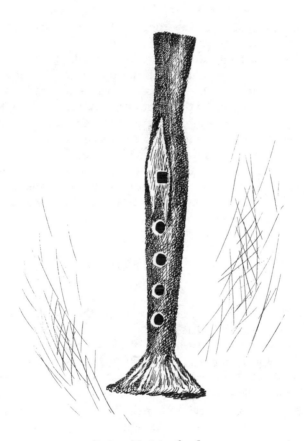

Ancient Mexican clay flute

ceremonies and is an object of importance beyond its musical service. Rattles are also of various types and associated with specific ceremonies. Gourd rattles (with pebbles inside the gourd) are used for Peyote ceremonies. Also used in North America are rattles made of deer hooves strung together, rattles made on a base consisting of a turtle shell, notched sticks held against a basket resonator and rubbed with another stick, and wooden bells.

The South American Indians have a larger variety of rattles, but they are particularly distinguished from the North American tribes in their development of panpipes and of chordophones (string instruments). Panpipes made of fired clay and of wood seem to have been used in the highlands of Peru and Bolivia for centuries. Some have pipes up to five feet tall. The number and arrangement of pipes vary, but, interestingly enough, this type of instrument has been altered and its scale made to fit Western popular music, so that some of the present-day Indians of Peru, for example, use them to play tunes in the prevalent Hispanic style. Although there is inconclusive evidence that some North American tribes used hunting bows to play simple tunes, the musical bow, played in much the same ways as in Africa, appears among several South American tribes, including the simple Araucanians of Patagonia. The high cultures of Peru, Colombia, and Mexico had rather elaborate instruments of various sorts, but we know little about the music produced on them.

STYLES BY AREA IN NORTH AMERICA

The distribution of musical styles among the North American Indians coincides more or less with that of the culture areas. There appears to be, however, a somewhat smaller degree of correspondence here than there is in Africa. In North America (north of Mexico) there are six main areas; in some cases these cannot be distinguished on the basis of single pieces of music, and the distinctions among them are statistical, that is, they depend on the frequency of a given trait rather than its simple presence or absence.

1. The Northwest Coast-Eskimo area contains, besides the areas mentioned, the Salish Indians in the interior of British Columbia and in the state of Washington. Although these groups have little in common cultur- ally, they seem to be among the most recent immigrants from Asia. Their music is characterized by nonstrophic forms, by complex and sometimes nonmetrical rhythmic organization, by the prominence of small intervals such as minor seconds, and by a relatively small range in the melodies. The melodic contours in Eskimo music tend to be undulating, whereas they are more frequently of a pendulum type in Northwest Coast and Salish music. One important characteristic is the use of rhythmic motifs in the

percussive accompaniment. Generally, in Indian music, drums and rattles follow a simple pulse. But in the Northwest Coast-Eskimo area, designs such as ♪♪♪♩ or ♪♪ ♪ are found. Despite this shared feature, however, the Eskimo music is generally simple whereas that of the Northwest is complex and, in its relative wealth of instruments, indicates some relationship to the culture of the Mexican civilizations.

2. The California-Yuman area, consisting of tribes in central California and of the Yuman-speaking tribes of the extreme southwestern United States, is characterized by singing in a relatively relaxed manner. Most Indian tribes use a tense, harsh vocal technique, but here the singing is more in the style of Western or Central European folk singing. The songs are not in strophic form; rather, they consist of two or more separate sections or phrases which are repeated, alternated, and interwoven without a predetermined pattern. The most characteristic feature of this area is the so-called *rise*, a form discovered and labeled by George Herzog.[3] The rise itself is a section of a song that is slightly higher in pitch than the rest of the song if not very obviously so. The Yuman Indians recognize this feature and use a word roughly translated as "rise" to indicate it. The rise is found in most songs of the California-Yuman area, and also elsewhere, mainly along the coasts of North America. It is found in some 20 or 30 percent of the songs of some Northwest Coast peoples, and in those of the Southeastern Choctaw, in 10 to 20 percent of the songs of the Northeastern Penobscot and the Northwestern Nootka, and in less than 10 percent of the repertory of the Southeastern Creek, Yuchi, and Tutelo.

3. A third area is centered in the Great Basin of Nevada, Utah, and northern interior Canada, basically a desert area with simple hunting and gathering cultures. The style of the music here became the style of the Ghost Dance songs further to the east. Singing is in a relatively relaxed manner, melodic range is small, and the typical form is that of paired phrases, with each phrase repeated once. In the northwestern part of the area, some tribes with even a simpler style—the Modoc and Klamath, for example—have many songs consisting of a single repeated phrase. This kind of form is found in traditional musics throughout the world, and there are a few Indian tribes such as the previously mentioned Sirionó of Bolivia whose entire repertories don't go beyond this level of simplicity. But it seems possible that the simple repetitive forms of the Modoc and Klamath are historically related to the somewhat more complex but still essentially repetitive forms of the Great Basin proper. Because of long-standing contacts with the Plains Indians, the Great Basin tribes also have songs in the Plains

[3] George Herzog, "The Yuman Musical Style," *Journal of American Folklore*, LXI (1928), 183–231.

style. And an interesting exception to the tendency of Indian songs to be short and to eschew narration is the existence, among the Ute, of some songs that serve as vehicles for reciting tales. These narrative songs do not have strophic forms (as do European ballads), but continue in unstructured fashion, liberally repeating and varying a few basic musical motifs. Example 8-3 illustrates the Great Basin style.

4. A fourth area, the Athabascan, seems to coincide with a language family by the same name. It consists of the Navaho and Apache tribes and, possibly, of another group of tribes, the Northern Athabascans in Western Canada. Though these northern tribes have for centuries been separated from the Navaho and Apache by a thousand miles, there is evidence that the musical styles of the two areas are related. The music of the Navaho is the most complex of this area, perhaps because it has been greatly influenced by the neighboring Pueblo tribes. Its melodies have a large range, a pendulum-like melodic movement, and large intervals; there is liberal use of falsetto. The Apache songs tend to have smaller range and tenser singing. What relates the two musics is the form—usually nonstrophic and resembling that of the California-Yuman tribes—and the rhythmic structure, in which meter is rather well established but changes frequently and suddenly. The note values in each song are few, usually just two, quarters and eighths, and it seems likely that the style of Peyote music, as previously described for the Arapaho, is in this respect based on the music of the Apache, from whom the use of Peyote for ceremonies had spread to the other tribes. Example 8-4 is a Navaho song.

5. The Plains-Pueblo area takes in two of the most important cultural groups, the Plains Indians (Blackfoot, Crow, Dakota, Comanche, Kiowa, and others) and the Pueblo Indians. The most recent aboriginal form of living of the Plains Indians was nomadic; their economy was based on the buffalo. Their loose political and ceremonial structure contrasts with the elaborate organization of life and religion among the Pueblo Indians (Hopi, Zuni, Taos, and others), and in recent centuries there has been only slight contact between these two groups. Yet their music shares some important characteristics, particularly the great amount of tension in the singing and the two-part song form, which was previously described for the Arapaho.

EXAMPLE 8-3. Paiute Indian song, transcribed by Bruno Nettl from the recording *Great Basin: Paiute, Washo, Ute, Bannock, Shoshone* (Library of Congress AAFS L38), recorded and edited by Willard Rhodes.

EXAMPLE 8-4. Navaho Indian Enemy Way ceremony song, from David P. McAllester, *Enemy Way Music* (Cambridge, MA: Peabody Museum of Harvard University, 1954), song no. 35.

The use of terrace-like melodic contour, gradually descending and leveling off on a long, low tone, is also typical (although the Pueblo songs often precede this form with a low-pitched introduction). The area directly east of the Plains, including the Pawnee and the Eastern Woodland tribes such as the Menomini, Chippewa, and Winnebago, shares the main traits of the Plains but adds some characteristic ones of its own. Typically the Plains songs do not have strongly pronounced metric units, nor are repeated rhythmic patterns or motifs usually evident. Among the tribes to the east, however, repeated rhythmic motifs can be identified, and a good many songs have elements of isorhythmic form—a rhythmic pattern repeated several times, with different melodic content each time. This practice is also found here and there among the typical Plains tribes. Example 8-5 presents an Arapaho song.

6. The eastern portion of the United States and southern Canada may be considered as one musical area, although it is only sporadically known. Perhaps the most distinctive feature is the development of respon-

EXAMPLE 8-5. Arapaho Sun Dance song, from Bruno Nettl, *Musical Culture of the Arapaho* (M.A. thesis, Indiana University, 1951), p. 100.

Song is repeated four times. Drum begins before the singers.
* Women enter here in repeat.
⊕ During last rendition, women finish alone, without drum.

sorial singing—shouts thrown back and forth between leader and chorus, probably as a result of rudimentary rounds. Forms are frequently elaborate and composed of several phrases, some of which recur. Thus the Eagle Dance ceremony of the Iroquois has many songs with the form of AABAB, in which section A is always accompanied by quick shaking of a rattle, while B has slower percussive accompaniment. Similarly, some of the southeastern tribes have social dances accompanied by groups of songs strung together in series that are repeated and interwoven in intricate sequences. Vocal quality is tense, and melodic contour usually descending, though not in the predictable terrace patterns of the Plains. The tribes living in the Gulf of Mexico area seem to have had, before the advent of the whites, a very complex culture related to that of the Aztecs, and it is possible that their music was similarly more complex. But little of this remains. Example 8-6 is an Iroquois song, an example of music from the Eastern area.

The level of musical complexity among these areas varies. Pueblo, Eastern, and Northwest Coast are the most complex and developed, and the Great Basin is, on the whole, the simplest. Although the musical areas do not correspond precisely to the culture areas, they do coincide at various major points. Such easily defined culture areas as the Plains and the Northwest Coast have a unified musical style. The greatest cultural diversity as well as the greatest musical variety is found in the western part of the continent. On the other hand, the large number of language families found in North America do not coincide in their geographic distribution with either the musical or the culture areas.

EXAMPLE 8-6. Iroquois thanksgiving ritual song, from Wallace Chafe, *Seneca Thanksgiving Rituals* (Washington, DC: Bureau of American Ethnology, Bulletin 183, 1961), p. 66.

INDIAN MUSIC OF LATIN AMERICA

It is interesting to find some of the North American stylistic traits paralleled in South America. This is true of the terrace-shaped melodic contours of the Plains tribes, which are found also among tribes in northern Argentina. But in contrast to North America, the South American Indians seem to have developed some polyphony to the level of definite intention; thus the tribes of Tierra del Fuego occasionally sing in parallel fifths.

The Latin America area produced several Indian cultures whose technology and whose social and political organization were considerably higher than those of most nonliterate tribes, which were, in fact, comparable to some of the ancient civilizations of Europe and Asia. We are speaking, of course, of the Mayas of the Yucatán peninsula (who developed a kind of written communication), the Aztecs, and some of their predecessors, the Inca of Peru, and the Chibcha of Colombia. Archeological evidence indicates that they had rather elaborate musical practices and styles. Their instruments were larger in number than those of other tribes. Pictorial representations of groups of instrumentalists indicate that playing in ensembles was a common practice. The Mexican cultures, though together they span hundreds of years, seem to have used essentially the same instruments. Prominent were the *teponatzli*, a log drum with a slit similar to some of the West African signal drums; the *tlapitzalli* (our names here are the Náhuatl forms—this is the language of the Aztecs), a true flute with four finger holes, made of clay, reed, or bone, with major seconds and minor thirds as the main intervals; the *huehuetl*, a kettledrum which was produced in several distinct sizes and pitches; a conch-shell trumpet; rattles; and rasps. The Incas added to these types a large number of ocarinas, flutes with varying numbers of finger holes (three to eight), and panpipes. The identity of tuning of some Peruvian panpipes with some of Oceania has been a factor in the debate about the possibility and nature of contact between native South America and Oceania.

According to early Spanish accounts of the remnants of Aztec culture,[4] the Aztecs recognized only religious music, and musical life was largely in the hands of a professional religious caste. Some instruments themselves had divine power. Music was normally performed by groups in concert, and responsorial singing was heard. Musicians were trained rigidly, and performances had to be completely accurate in order to please the deities; performers who made errors, such as missed drumbeats, were punished.

Before their discovery by the Spaniards, the Inca evidently had an even more elaborate musical culture than the Aztecs. The ruler had specially trained musicians for entertainment at his court. A school of music was instituted at Cuzco by the Inca Roca about 1350,[5] and in the fifteenth century the Inca Pachacuti ordered the collection of narrative songs about the deeds of the earlier Inca rulers; these were organized in song cycles.

THE WORDS OF INDIAN SONGS

The words of Indian songs are of considerable interest, for they frequently fit into the musical structure in unexpected and interesting ways. For example, the Plains Indians, with their two-part song structure, have developed a rather dramatic but simultaneously utilitarian way of setting

[4] See Robert Stevenson, *Music in Mexico* (New York: Crowell, 1952), pp. 14–19.

[5] Robert Stevenson, *The Music of Peru: Aboriginal and Viceroyal Epochs* (Washington, DC: Pan American Union, 1959), p. 39. The music of the Aztecs and Incas is discussed further by Stevenson in *Music in Aztec and Inca Territory* (Berkeley: University of California Press, 1968).

words to music. Most of the song is taken up with syllables such as "he-he" or "ho-ho," but recognizable words appear at the beginning of the second section, which starts again (as does the first) on a high note and works its way downward. The text's structure does not have the characteristics, such as rhyme or meter, of European poetry; it is rather like prose, although nonlexical syllables (vocables) sometimes appear between words and even between the syllables of one word, presumably in order to keep the stressed syllables on stressed musical beats. The text does not fill the whole second part of the song; when it is finished, vocables are again used to fill in the rest of the melody. This kind of structure gives considerable flexibility to the composer or poet, who is able to substitute new words for old in the same tune, or to make slight changes in the words in order to keep up with the times. Thus warriors of the Plains would report on their exploits in such songs, and the same tune could be used for various exploits. After World War I, in which many Indians served as soldiers, old tunes with new words recounting stories of the war began to appear. Such words as Germany and an Arapaho word for submarine began to appear in the songs. Frequently these songs used texts from the tribal wars, but simply substituted German soldiers for Indian tribes, for example, "The German officer ran and dragged his blanket along." The following are song texts of the Arapaho:[6]

Woman, don't worry about me; I'm coming back home to eat berries.
I am the crow; watch me.
The bird has come; it makes yellow the sky.
Young man, be brave; you're going to a dangerous place; your chieftainship will become famous.
Really it is good to be young, for old age is not far off.
The Ute Indian, while he was still looking around for me, I scalped him alive.
Young man, it is good that you are going to war.

Elsewhere among the North American Indians, however, nonlexical syllables are not so prevalent, and entire tunes are supplied with words; the subjects range from serious thoughts about the gods, to lyrical complaints about the weather, to frivolous love songs. But the songs using vocables occupy an important role, analogous perhaps to instrumental music. There are entire bodies of song of this type. The famous night chant of the Navaho, the "yeibetchai," includes a group of songs sung by masked dancers in falsetto without recognizable words. Many of the Peyote songs use only vocables, but, interestingly enough, they use special patterns such as "yowitsini," "heyowitsi," and "heyowitsinayo," which can easily be identified as belonging to the Peyote. Some of the Indian texts are long and elaborate; the Navaho

---

[6] Collected by Bruno Nettl.

songs may enumerate holy people, places, or things in great numbers. More commonly, however, a short sentence or phrase is repeated several times.

INDIAN MUSIC IN MODERN AMERICA

Considering the small number of Indians and the tremendous impact of Western culture on their lives, it would be surprising if their music had remained uninfluenced by that of the West, and particularly by Western thought and ideas about music. The effect of Westernization can be seen in many, sometimes contradictory, ways. It is important, first, to reiterate an important difference between North and Latin American Indian cultures. The Indians of Latin America, who in several countries now make up the bulk of the Spanish- or Portuguese-speaking population, have learned Iberian folk music styles and have also developed styles that are to a considerable extent mixtures of European and Indian materials. For example, in the Andes of Peru, tunes in an essentially Hispanic style are played on the aboriginal Indian panpipes; many similar illustrations could be cited. On the other hand, in North America—probably because the Indians have largely been segregated—such a mixture of styles has not taken place. But there is a great deal of evidence that principles of musical thought, aesthetics, and social organization from the white Americans have made their mark in contemporary Native American musical culture. To be sure, many American Indians now participate in purely Western musicial practices, but they do not have, as a major part of their repertory, music that sounds both Indian and Western, although their way of singing the strictly Indian music may be influenced subtly by Western ideas of making music.

The fact that North American Indian and European musical styles have not merged is probably also due in part to the great difference between them, a difference verging on incompatibility (in contrast, for instance, to the greater compatibility between European and African musics). But despite the points made in the previous paragraph, there are some changes in style that have come about through Western music. More recent Indian songs appear to have an interval and intonation structure more like that of Western music than do older songs, and accompaniment of piano or guitar is occasionally found.

Even so, the influence of Western civilization on Indian music is most commonly felt in less direct ways, and this is true of both the historical and the contemporary Indian cultures. In Mexico and Peru, the relatively high developments of music were reduced to simpler levels and styles through the annihilation of the aboriginal ruling classes, and through the introduction of Christianity. In Central America, the presence of simple xylophone-like instruments facilitated the introduction of the African marimba. In North America, tribes with radically different cultures became neighbors and learned from each other. One example is the Shawnee tribe, which at the time of first white contact was located in the southeastern United States, but had probably come from the Northeast a few centuries before. The Shawnee tribe participated in the music of the Eastern musical area but was forced to migrate repeatedly and was finally located largely in Oklahoma, near the Plains Indians. Its repertory today contains songs in both the Eastern and Plains styles, simple songs of an older layer which the Shawnee may have brought with them from the Northeast and songs in the Peyote style. The spreading of the Peyote and Ghost Dance styles to tribes with other kinds of music, such as the Plains Indians, was also a result, though somewhat indirect, of the impact of Western culture, which caused the rapid spreading of new religions that were needed to cope with the drastically changed condition of the Indians, and which brought about the equally rapid distribution of musical styles. These kinds of indirect influences of Western civilization continue into the present.

Among the Indians of the United States, and of the Northern Plains in particular, music is developing and flourishing. Its role now is primarily that of a symbol of Indian identity, because it is one of the few aspects of Indian life into which whites have not penetrated, and which they are usually unwilling to take the trouble to imitate. Although Indians can hardly avoid trying to enter the Western economic and political systems, and although they have been converted religiously as a result of centuries of missionizing, there is little reason why they should not continue to sing in distinctively Indian musical styles. But many of the activities to which music was essential in the past are now gone—the traditional religions, war, the buffalo. On the other hand, the fact that Indians of various tribes have been thrown together on some of the reservations, and also their relatively greater mobility (along with other Americans), have added to a desire on their part to retain a single Indian identity, rather than a separate tribal identity, and has facilitated musical contact and exchange of materials among Indian peoples. All of this has led to a pan-Indian culture and musical style, based essentially on the culture of the Plains, as far as music is concerned, but distributed throughout a large part of the United States and Canada. In this culture, the older, largely ceremonial musics live on only as relics, to be occasionally dusted off and brought out for the sake of tradition, and living vividly only in the memories of older persons. (But there is evidence that each generation, as it grows older, begins to take an interest in this older material, so that it does not completely die out.)

Flourishing, however, is the music accompanying social dances. Here we find many songs being composed each year, and we see the development of a class of singers and drummers who are semiprofessional, admired not for the power which their knowledge of songs brings them but for their knowledge of a repertory, and for the excellence with which they perform it—a way of thinking about music typical of Western culture. We see Indians recognizing musical composition as a human rather than a supernatural act. We find older practices, such as the Sun Dance, translated into the modern powwow, which has the social functions of the old Sun Dance— bringing the tribe together and permitting social interchange, gambling, and athletic contests—but which no longer has the religious function. We find a higher degree of standardization of musical forms, due perhaps to the greater standardization in the forms of Western music known to the Indians—particularly hymns and country music—but also perhaps due to the need for learning songs from other tribes as quickly as possible. Large intertribal festivals in such places as Anadarko, Oklahoma, and Gallup, New Mexico, accelerate the intertribal contacts and provide a Western-style forum for star Indian musicians and dancers. Because Indian languages are no longer spoken by all Indians, and because speakers of various languages will sing a song together, there is an acceleration of the old Plains practice of singing songs without words, with nonlexical syllables only, or, occasionally, of singing Indian songs with English words. And Indian music has become, like Western music, something which expert musicians perform for an audience (both Indian and white), rather than as an integral part of many everyday activities. Record companies now issue discs primarily for an Indian market. All of this shows that Indian musical culture in North America is still very much alive, but that its functions and uses have changed as the lifestyles of the Indians have changed, in the direction of Western culture. Thus the role of music in Indian life is today very much like the role of folk music in the life of other minorities in North American culture.

BIBLIOGRAPHICAL AND DISCOGRAPHICAL NOTES

Because this chapter introduces the music of the Americas generally, besides covering American Indian music, some publications on the entire subject are cited here. Important reference works include Terry E. Miller, *Folk Music in America: A Reference Guide* (New York: Garland, 1986); David Horn, *The Literature of American Music in Books and Folk Music Collections* (Metuchen, NJ: Scarecrow Press, 1977); Edith Fowke and Carole Henderson Carpenter, *A Bibliography of Canadian Folklore in English* (Toronto: University of Toronto Press, 1981); Charles Haywood, *A Bibliography of North American Folklore and Folksong*, 2nd rev. ed., 2 vols. (New York: Dover, 1961); Ray M. Lawless, *Folksingers and Folksongs in America: A Handbook of Biography, Bibliography, and Discography*, 2nd rev. ed. (New York: Duell, Sloan &

Pearce, 1960; reprint Westport, CT: Greenwood Press, 1981); *Resources of American Music History*, ed. D. W. Krummel and others (Urbana: University of Illinois Press, 1981); and Gilbert Chase, *A Guide to the Music of Latin America*, 2nd ed. (Washington, DC: Pan American Union, 1962). *The New Grove Dictionary of American Music*, 4 vols., ed. H. Wiley Hitchcock and Stanley Sadie (London: Macmillan Press, 1986), contains several fine articles pertaining to folk and traditional musics of the United States. Bruno Nettl, *An Introduction to Folk Music in the United States*, 3rd ed., revised by Helen Myers (Detroit: Wayne State University Press, 1976), is a survey. A special Canadian issue of *Ethnomusicology*, Vol. XVI, no. 3 (September 1972), ed. Israel J. Katz, includes discussions of folk and Native American musics in Canada, as well as bibliographies and discographies.

Two attempts to show the various styles in North American Indian music are Helen H. Roberts, *Musical Areas in Aboriginal North America* (New Haven: Yale University Press, 1936), and Bruno Nettl, *North American Indian Musical Styles* (Philadelphia: American Folklore Society, 1954). The most prolific author on North American Indian music was Frances Densmore, and all of her publications, many of them published by the Bureau of American Ethnology, Smithsonian Institution, Washington, DC, are worth examination. Willard Rhodes, "Acculturation in North American Indian Music," in *Acculturation in the Americas*, ed. Sol Tax (Chicago: University of Chicago Press, 1952), is also important. Essays in the UCLA *Selected Reports in Ethnomusicology*, Vol. III, no. 2 (1980), an issue devoted to music of the North American Indian, exhibit a variety of approaches and focusses. Marcia Herndon, *Native American Music* (Norwood, PA: Norwood Editions, 1980), concentrates on the cultural context for music. A survey of recent developments relating to Pan-Indianism may be found in James H. Howard, "Pan-Indianism in Native American Music and Dance," *Ethnomusicology*, XXVII (1983), 71–82. Useful reference aids are Marsha Maguire, Pamela Feldman, and Joseph C. Hickerson, *American Indian and Eskimo Music: A Selected Bibliography through 1981* (Washington, DC: Archive of Folk Culture, Library of Congress, 1983); Marie-Françoise Guédon, "Canadian Indian Ethnomusicology: Selected Bibliography and Discography," *Ethnomusicology*, XVI (1972), 465–78; Beverley Cavanagh, "Annotated Bibliography: Eskimo Music," *Ethnomusicology*, XVI (1972), 479–87; and Dorothy Sara Lee, *Native North American Music and Oral Data: A Catalogue of Sound Recordings, 1893–1976* (Bloomington: Indiana University Press, 1979).

An excellent study of the music and musical culture of one American Indian tribe is Alan P. Merriam, *Ethnomusicology of the Flathead Indians* (Chicago: Aldine Press, 1967). Also of great interest is Robert Witmer, *The Musical Life of the Blood Indians* (Ottawa: National Museum of Man, 1982). Among the many studies of special problems and styles are the following: David P. McAllester, *Peyote Music* (New York: Viking Fund Publications in Anthropology, 13, 1949), and *Enemy Way Music* (Cambridge, MA: Peabody Museum of Harvard University, 1954); Bruno Nettl, "Studies in Blackfoot Indian Musical Culture," *Ethnomusicology*, XI (1967), 141–60 and 293–309, and XII (1968),

11–48 and 192–208; Charlotte Frisbie, "Vocables in Navajo Ceremonial Music," *Ethnomusicology*, XXIV (1980), 347–92; Thomas Vennum, Jr., *The Ojibwa Dance Drum* (Washington, DC: Smithsonian Institution Press, 1982) (a black and white 16-mm film, *The Drummaker*, is also available); Jill D. Sweet, *Dances of the Tewa Indians: Expressions of New Life* (Santa Fe: School of American Research Press, 1985); Richard Keeling, "Contrast of Song Performance Style as a Function of Sex Role Polarity in the Hupa Brush Dance," *Ethnomusicology*, XXIX (1985), 185–212; and George List, "Stability and Variation in a Hopi Lullaby," *Ethnomusicology*, XXXI (1987), 18–34. Ben Black Bear, Sr., and R. D. Theisz, *Songs and Dances of the Lakota* (Rosebud, SD: Sinte Gleska College, 1976), is a collaborative effort between a native Lakota singer and composer and a non-native scholar and singer; cassette tapes and a color videotape are available to supplement the printed material. Individual singers are the focus of *Navajo Blessingway Singer: The Autobiography of Frank Mitchell 1881–1967*, ed. Charlotte J. Frisbie and David P. McAllester (Tucson: University of Arizona Press, 1978), and of Judith Vander, *Songprints: The Musical Experience of Five Shoshone Women* (Urbana: University of Illinois Press, 1988), for which a sixty-minute cassette is available separately.

Several fine studies of Eskimo music have been published in the Canadian National Museum of Man Mercury Series, among them Thomas Johnston, *Eskimo Music by Region: A Comparative Circumpolar Study* (Ottawa: National Museum of Man, 1976); Maija M. Lutz, *The Effects of Acculturation on Eskimo Music of Cumberland Peninsula* (Ottawa, 1978), and *Musical Traditions of the Labrador Coast Inuit* (Ottawa, 1982); and Beverley Cavanagh, *Music of the Netsilik Eskimo: A Study of Stability and Change*, 2 vols. (Ottawa, 1982), accompanied by an eight-inch disc. Ramon Pelinski, Like Suluk, and Lucy Amarock, *Inuit Songs from Eskimo Point* (Ottawa: National Museum of Man, 1979), is a songbook accompanied by one nine-inch disc.

Among the important publications on Indian music in Latin America are Robert Stevenson, *Music in Aztec and Inca Territory* (Berkeley: University of California Press, 1968); Marguerite and Raoul d'Harcourt, "La musique des Aymara sur les hauts plateaux boliviens," *Journal de la Société des Américanistes*, XLVIII (1959), 5–133; Karl G. Izikowitz, *Musical and Other Sound Instruments of the South American Indians* (Göteborg: Elanders, 1935; reprint Wakefield, Yorkshire: SR Publishers, 1970); John M. Schechter, "The Inca *Cantar Historico*: A Lexico-Historical Elaboration on Two Cultural Themes," *Ethnomusicology*, XXIII (1979), 191–204; Anthony Seeger, "Sing for Your Sister: The Structure and Performance of Suyá Akia," in *The Ethnography of Musical Performance*, ed. N. McLeod and M. Herndon (Norwood, PA: Norwood Editions, 1980), pp. 7–42; and Dale A. Olsen, "Towards a Musical Atlas of Peru," *Ethnomusicology*, XXX (1986), 394–412. Other pertinent sources are listed in the bibliographical notes for Chapter 9.

The Library of Congress has issued a number of recordings made from Frances Densmore's and Willard Rhodes's collections in its series *Folk Music of the*

United States. North American Soundchief Enterprises has issued recordings, primarily of Plains Indian music, in a series *Songs of the Red Man.* This series, and the recordings issued by Indian House, Taos, NM, and by Canyon Records are for use by scholars as well as American Indians interested in hearing songs of their own heritage. As a sample of discs available on the Indian House label (with notes by Tony Isaacs), we mention the following: *Cheyenne Peyote Songs,* IH 2201–2; *Kiowa Gourd Dance,* IH 2503–4; *Flute Songs of the Kiowa and Comanche: Tom Mauchahty-Ware,* IH 2512; *War Dance Songs of the Kiowa,* performed by the O-ho-mah Lodge Singers, IH 2508–9; *The Klagetoh Swingers: Navajo Songs about Love,* IH 1509–10; and *Turtle Dance Songs of San Juan Pueblo,* IH 1101. Also recommended are *Indian Music of the Canadian Plains,* Folkways P 464; *American Indians of the Southwest,* Folkways FW 8850; *Music of the Sioux and Navaho,* Folkways 4401; *Songs of Earth, Water, Fire and Sky: Music of the American Indian,* New World Records NW 246, and *Songs of Love, Luck, Animals and Magic: Music of the Yurok and Tolowa Indians,* New World Records NW 297, both produced by Charlotte Heth; *A Cry from the Earth: Music of the North American Indians,* Folkways FC 7777, ed. John Bierhorst; *Kwakiutl: Indian Music of the Pacific Northwest,* Folkways FE 4122 and *Nootka: Indian Music of the Pacific Northwest Coast,* FE 4524, both with extensive notes by Ida Halpern; *Washo-Peyote Songs: Songs of the American Indian Native Church— Peyotist,* Folkways FE 4384, recorded by Warren L. D'Azevedo; *American Indian Music of the Mississippi Choctaws* (2 discs), available from the Music Department, Choctaw Central High School, Philadelphia, MS 39350; and *Choctaw-Chickasaw Dance Songs* (2 discs), Sweetland Productions (Buster Ned, Chairman, Choctaw-Chickasaw Heritage Committee, Box 44, Mannsville, OK 73447). Inuit music is recorded on *Inuit Games and Songs,* Philips 6586 036, produced under the direction of Jean-Jacques Nattiez, and on *Music of Hudson Bay and Alaska,* Folkways FE 4444, collected by Laura Boulton.

The *Serie de Discos,* INAH 1–23, available from the Instituto Nacional de Antropología y Historia, Córdoba 45, México 1, D. F., México, includes field recordings of Indian music from various regions in Mexico. Indian music of Latin America is also presented on *Anthology of Central and South American Indian Music,* Folkways FE 4524 (2 discs); *Modern Maya: The Indian Music of Chiapas,* Folkways FE 4377 and 4379, recordings and commentary by Richard Alderson; *Mexico: Fiestas of Chiapas and Oaxaca,* with notes by Walter F. Morris, Jr., Nonesuch H-72070; *Music of Guatemala,* Folkways FE 4213; *Music of the Maya-Quichés of Guatemala,* Folkways FE 4226, recordings and notes by Henrietta Yurchenco; *Songs of the Face of the Earth: Ancestor Songs of the Tzutuhil-Maya Indians of Guatemala,* recorded and with notes by Linda Lee O'Brien, Ethnodisc recordings ER 45150-51 (2 cassettes, available from Pachart Publishing House, P. O. Box 6721, Tucson, Arizona 85733); *Music of the Jivaro of Ecuador,* Folkways FE 4386, recordings and commentary by Michael J. Harner; *Music of the Venezuelan Yekuana Indians,* Folkways FE 4104, with notes by Walter Coppens and Isaias Rodríguez; *Wayãpí Guyane,* recordings of Amerindian music of French Guiana

with commentary by Jean-Michel Beaudet, SELAF/ORSTROM CETO 792
(available from Earth Music, P. O. Box 2103, Norwalk, CT 06852); *Instruments
and Music of Bolivia*, Folkways FM 4012; *Musik im Andenhochland/Bolivien*,
recordings and commentary by Max Peter Baumann, Museum Collection
Berlin (West) MC 14; *Mountain Music of Peru*, Folkways FE 4539; *Indian
Music of the Upper Amazon*, Folkways FE 4458; *Music from the Mato Grosso*,
Folkways 4446; *Brésil: Musiques du Haut Xingu*, Ocora 558.517, recorded
by J. F. Schiano; and *Música indigena: A arte vocal dos Suyá*, Edições Tacape
T007, recordings and notes by Judith and Anthony Seeger (available with an
English translation of the notes from A. Seeger, Archives of Traditional Music,
Maxwell Hall 057, Indiana University, Bloomington, IN 47405).

NINE

LATIN AMERICAN FOLK MUSIC

by Gerard Béhague

The Latin American continent and the Spanish Caribbean area present, on the whole, cultural traits obviously inherited from the Iberian Peninsula, but the Iberian-American folk music traditions reveal varying aspects of that old heritage. Many parts of what (for the sake of convenience) is generally called Latin America are virtually devoid of any Latin cultural elements; this is true of numerous tropical-forest Amerindian cultures whose contacts with European traditions have been sporadic over the centuries or relatively recent. Moreover, in many cases the prevailing cultural influences are Afro-American and not Latin American. In addition, other non-Iberian Europeans who settled in Latin America brought with them folk music practices and genres that influenced other traditions but also underwent considerable change over a period of time. To the strong social stratification that character-izes the large majority of Latin America's social organization corresponds a variety of musical expressions that often involve rural and urban societies and their frequent interpenetration. The study of folk music in individual countries or territories is, therefore, bound to be somewhat artificial, although common and general cultural traits do exist in very large geographical areas, such as the areas occupied by the Inca Empire in pre-Columbian times, which extend from western Argentina and northern Chile to the highlands of northern Ecuador, or in the areas of predominantly Afro-American populations, found in Brazil, Trinidad, Cuba, the Dominican Republic, and Puerto Rico, and Western Colombia, Ecuador, and Venezuela with their analogous developments. In such areas, a geographical approach to the study of folk music could be justified. Numerous folk song and dance music genres in the various areas exhibit similar features and functions resulting from their common history. In these cases, an approach by genres might well yield significant results.

The degree to which a single culture predominates—Iberian, Amerindian, or African—varies greatly among the nations, and, within nations, among regions. For example, in Bolivia, where people of pre-Columbian Indian descent represent about 70 percent of the total population, Aymara- and Quechua-speaking native peoples in the *altiplano* area have traditional music, but typical mestizo (a term designating culturally and racially mixed groups in Latin America) folk music predominates in the valleys and the eastern provinces. Mestizo music is often characterized by Spanish-related tunes and song texts in Spanish but uses Indian instruments and accompanies dances of Indian origin. Conversely, it is not uncommon to find rather isolated highland Indian peasant groups using string instruments clearly of Spanish derivation, such as the ubiquitous *charango* developed by the Indians (an instrument with five courses of double strings, made in its most rustic form out of an armadillo shell) and the diatonic harp. As opposed to Indian music of tropical-forest cultures (Mato Grosso and the whole Amazon basin and the main adjacent areas in eastern Peru, Ecuador, southeast Colombia, and southern and eastern Venezuela), Indian music of the Andean countries represents, as a whole, a dominant ingredient of the folk music traditions of the area. Mexican and Central American Indian cultures present a wide variety of social organization and greatly varied mixtures with other cultural groups, so that the resulting continuum ranges from agriculture-based tribal groups with a considerable music continuity to highly homogeneous native enclaves in close contact with mestizo music, to strongly acculturated, Westernized native communities with little or no retention of traditional music of their ancestors. Finally, there are also instances in which Indian music operating in ritual contexts exhibits clear native traditional styles while nonritual musical expressions in the same group follow the prevailing mestizo style of the particular area. This is the case, for example, of the Tarascans (also known as Purépecha) of Michoacán, Mexico. In the transfer of Iberian or African material to the Americas, *syncretism* accounts for the creation of certain forms—that is, features of the two cultures that are similar or compatible grow into a new combined form—and the preservation or rejection of others. It is, therefore, accurate to assume that genuine Latin American folk music traditions are the result of mestizo cultures.

The actual history and ethnohistory of a given country or area should also be considered in accounting for specific stylistic traits and functional features. A case in point would be a comparative historical study of such Caribbean islands as Haiti, Jamaica, and Trinidad. Although a large majority of the population of all three countries is of African descent, the countries were at various periods of their history under the political and cultural domination of Spain, France, and Great Britain. In the case of Trinidad, although France actually never dominated her, French influences (e.g., Trinidadian creole) have been considerable. In addition, the Western African cultures transferred to those areas and brought together by chance had quite diverse origins: predominantly Ewe and Fon (Dahomey/Bénin) in the case of Haiti, mostly Yoruba (Nigeria) and Ashanti (Ghana) in Jamaica and Trinidad. The problem becomes exceedingly intricate when one considers the immigration of East Indians and Chinese to Trinidad, Guiana, and Surinam, or that of Japanese, Germans, and Italians to Peru, Brazil, Uruguay, and Argentina.

The Latin American and Caribbean folk music arena is, then, a very complex one, and a macroscopic exposition can only be contemplated here, with but a few illustrations of representative examples of the various traditions rather than a survey of the entire wealth of song, dance, and instrument types. For the sake of clarity, albeit somewhat arbitrarily, we should distinguish between the Iberian related folk music genres, on the one hand, and mestizo folk genres, on the other, with either Indian-Hispanic or Afro-Hispanic prevailing, depending on the specific area. Hispanic-American and Luso-Brazilian folk musics have maintained enough of their Iberian heritage to allow us to refer to their common general style and functional characteristics. Afro-American music in Latin America is discussed in Chapter 10.

SOUTH AMERICA

Folk Songs

Examples of autonomous folk song genres are relatively few in South American folk music, because song functions in conjunction with dancing in a very high proportion of the repertories. Throughout the continent we find a multitude of song types derived from the old Spanish *romance*, a narrative song form dating back to the early Renaissance, typically based on eight-syllable lines and four-line stanzas (known as the *copla* poetic form, with rhyming schemes of ABCB, known as *rima romancera*). Under different local names, *romances* have been preserved, sometimes in their original form (e.g., in the Chocó province of Colombia) and sometimes with significant variations which reveal the characteristic feeling and world view of the mestizos of a given region. Improvised *coplas* of a narrative nature frequently replace the *romance* as the ballad genre (although they are derived from it), especially in Colombia, the Andean countries, and Argentina. Typically, *romances* and *coplas* describe, in an epic lyrical manner, famous historical events of a region, the feats of a folk hero, or episodes of daily life. Apart from their poetic and musical value, they often provide significant sociological data, frequently expressed in metaphorical language. Example 9-1 shows two versions of a traditional *romance* known in Lima, Peru. Entitled *La esposa difunta o la aparición*, its origin has been traced to sixteenth-century Spain. The regular two- and four-bar phrases and their isometric structure are characteristic of Spanish folk song. Literary versions of the same *romance* have been collected in New Mexico, California, Mexico, Nicaragua, Cuba, the Dominican Republic, Puerto Rico, Venezuela, Ecuador, and several provinces of Argentina, thus attesting to the wide diffusion of the *romance* tradition in Latin America.

Other folk songs, such as the Argentine and Chilean *tonadas* and *tonos*, have maintained other old Spanish literary forms. The *glosa* and the *décima* are, respectively, a quatrain which sets the basic subject or story, and a development of the basic subject in a stanza of ten octosyllabic

EXAMPLE 9-1. Two versions of the romance *La esposa difunta o la aparición*. From Emilia Romero, *El romance tradicional en el Perú* (Mexico: El Colegio de México, 1952), p. 89.

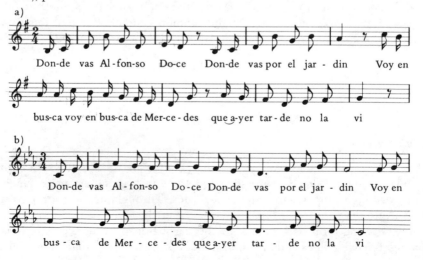

lines. This structure, combining both *glosa* and *décima*, is found in Chilean, Peruvian, Ecuadorian, and Colombian *décimas*, Argentine *estilos* and *cifras*, and in many other genres, such as the *guabina* of Colombia or the *romances* and *xácaras* of Luso-Brazilian folk music. The classical rhyme scheme of the Spanish *décima*, ABBAACCDDC, known as *décima espinela* (after Vicente Espinel who first introduced it in the sixteenth century), prevails in most of the folk song types mentioned.

Actual Iberian folk melodies still extant in Spain and Portugal today, however, are very rare in Latin America. Children's songs (particularly round-play songs and lullabies) seem to be the notable exceptions, for many of them remain basically the same in both areas. The problem of determining the sources of Iberian tunes in Latin American folk music is generally unsolved. But we can say with some certainty that the tunes sung in Latin America are for the most part not simply imports from Spain and Portugal, although the texts more frequently are. They are more usually songs either composed in Latin America in the styles brought from Europe, or brought from Europe centuries ago but so changed by oral tradition that their European relatives can no longer be recognized: Or perhaps it is the European tunes that have undergone change. This situation is paralleled in certain aspects of Afro-American music traditions in Latin America and the Caribbean, particularly those musics that function in African-related religious activities. On the other hand, the traditions of European minority groups living in South America—Germans, Eastern Europeans, Italians—present a different picture, because they have preserved many of the songs brought from Europe, but have not to a large extent created new material in the corresponding styles.

An extensive study of the Chilean *verso*[1] (also known as *canto a lo poeta*), a traditional type of sung poetry, has conclusively shown stylistic similarities with Spanish medieval and Renaissance genres (*cantigas, villancicos*), especially regarding modality, cadential practices, and both strict and free metrical and rhythmic styles. The folk *poetas* or *cantores* perform *versos* accompanying themselves with a guitar or more commonly the *guitarrón* (not to be confused with the Mexican instrument of the same name), an older type of guitar of 25 strings, 21 of them grouped in five courses, the remaining four strings directly attached in pairs to the table of the sound box on each side of the neck. Quite apart from their poetry, which ranges from biblical stories to Spanish historical and legendary accounts of the Middle Ages, the musical behavior of the folk *cantores* reveals striking similarities to the Spanish medieval *juglar* and other European types of troubadour.

---

[1] María Ester Grebe, *The Chilean Verso: A Study in Musical Archaism* (Los Angeles: Latin American Center, University of California, 1967).

Archaic musical elements are also found in the *cantoria* (generic term for poetic singing of a predominantly narrative nature) of Northeast Brazil, as well as in some folk melody types associated with the *desafio* (literally "challenge"), used in singing contests, with frequently improvised texts consisting of questions and answers and performed by two singers, often in antiphonal structure with instrumental interludes (by a *viola*—a folk guitar of five courses of double strings) between the vocal sections. The most common literary form of *desafio* in Brazil is the six-line heptasyllabic stanza, common in Portuguese folk poetry. One of the most popular song types associated with the *desafio* as well as with several dances, such as the *coco*, is the *embolada*, found throughout Brazil's hinterland but originally from the Northeast. Mostly improvised, it is generally declamatory in character and presents a characteristic refrain in addition to the six-line stanza. As in many Brazilian songs, the refrain makes use of alliteration, assonance, and onomatopoeia in a syncopated melodic line with many repeated tones and an unusually fast tempo. The text of the *embolada*, based on stereotyped models, comments on local customs and criticizes figures and events of the community in a very humorous, satirical, and provocative manner. During the 1950s, the *embolada* began to penetrate urban areas, where it has been used mostly as a chronicle of current events. But, as a whole, the *desafio* and *embolada*, together with songs of praise (*louvações*) constitute the main bulk of the folk song repertory of northeastern Brazil. This particular tradition is referred to in Brazil as the *caboclo* tradition, that is, mestizo tradition combining traits and values inherited from the Portuguese and some local Amerindian cultures. In this tradition, we generally find modal melodies, with frequent occurrences of the Lydian and Mixolydian modes. In addition, a mode consisting of a major diatonic scale with the fourth degree sharpened and the seventh flattened often appears in the *caboclo* repertory.

Song genres similar to the *desafio* and forming part of the song-duel tradition of southern Europe are widely used elsewhere in South America; they are called *contrapunto* and *cifra* in Argentina, *payas* in Chile, and *porfias* in Venezuela.

Folk songs of lyrical character whose subject matter is associated with expressions of love abound in South American folk music. Generically known as *tonadas* in the Spanish-speaking countries, and *toadas* in Brazil, they appear, typically, in four-, five-, or ten-line stanzas, sometimes incorporating a refrain. The Argentine *estilo* will serve as an example. According to Isabel Aretz, the *estilo* is a well-defined lyrical song genre made up of two melodic ideas, the "theme," properly speaking, and a somewhat faster strain known as *alegre*.[2] The overall form of the song is ternary, ABA.

[2] Isabel Aretz, *El folklore musical argentino* (Buenos Aires: Ricordi Americana, 1952), p. 144.

The text of the *estilo* is generally set in quatrains or *décimas*. In the Cuyo province of Argentina as well as in Chile, the *estilo* is known as *tonada*, and in the northern provinces it is called *verso* or *décima*. The *estilo* is also common in Uruguay. Example 9-2 illustrates the characteristics of this folk song species: guitar accompaniment (both picked and strummed styles), vocal duet in parallel thirds, and the theme and alegre sections.

An interesting example of folk song in South America is the Brazilian *modinha*, for its origin has been traced to cultivated musical circles in eighteenth-century Portugal and Brazil. It is a love song type whose actual printed examples from the late eighteenth and the nineteenth centuries reveal a strongly sentimental and at times melodramatic character, fairly similar to salon music of the period. *Moda* (diminutive: *modinha*) is a generic term applied vaguely in Brazil and Portugal to a song or a melody. (The *moda-de-viola*, however, is a folk song type known especially in the rural areas of the central and south-central states. Its Portuguese antecedents are most obviously seen in the duet singing in parallel thirds and the folk guitar (*viola*) accompaniment. The nature of the texts (in pentasyllabic and heptasyllabic verses) reveals very often a narrative, satirical, and, less frequently, sentimental and amatory character, with strong reminiscences of the Iberian *romance*.) The Brazilian *modinha* became folklorized only in the latter part of the nineteenth century, when it gradually lost its original Italian operatic flavor and became a simple sentimental song. In the course of its popularization it acquired simpler structures, such as ABACA, or a refrain and a stanza, and the Spanish guitar became its inseparable accompanying instrument. With its cultivated origin, the *modinha* clearly illustrates the direct transplanting of European musical culture into the popular music of Brazil.

A fairly important body of folk songs in South America comes from folk and popular religious customs accompanying the liturgical calendar of the Catholic church. Here again, the repertory exhibits a close relationship with the Iberian Peninsula. Brought to the New World by Spanish and Portuguese missionaries, hymns and songs of praise are still found today and variously known as *alabados*, *alabanzas*, *salves* (hymns of praise) in Spanish, *cantigas de romarias* (songs of pilgrimage) in Portuguese. Most of these are predominantly modal and follow the traditional pattern of folk hymn singing, that is, alternation of refrain (*estribillo*, performed by chorus) and stanza (*copla*, performed by one or two soloists). In the Chocó province of Colombia, inhabited mostly by black Colombians, *alabados*, *romances*, and *salves* are performed antiphonally at various wakes for an adult (*velorios de muerto*) or a child (*velorio de niño* or *gualí*) to pay tribute to the dead person; the text is improvised and frequently alludes to the life story of that person. In responsorial style, these songs maintain an archaic character through the modal structures of the solo lines and polyphonic choral responses in parallel fourths and fifths.

EXAMPLE 9-2. *Estilo.* From Isabel Aretz, *El folklore musical argentino* (Buenos Aires: Ricordi Americana, 1952), p. 147.

Numerous religious folk songs are associated with the Christmas season. Thus the traditional Spanish *villancico* has developed into many folk song genres, known as *aguinaldo, adoración, coplas de Navidad, esquinazo,* and others in the various countries of Latin America. Although most of this body of songs obviously relates to its Spanish counterpart, it also displays many mestizo or *criollo* characteristics. For example, the Venezuelan *villancicos* and *aguinaldos* present a regular meter in 2/4, 6/8, or 3/4, regular phrases of two- and four-bar lengths, major and minor mode or bimodality, melodies in parallel thirds with a range not exceeding a sixth, almost total absence of modulation and chromaticism, and syllabic setting of the text.[3] All of these features are part of the Hispanic Christmas *cancionero.* But most *aguinaldos* differ from the Spanish *villancico* in rhythmic structure. In addition to the indispensable *cuatro* (a small four-string guitar, not to be confused with the Puerto Rican instrument of the same name), they are accompanied by various percussion instruments, such as a double-headed drum (*tambora criolla*), a friction drum (*furruco*), a shaker-rattle (*chineco*), a *güiro*-type rattle (*charrasca*), and maracas. This accompaniment is typically based on the alternation of binary and ternary rhythmic figures, so common in mestizo dances such as the *merengue* and the *guasá.*[4] The melodies of the Venezuelan *aguinaldos* tend also to be more syncopated than the Spanish *villancico.* Example 9-3 shows some of the features of the Venezuelan *aguinaldo.*

Work songs also constitute an important part of the South American folk song repertory. As the predominant rural work is agricultural—farming and animal raising—the various genres of work song naturally reflect that activity. The Spanish *zafra* song refers to the olive harvest in Spain, and the same term is generally used for the sugar cane harvest in the Caribbean and for any type of agricultural work in the Atlantic coastal area of Colombia. Colombian *zafras* are performed either by one man answered by others with typical cries ("gritos"), or by two or more men in alternation. The *copla* forms the most common basis for the texts of the songs, although interjections, the addition of syllables at the beginning and ending of verses, and the occasional insertion of new verses frequently give the performances an improvisatory character. In this same area of Colombia, cattle-herding songs, known as *vaquerías,* are performed in responsorial fashion between various *vaqueros* walking or riding in front and in the rear of the herd. According to George List, the terms *zafra* and *vaquería* refer in the strictest

---

[3] Isabel Aretz, *Cantos navideños en el folklore venezolano* (Caracas: Casa de la Cultura Popular, 1962), pp. 40–42.

[4] Ibid., p. 92.

EXAMPLE 9-3. Venezuelan *aguinaldo*. From Isabel Aretz, *Cantos navideños en el folklore venezolano* (Caracas: Casa de la Cultura Popular, 1962), p. 111.

sense to styles of singing, not to song genres.[5] The two are similar in their rather free form, which is made up of various improvised combinations of melodic patterns, and in the style of vocal production, which favors a very high tessitura. A similar type of herding song is the Brazilian *aboio de gado* performed by *vaqueiros* of south-central and Northeast Brazil. The *aboio* is stylistically different from its Portuguese counterpart in that it is made up of nonlexical syllables, involves no recurrent pulse, and is sometimes sung in parallel thirds in the highest tessitura with sustained tones and

[5] George List, *Music and Poetry in a Colombian Village: A Tri-Cultural Heritage* (Bloomington: Indiana University Press, 1983), p. 308.

vocal *glissandi*. The *aboio da roca*, another type of Brazilian work song, differs from the cattle-herding genre in function (for general agricultural labor contexts) and style (strongly emphasized rhythmic pulse matching the pace and rhythm of the labor).

Autos and Dramatic Dances

Many of the Latin American Christmas and other religious songs are associated with popular dramatizations of the corresponding liturgical feasts, such as the Nativity and the journey of the Three Kings, the Lent and Easter cycle, and the Holy Cross ("Santa Cruz") observance, as well as with processions of various kinds and purposes. Such festivities are known throughout the continent and are variously called *auto sacramental, posadas, pastoris, folias de Reis*, and so on. Dance and choreographed dramatic representations form an integral part of such revelries.

True rituals associated with the Roman Catholic feasts and the commemoration of saints' days, offering examples of cycles of syncretic feasts, are quite common in Latin America and the Spanish Caribbean. Among these, Carnival is the most popular. Many folk dances and songs function within the summer and winter cycles of feasts, such as St. John's Day or feasts to the Virgin, in which syncretism with Indian or African deities is often present. In Brazil, for example, there exist many dramatic dances (*bailados*) whose central subject is always religious. Conversion is the main theme of such dramatic dances as *congada, marujada*, and *moçambique*, whereas *quilombo, caiapó, cabocolinhos*, and *lambe-sujo*, among others, are concerned with resurrection. Most of these dances appeared during the colonial period as a result of the Iberian catechization. In this process, the medieval crusades represented in the Peninsula as dances of Christians and Moors (*Danza de Moros y Cristianos*) were incorporated in similar dances in Hispanic America, where the native infidels became the "Moors." In Brazil, specifically, the Jesuits were responsible for diffusing many of these dances and for giving them unity and uniformity. Indeed, the *congada*, for example, is known all over Brazil. It combines elements of the popular religious theater of the Peninsula with Afro-Brazilian traditions and customs, such as the coronation of Black Kings during the slave period. But in spite of its name and the fact that blacks participate in it in large numbers, the history of the dance suggests that it is not of African origin, but simply "a remembrance of the *Chanson de Roland* (the medieval French *chanson de geste*) wisely turned to the advantage of the catechist."[6] A consideration of the musical components of this dramatic play points to the absence of

---

[6] Alceu Maynard Araújo, *Folclore nacional*, Vol. I (São Paulo: Edições Melhoramentos, 1964), p. 216.

any particularly evident African element, although the call-and-response pattern is often found, and drums frequently accompany the chorus. The songs accompanying the cortege, which is led by the main characters (including Roland himself and Charlemagne, among others), show typical traits of Portuguese folk songs. The text of the play always appears in verse rather than prose, resulting in the adoption and transformation of the main incidents of the medieval epic poem. A number of dramatic dances also refer to the great maritime exploration of Spain and Portugal in the fifteenth and sixteenth centuries, but always in conjunction with their civilizing mission of converting the native populations of the conquered territories.

Folk Dances

In the category of secular folk and popular dances the Latin American countries enjoy a well-known distinction. Many such dances originated in the Iberian Peninsula, and although they have undergone considerable changes in the New World, choreographic traits specific to much Spanish folk dancing, such as shoe tapping (*zapateado*) or finger snapping, remain significant in many dances. This is the case in the Argentine *chacarera*, whose actual origins have not been fully elucidated. The name of the dance is derived from *chacra* meaning "farm" (from the Quechua *chagra*—"cornfield"); thus it is believed that the *chacarera* was probably created by the farmers of the plains (*pampas*) in the province of Buenos Aires, although it is used in almost all Argentine provinces. The choreography includes stamping of the feet and snapping of the fingers. Musically, Spanish ancestry is evident in the hemiola rhythm of the instrumental introduction, generally six or eight measures long. The rhythmic pattern of the introduction is $\frac{6}{8}$ ♩ ♫♫♫ $\frac{3}{4}$ ♩ ♩ ♩ ♪, and that of the vocal part which follows is $\frac{6}{8}$ ♫♩ ♪ ♩ ♪ ♫♫♫♫ ♪ ♩ ♩ ♩; both are very common in Spanish folk music.[7] The vocal part is generally sung by one soloist, although trios began to gain popularity in the late 1940s. The text, of good-humored, satirical, or comic character, consists of four quatrains of octosyllabic lines, coinciding with the six figures of the dance. The *chacarera* also appears in exclusively instrumental versions; the instruments used are harp, guitar (*punteado* style), violin, or accordion, with a drum accompaniment.

One of the most important *criolla* (i.e., native, indigenous) dances of the Argentine countryside is the *gato*. Not only is it widespread, but other dances derive from it. Here also the Spanish heritage comes to light. Dance figures include shoe-tapping steps performed by women. Much like female *flamenco* dancers, the women lift their long skirts to show their agile foot movements. Another familiar choreographic figure is the so-called

[7] Cf. Isabel Aretz, *El folklore musical*, pp. 202–205.

escobillado (or *escobilleo*), a very fast foot movement performed by men, consisting of swinging one foot after the other with scraping of the ground. Rhythmically and formally, the *gato* presents singular features. The text of the sung *gato* follows the form of the *seguidilla*, a four-line verse pattern in which the second line is assonant with the fourth. But the lines of the *gato* are of seven and five syllables, in alternation. This textual irregularity creates, in a strict syllabic setting, a rather uneven melodic phrasing. In actual performance, however, the difficulty is surmounted by anticipating the last accent of the seven-syllable line and by augmenting the note values in the melodic phrase corresponding to the five-syllable line. The *gato* vocalist plays an accompaniment on the guitar. The specific Spanish guitar technique known as *guitarra rasgueada* (strumming) is used here consistently, in a 6/8 meter. Picked guitar (*punteada*) is used only in the prelude and interludes. Characteristically, the rhythmic formula of the *gato* alternates between 6/8 and 3/4 meters (the hemiola rhythm again). Generally, the sung *gato* is made up of four melodic phrases, repeated with some minor variants in the following order: prelude, AABB, interlude, AB, interlude, CD (in which prelude and interludes are strictly instrumental). Whenever it is sung in duet, parallel thirds prevail, as is characteristic of Iberian folk polyphony.

Among the many Argentine folk dances for couples, the *zamba* should be mentioned. Together with such dances as the *aires* and the *lorencita*, it is a "scarf dance" (*danza de pañuelo*). According to Carlos Vega and Isabel Aretz, there exists in Argentina (and in Chile, Peru, and Ecuador for that matter) a truly symbolic code involving the use and function of the scarf. The *zamba* has a rather obscure history. An old colonial Peruvian *criolla* dance known as *zamacueca* or *zambacueca* (today *marinera* in Peru) was introduced into Argentina during the first half of the nineteenth century. Out of this dance emerged the *zamba*, on the one hand, and the *cueca* on the other. The latter became one of the most familiar dances of Chile and Bolivia. In the western provinces of Argentina the name *chilena* was used to designate the Chilean *cueca*. Thus the three names *zamba*, *cueca*, and *chilena* have survived and have, nowadays, specific meanings. Choreographically, *zamba* and *cueca* differ considerably. Although the basic figures are similar, the overall development of one dance departs from the other. The *cueca* allows extemporized shoe tapping, whereas the *zamba* adheres more strictly to less vivid and traditional figures.

Musically, the *zamba* and the *cueca* have the same general form but present different melodic types. Both show preference for four musical phrases, the last two of which are repeated. They both start with an eight-measure introduction and end with a coda in which new melodic material is presented. The prevailing meter is 6/8, with subdivisions of ternary and binary figures. The *zamba* is essentially instrumental, although vocal versions also exist. Traditionally, the performing ensemble includes the violin for the melody, the guitar for harmonic support, and the drum (*bombo*) for accompaniment. Since the 1940s, the accordion has tended to substitute for the violin. Older *zamba* melodies tend to exhibit a modal ambiguity, due to the alternation of major and minor thirds, or that of B natural and B flat in the Dorian mode; the melodic minor scale also appears. More recent melodies adhere strictly to the major mode; so do *cueca* melodies, which tend, however, to end on the fifth degree of the scale. But it is in their rhythmic cast that *cuecas* differ intrinsically from the *zamba*. For the *zamba* the basic rhythmic formula for both accompaniment and melody is ♮ [musical notation], but a ¾ [musical notation] accompaniment figure occurs rather frequently. *Cuecas* are essentially vocal and their texts follow the *seguidilla* form, resulting in the same metric irregularity observed in the *gato*. Only the guitar accompanies the *cueca*, with the occasional addition in the western provinces of the *charango*, under the influence of the Chilean and Bolivian *cueca*. The accompaniment consists typically of a regular strumming in 6/8 ([musical notation]) creating cross-rhythmic effects with the vocal line.

The Chilean *cueca* presents a more complex poetic and musical structure. Although it consists of two musical phrases, A and B, these are set to a text made up of three elements: a quatrain (*cuarteta*) of octosyllabic lines, followed by a *seguidilla* of seven heptasyllabic and pentasyllabic lines with frequent repetition of the fourth line, and a final pair of lines (*pareado*), made up of either the last two lines of the *seguidilla* or of new text. In actual performance, a number of extemporized stock verbal interjections, known as *muletillas* (such as "Caramba" or "Mi vida") may be added at will in any of the three basic components. These additions and repetitions frequently result in six musical phrases (ABB-ABB) for the *cuarteta*, and six phrases for the *seguidilla* (ABB-AB) and *pareado* (A), taken together. Each of the choreographic parts of the *cueca* corresponds to one of the literary units: the initial figure to the *cuarteta*, two *vueltas* to the *seguidilla* and the final figure to the *pareado*.[8]

Many Brazilian folk songs and dances also exhibit considerable European retentions. For example, many of the round-dance types used in the *fandangos* are popular rural revelries in which regional dances, such as the *tirana*, *tatu*, *balaio*, *recortado*, *chimarrita*, and many others, are performed. One of the most frequent components of these dances is shoe tapping; another, in the state of Rio Grande do Sul, is the use of castanets. Thus *fandango* was transformed in Brazil into a generic term, which suggests that the Spanish dance of the same name was once popular there, as it was in Portugal. The numerous designations for these dances derive from

---

[8] Cf. Samuel Claro Valdés, *Oyendo a Chile* (Santiago: Editorial Andres Bello, 1979), pp. 56–58.

the song texts. Typically, the singing, which alternates stanza and refrain and is always in parallel thirds, is the responsibility of the *viola* players. In the coastal area of the southern states, the fiddle is common, and in Rio Grande do Sul the accordion has become a popular accompanying instrument of the *fandango* dances.

In Venezuela, one of the most typical mestizo dances and songs is the *joropo*, the "national dance" of that country. The term itself has a generic sense of music for dancing. According to the Venezuelan ethnomusicologist Ramón y Rivera,[9] there are four main categories representing the music used to sing or dance the *joropo*: the *corrido*, *galerón*, *pasaje*, and *golpe* (the last two for accompanying the dance). As a result, the melody of this dance presents greatly diversified aspects. But the urban *joropo*, which is cultivated by many popular composers and has significantly penetrated the rural regions as well, is a fast dance in triple time, with a strongly syncopated accompaniment and frequent hemiola effect. Its choreography (for solo couple) seems to be analogous to that of the Colombian *pasillo* and *bambuco*. The latter is one of the most representative dances of the Colombian mestizo; it also alternates 3/4 and 6/8 meters. The text of the *bambuco*, Spanish-derived, consists of four octosyllabic lines with an occasional refrain, and its accompaniment calls for Spanish-related folk instruments, such as the *tiple*, the *bandola*, and the *requinto* (respectively, a small guitar, a mandolin, and another guitar still smaller than the *tiple*).

The Andean Area

The territory formerly occupied by the Inca Empire (from the northern highland and coastal areas of Ecuador to the Chilean river Maule and northwestern Argentina) includes numerous folk and primitive musical traditions that either form part of various Indian cultures or of the varied mestizo cultures greatly influenced by those of the Indians. Music and dance in the ancient empire known as "Tahuantinsuyo" can be only partially documented through the study of archaeological musical instruments, iconographic evidence of various kinds, and the writings of the Spanish chroniclers and lexicographers of the sixteenth and early seventeenth centuries. Such studies have revealed a relatively greater sophistication in relation to instrument making in comparison with the musical cultures of South American tropical-forest Indian tribes. In his study of instruments used by the Incas and their predecessors (especially the Nazca, Mochica, and Chimú tribes), Robert Stevenson has conclusively shown that the ancient Andean peoples had, at the time of the Spanish conquest, the most advanced musical culture

---

[9] Cf. Luis Felipe Ramón y Rivera, *El joropo: Baile nacional de Venezuela* (Caracas: Ministerio de Educación, Dirección de Cultura y Bellas Artes, 1952).

of the whole American continent.[10] Not only did they know five- and six-hole flutes with unequal finger holes, fourteen- and fifteen-tube *antaras* (panpipes made of clay), double-row panpipes with unequal pipe growth, and cross flutes, but their instrument making proves their intent to use predetermined pitches. In Peru, the oldest archaeological instruments are approximately seven thousand years old. Today, in the Andean area there is hardly any village or town (even in the mestizo villages) that does not have a kind of traditional music with elements of Indian musical provenance. The widespread use of pre-Columbian instruments such as the panpipe (called *sicu* by the Aymaras, *antara* by the Quechuas, and *zampoñas* by the mestizos) and vertical flute with whistle mouthpieces (*pincollo, pincullo*) attests to that influence. The ubiquitous end-notched flute known as *quena* (or *kena*) is used along with European types of double-headed drums in processions for Catholic saints, and in social dances and festivals, along with post-Columbian indigenous instruments such as the *charango*. The pipe and tabor tradition, although well known in medieval and Renaissance Europe, is a constant occurrence in the area in both pre- and post-Columbian periods.

In Bolivia, Peru, and Ecuador, it is very difficult in many contexts of music making to separate the musical elements of Indian origin from those of the European folk tradition. Acculturation began in the sixteenth century; it was consciously fostered by the Catholic missionaries who realized that the survival of Christianity depended in part on its absorption of native elements, and therefore used music as one of the most effective tools of conversion. The elements of the two cultures combined to form inseparable units. Many of the tunes are European in style and structure, but a very large number make use of tetratonic and pentatonic scales. The introduction of European-derived diatonic scales in modern times has required adjustments in the construction of instruments. Thus today six-hole (sometimes seven-hole) *quenas* are more common than the three- and four-hole models. In addition, European string instruments (violin, guitar, harp, and mandolin) have, to a a great extent, modified the original character of highland Indian music, although these instruments are performed in a uniquely Indian manner and represent an important aspect of Indian aesthetic systems. European harmonic patterns have thus been added to a music that was probably essentially monophonic. These patterns form today the basic support for melodies of clearly non-European character.

In their study, the d'Harcourts analyzed the various modes used in Quechua music.[11] Out of some two hundred melodies collected in the high-

---

[10] Robert Stevenson, *Music in Aztec and Inca Territory* (Berkeley and Los Angeles: University of California Press, 1968), pp. 243–58.

[11] Raoul and Marguerite d'Harcourt, *La musique des Incas et ses survivances* (Paris: Paul Geuthner, 1925), pp. 141–54.

lands, the majority show a descending progression and are built on the pentatonic scale without semitone, G-E-D-C-A, where the highest tone tends to act as a dominant. Although hundreds of songs in the highland Andean area present this melody type, the d'Harcourts's pentatonic thesis is far too exclusive to do justice to the general Andean Indian melodic system. Although mestizo melodies (partly based on the European diatonic scale) abound, all tunes maintain a modal flavor, a prevailingly descending tendency, large intervals, and few modulations. Rhythmically, Indian traits also prevail. Duple meters, with binary and ternary divisions, are the most frequent, especially a dactylic formula for percussion accompaniment. Syncopated melodic lines are also very common in pure song genres, such as the *yaravi*, and in dance types, such as the *huayno*. Particularly important in the latter is the syncopation of ♫♩ together with ♩♫ . Although the same syncopation occurs in most Afro-American music in Latin America, the resulting effect here is quite different, partly because the first note of each beat tends to be strongly accented. Another rhythmic peculiarity of many Andean melodies is an emphasis on shorter note values when they occur at the beginning of a beat. Example 9-4, taken from the d'Harcourts's study, illustrates these peculiarities. Meters of 6/8 are also common and frequently used in alternation with 3/4 (again the hemiola we noted in Argentine dances). Triple meters are found in mestizo music in which Spanish elements appear more clearly, but tunes of song types of Indian descent, such as the *yaravi*, are also often cast in triple meter. Finally, many Indian and mestizo song melodies are of a nonmensural nature.

Typical accompanimental figures of the Andean area represent an unmistakably Indian percussion style. This style consists, for the most part, in a straightforward, systematic repetition of the simplest figures. In addition to the dactylic rhythm in 2/4 already mentioned, the percussion presents the following figures: ¾ ♩ ♫♩ and ⅝ ♩ ♪♪♩ . In some instances, such as the *cachua* (or *kashua*) dance of the Aymaras of southern Peru and northern Bolivia, the percussion accompaniment, whether with harp, *charango*, or guitar, also presents distinct features. Among these, one particularly favored pattern, which can be considered as a true trademark of the Andes, is a series of arpeggios based on two fifths, with roots a minor third apart,

EXAMPLE 9-4. Rhythmic formulas of Andean music. From Raoul and Marguerite d'Harcourt, *La musique des Incas et ses survivances* (Paris: Paul Geuthner, 1925), p. 156.

presented in a rhythmic figure of an eighth followed by two sixteenths (Example 9-5). This pattern represents the basic accompaniment of many dances, such as the *huayno* (*wayno*), *carnaval*, *pandilla*, and *pampeña*, to name a few.

Strophic form dominates much of Quechua and Aymara music. The simplest types of variation are fairly common as well. Improvisation exists but does not have a major role. Mestizo songs or tunes tend to be in binary or ternary structures, with parallelism in thirds. Aymara instrumental ensembles, on the other hand, very often present the melody doubled at the fourth and the octave, especially in the *sicus* ensembles. The *sicus* are played in pairs in a hocket technique and are designated according to their size and tuning, such as *tayka-irpa* ("leading mother") for the larger size.

Many indigenous dances of the Aymara and Quechua Indians, including pantomime dances, have become traditional for celebrating Catholic religious feasts as well as their own rituals. For example, the patronal fiesta of the Virgen del Carmen in the town of Paucartambo in the province of Cuzco, Peru, is celebrated in mid-July and involves Indians and mestizos in various combinations of pre-Columbian and Spanish traditions of dances and songs. Various dance ensembles, such as the Capac Chunchos, Qollas, Capac Negros, Majeños, Waka-Waka, K'achampa, Qoyacha, and Saqras, representing different Indian or mestizo groups, participate in the festivities as a demonstration of their dedication to and close association with the patron saint. Music for the various dances is provided by *orquestas* (bands made up of *quenas*, violins, diatonic harp, accordion, and drums) performing popular *huaynos* and *marineras*, brass bands, or more specifically regional ensembles, such as those for the accompaniment of the Chunchos that include one or two *pitus* (a six-hole cane transverse flute about two feet long), a *tambor* (wooden snare drum), and a *bombo* (a wooden bass drum). The Chunchos and Qollas ritual battle dance in the fiesta symbolizes the traditional dichotomy between Christians (Spaniards) and Indians and reinforces the dualistic opposition of the groups, expressing concurrently the meaning of the fiesta as group solidarity and communal prosperity through

EXAMPLE 9-5. Accompanimental patterns of Andean dance music. From Raoul and Marguerite d'Harcourt, *La musique des Incas et ses survivances* (Paris: Paul Geuthner, 1925), p. 162.

a significant reciprocal relationship with the Virgin. Numerous other dramatic dances are reminiscent of events from the Conquest period or of the glory of the past. The well-known *Baile del Inca*, for example, reminds one of Atahualpa's cruel death. Ritual Indian dances of both Quechua and Aymara people are closely connected with the agricultural labor cycle. The dance of *Wipfala*, for example, is associated with the agrarian rituals (to the deity of the earth, Pachamama) and is preferably performed during the harvest season and on August 15 (Assumption Day).

Among the principal social dances of the Andes is the *huayno* (commonly called *huayño* in Bolivia), popular among Indians and mestizos from northern Argentina to Ecuador, where it is known as *sanjuanito* (this term could be derived from the diminutive "huaynito" rather than San Juan). Although an Indian dance, it has been adopted by mestizos of the highlands as their own. The Aymara and Quechua *huaynos* retain their aboriginal character in both functions and styles. Vocal Indian *huyanos* are generally sung in the native languages, although lyrics in both Spanish and Quecha, for example, are not uncommon. Aymara *huaynos* are almost exclusively instrumental, performed by *sicuris* bands or *pincullo* or *tarka* ensembles. In lively tempo, the *huayno* appears most of the time in duple meter and in binary form, consisting of two phrases (AB) of equal length (generally four measures each) repeated *ad libitum*. Versions alternating triple and duple meter (or compound duple), or simply alternating binary and ternary divisions in a single meter, are fairly frequent. Many tunes associated with the dance take a pentatonic mode (G-E-D-C-A) as their basis. Example 9-6 shows one of the most typical versions of the *huayno*, from the Cuzco area.

Another Peruvian dance widespread throughout the country is the *marinera*, historically related to the *zamacueca* or *zambacueca*, and, like the Argentine *zamba* or the Chilean and Bolivian *cueca*, a *danza de pañuelo* or "scarf dance." The *marinera* is known in both rural and urban areas and in several regional styles, such as the *marinera serrana* (from the *sierra* or highland), *marinera norteña* (northern) (also known as *tondero* on the northern coast), and *marinera limeña* (from Lima). Labeled *chilena* in the nineteenth century, the name *marinera* is supposed to have become more common following the Pacific war with Chile (1879), as a tribute to the Peruvian navy ("marina"), because the retention of the name *chilena* for a Peruvian national dance would have been embarrassing. (Peru lost the war.) Although the regional variants reveal different melodic types and characteristic regional ensembles, the *marinera* is set in a predominantly 6/8 meter with occasional hemiola. The *limeña*, of a somewhat slower tempo than the others, is generally performed by voices with guitars and *cajón* (wooden box drum), includes an extra section called *resbalosa*, and involves shoe tapping and hand clapping. The *norteña* is faster than the *limeña* and can

EXAMPLE 9-6. The typical *huayno kaypipas*, from Cuzco, Peru. From *Cancionero andino sur*, ed. Consuelo Pagaza Galdo (Lima: Casa Mozart, 1967), p. 13. Collected by Consuelo Pagaza Galdo and transcribed by Rodolfo Holzmann.

be differentiated from the *tondero* by the addition of a *triste* (a mestizo love song of the *yaravi* type) preceding it and a *fuga* following it. The *serrana* has numerous variants and generally concludes with a *fuga de huayno*.

Afro-Iberian Folk Music

The other major South American folk musical tradition derives from varying degrees of combination of African and Iberian styles. This tradition is particularly significant in Brazil, Colombia, Venezuela, Surinam, Guyana, and French Guiana, and to a lesser extent in Uruguay, Argentina, and the lower coastal regions of Peru and Ecuador.

The special character of Brazilian folk music is largely due to the importance of the black population in much of the national folk culture as a whole. Not only do the black communities have their own traditions, which often revolve around styles that are still very close to their African ancestry, as we indicate in Chapter 10; the folk music of the Brazilian mestizos and whites, in many instances, can hardly be distinguished from that of the Afro-Brazilians, because they both result from basically identical syntheses. The Afro-Brazilian components are especially recognized in the driving rhythms, the particular performance practices, the explicit importance of percussion instruments, and the deep integration of music performance in a sociofunctional context. The emphasis on dancing can also be interpreted as a result of the same syntheses. The number of distinct Brazilian folk dance forms of Luso-African derivation is striking. Among these, the best known are *batuque*, *samba*, *jongo*, *côco*, *lundu*, *baiano*, and some purely urban types, such as the *samba de morro*, *samba de enredo* (associated with Rio's samba schools), *maracatu*, *maxixe*, and *choro*, among many others. All Afro-Brazilian folk dances include specific choreographic traits, such as tapping, marked movement of the hips and the shoulders, and *umbigada*. *Umbigada* (from the Portuguese *umbigo* meaning navel) is the most characteristic choreographic element of these dances, a sort of "invitation to the dance" manifested by the symbolic touching of the couple's navels, through a pelvic thrust. When there is no *umbigada* in a given dance, the dance generally belongs to the mestizo folk or urban tradition, or has an Hispanic origin. The *umbigada* is therefore a diagnostic trait defining the different origins of these dances.

Samba (probably from the African Kimbundo language *semba* meaning *umbigada*) is a generic term designating, along with *batuque*, the choreography of certain round dances imported from Angola and the Congo area. We should distinguish between the various rural versions of the folk *samba* and the popular urban dance which developed only after World War I and became the national dance of Brazil. The folk versions, especially from the states of Bahia, Rio de Janiero, and São Paulo, have different musical characteristics from the urban versions, although responsorial vocal performance and highly syncopated accompanimental rhythms are common to both. The vocal line of the rural version from São Paulo (*samba rural* or *samba campineiro*), as studied by the Brazilian musicologist, Mário de Andrade, tends to be divided into irregular patterns: three to five units for the stanzas, four to seven for the refrain, with variants. In São Paulo, the *samba* moved from an Afro-Brazilian to a *caboclo* realm, which is reflected in the frequently vocal performance in parallel thirds, and the instrumental accompanying ensemble which includes *violas* (folk guitars), *adufes* (square tambourines without jingles), and regular tambourines. The melodies rarely go beyond the range of a sixth. The Bahian *samba*, particularly the types known as *samba de roda* and *samba de viola*, follows the formal pattern of alternation of stanzas (soloist) and refrain (chorus) and presents a wider variety of choreographic traits than its southern counterpart. In it, highly syncopated figures are common, in both melodic lines and accompaniment, with numerous improvisations based on the following rhythmic figures: $\frac{2}{4}$ ♩♪♪ , ♫♪♫ , and the superimposition of the dotted figure on regular pulsations of four sixteenths. The *samba de roda*'s accompanying ensemble includes in general one or two drums (of the *atabaques* type, i.e., conga type), a tambourine, a guitar, a rattle (shaker) or *agogô* (two-coned bell), and sometimes one or two *berimbaus* (musical bows). For the *samba de viola*, on the other hand, in addition to a drum, a tambourine, a triangle, and a *prato e faca* (dish and knife), the *violas* represent the central instruments of the ensemble, hence the designation of this genre.

A peculiar variety of *samba* which developed mostly in the city of Rio de Janeiro and was the forerunner of the urban Carnival dance is the *samba de morro*. Cultivated among the poor people inhabiting the hillside slums (*favelas*) of the city (*morro* means "hill" in Portuguese), this type preserves some aspects of the folk *samba*: responsorial pattern, with solo part often improvised; mostly two-part form; and accompaniment predominantly by percussion instruments with guitars, *cavaquinhos* (small four-string guitars, ukelele-like), snare drums, and other drums added later to the Carnival *samba*. Example 9-7 is a typical *samba de morro*, transcribed from a field collection made in the late 1930s. It shows most of the rhythmic-melodic patterns of the rural *samba*, that is, repeated notes, intervallic skips within a melodic progression up to the sixth, offbeat phrasing of accents (represented in notation by ties across beats), frequent descending melodic movement, and the contrasting regularity of the solo part.

Many varieties of urban *samba* have developed since the 1930s, with specific social functions, such as the *samba de partido alto* (cultivated by *samba*-school composers), *samba de breque* ("break" samba of highly syncopated rhythm), *samba-canção* (with romantic emphasis), *samba de gafieira* (exclusively instrumental for large ballroom orchestras), *sambalanço* (of the 1950s under jazz influence), and *bossa-nova* renditions of older classical genres.

Afro-American musical traits are quite prominent in some aspects of Peruvian, Colombian, and Venezuelan folk music. In Peru, although the black population (concentrated in the coastal region) represents a very small minority (less than 1 percent of the total population), Afro-Peruvian musical genres are fairly numerous. These genres, however, form an integral part of the *criolla* folk tradition. Only since the 1960s has there been in Peru the attempt to differentiate between the *criolla* and Afro-Peruvian traditions, as a result of black ethnicity. The revitalized "Africanized" elements of such *criolla* forms as the *marinera* and the *vals*, and the revival of predominantly black dance forms, such as the *festejo*, constitute the basis of these neo-Afro-Peruvian musical expressions, whose historical authenticity has been questioned but whose vital *raison d'être* can hardly be doubted.

Marked black musical influence in Colombia and Venezuela is to be found above all in the coastal regions which properly belong to the Caribbean area. The most authentically African drumming and dancing in Venezuela comes from the states of Zulia, Mérida, and Trujillo, along Lake Maracaibo, and the coastal areas of Miranda and the Distrito Federal. Most of the percussion instruments have an almost exclusively accompanimental

EXAMPLE 9-7. Brazilian *samba de morro*. From Egydio de Castro e Silva, "O samba carioca," *Revista brasileira de música*, VI (1939), 49–50. (*Surdo* is a low-pitched drum, *cuíca* a friction drum, *pandeiro* a tambourine, and *tamborim* a tabor-like instrument.)

function. Among these instruments, three types of drum should be mentioned: the *mina* drum (or *tambor grande*), more than six feet tall, with a single head fastened by ropes and wedges; the *curbata* drum, of the same family but smaller; and the *tambor redondo* ("round drum"), double-headed and always played in a battery of three (these round drums are also called *culepuyas*). These drums accompany the songs known as *tonadas de tambor* (in responsorial performance style, the singers also playing maracas) and dances in the celebration of the festivities of St. John in the Barlovento region. Bamboo stamping tubes, called *quitiplás*, are also part of the African heritage of Venezuela. The fact that a significant body of Afro-Venezuelan folk music is used in connection with Catholic feasts (such as those of St. John, St. Peter, and St. Benedict) is again indicative of the strong local cultural blending.

Song and dance genres of the Colombian Atlantic coastal area also reveal a marked African presence, combined with Spanish and Amerindian elements. The main folk dance of the region is the *cumbia* (also known in Panama), performed at night by couples as a round dance, to the accompaniment of either the *conjunto de cumbia* or the *conjunto de gaitas*. The first ensemble includes a *pito* or *caña de millo* (a transverse type of clarinet similar to West African millet cane clarinets) that provides the melody, and percussion instruments: *tambor mayor* and *llamador* (single-headed drums, large and small, an African derivation); *bombo* (double-headed bass drum); and *guachos* (tubular rattles) or maracas. The *conjunto de gaitas* consists of a pair of duct flutes (*gaitas*, one "male" and the other "female," of Indian origin according to George List[12]), a *tambor mayor*, a *llamador*, and a maraca. Although the folk *cumbia* used to be strictly instrumental, sung *coplas*, performed by one of the percussionists, have become very common. The music of the *cumbia* displays disjunct relationships between the various parts resulting in polyrhythmic activity, typical of much Afro-Caribbean music. The same occurs with the music of two other dances of the area, the *bullerengue* (which includes a vocal soloist and a female chorus), and the *danza de negros*, a male Carnival dance. The traditional dances and songs of the Pacific lowlands of Colombia retain strong African elements as well, particularly in the performance of the main secular ritual, the *currulao* (see Chapter 10).

MEXICO, CENTRAL AMERICA, AND THE CARIBBEAN

Mexico and Central America

That the high Indian cultures of the Aztecs and Mayas in pre-Columbian Mesoamerica developed a fairly sophisticated musical system is demonstrated by archaeological evidence, the testimony of early Spanish missionaries, and the study of Mexican codices and Indian language lexicons. At the time of the Spanish conquest (1521), the Aztecs in central Mexico ruled over a large confederation of peoples, and their empire extended to present-day El Salvador. From their own conquest of older Indian cultures (including the Mayas), they inherited numerous ideas of instrument making and performance techniques. According to the Spanish chronicles and to iconographic evidence, they knew percussion and wind instruments but no string instruments. Among the percussion instruments, the slit drum (or two-key xylophone) known as *teponaztli* in Náhuatl (the language of the Aztecs) and *tunkul* in Mayan, and the cylindrical drum, *huehuetl*, occupied a special place in their worship. Wind instruments included vertical whistle flutes and end-blown flutes as well as trumpets made of clay, wood, and other

---

[12] *Music and Poetry in a Colombian Village*, p. 93.

materials. Multiple flutes (from two to four pipes with a common mouthpiece) from the Teotihuacán cultural horizon (A.D. 400–600) indicate the existence of the concept of harmony in the sense of systematically simultaneous sound production. These flutes, however, are so unusual that they might have been associated with special religious events or ceremonies and perhaps were not part of daily music making. As in the Inca area, the pipe and tabor combination was apparently very common and has been retained in numerous contemporary Indian musical cultures.

The Mexicans distinguish between the traditions of *música indígena* (Indian music) and *música mestiza*. There is a wide continuum of greatly diversified styles and practices among the numerous Indian musical traditions of the twentieth century, from the primitive tribal groups of the Seris, Huicholes, Coras, and Tarahumaras in northern, northwest, and western Mexico, to the Tarascans and Mazatecs in Michoacán and Oaxaca, the Toto-nacs and Otomíes in Vera Cruz and Puebla, to the Mayan-speaking Tzotzil, including the Chamulas of Chiapas, to name but a few. These groups reveal varying degrees of preservation of their traditional music and of acculturation with the predominant mestizo musical styles and genres. The Indian communities retain their native musical styles, to a great extent, in their traditional sacred or secular rituals. Such is the case of the Tarascans (or Purépecha) who preserve in their *fiestas* the pipe and tabor preference, certain scale formations, rhythmic uniformity, and higher register and tense vocal style, among other features. They are, at the same time, some of the most accomplished string instrument makers and performers. Their major vocal genre, the *pirécua*, sung in Purépecha and Spanish languages, exhibits some typical Spanish traits, such as parallel-third or -sixth polyphony and metrical organization in triple or compound duple meters. The Chamulas, on the other hand, have made string music (violin, harp, guitar) their specialty, in full three-part harmony and even some systematic contrapuntal imitation, obviously learned from the early missionaries. They frequently sing in falsetto, a practice rare among Indian communities, who do tend to emphasize, however, the highest range of the voice.

The early missionaries in Mexico evidently tried hard to suppress the native Indian musical culture. Although they did not entirely succeed, as a result of their effective work much of the folk music of the Hispanic tradition found its way into the culture of almost all Mexican Indian groups. For example, obvious traces of Gregorian chant intonation and of old European modal melodies can be found nowadays in the shamanic chanting and singing of the Mazatec Indians. In addition, as Vicente Mendoza, a well-known authority on Mexican music, has shown, songs of the Otomí Indians of northeast Mexico follow the characteristic triplet figurations of Spanish folk song and have elements of major tonality emphasizing tonic and third.[13] Other Otomí songs give even greater evidence of European influence in their parallel thirds and sixths. Concurrently, these songs retain traditional Indian traits, such as small range and short melodies, with but a few tones. Regardless of the origins of the varied elements of their musical expressions, contemporary Indian groups have fully assimilated them as integral parts of their cultures.

Despite its strong Indian roots, Mexican folk music derives substantially from its Spanish heritage. This Hispanic domination is not only the result of the remarkable early missionary work in Mexico but also of the Indians' highly praised aptitude to learn and assimilate European music. Mestizo folk music exhibits a variety of scales, but the classic European major and minor modes predominate, especially in the various regional *sones* and other song types. Iberian folk polyphony (parallel thirds and sixths) constitutes a conspicuous trait of Mexican and Central American folk music in both instrumental and vocal performances. Likewise, Spanish popular literary forms (*décima*, *copla*) are the most frequently found in Mexican folk songs.

Several *membranophones* (instruments such as drums in which a stretched skin or membrane is the sound-producing agent), idiophones, and aerophones of pre-Columbian origin are still in use in contemporary Mexico. The *huehuetl* is still played in central, southern, and southeastern Mexico. The *teponaztli* is even more widespread. Turtle-shell rasps still accompany *sones* in the Isthmus of Tehuantepec. Whistle flutes, vertical flutes with varying numbers of finger holes, and panpipes are found throughout Mexico. The African-derived *marimba* is especially popular in Oaxaca and Chiapas, and in Guatemala. All other folk instruments are derived or adapted from European instruments. Particularly conspicuous are string instruments, including the standard violin, diatonic harp (the largest one of 35 strings), and a large number of instruments relating to the Spanish *vihuela* and guitar families, among them, besides the standard guitar, the *vihuela* (five-string with convex shape), *jarana* or *guitarra de golpe* (five-string small guitar), *requinto* (six-string guitar somewhat smaller than the classic guitar), *cuatro*, *guitarra huapanguera* (eight strings in five courses, three double courses and two single), *guitarrón* (large five-string bass guitar), *bajo sexto* (twelve-string guitar in six double courses), mandolin, and psaltery. The accordion (primarily the diatonic, button type) is the principal instrument of the northern *conjuntos* (or ensembles) but also appears as far south as Chiapas. The tradition of the brass band has proliferated throughout the

---

[13] Vicente Mendoza, "Música indígena Otomí," *Revista de Estudios Musicales*, Vol. II, nos. 5–6 (1950–51), 527.

country. Such bands constitute a matter of civic pride in all communities. In some places they tend to replace the traditional regional *conjuntos*.

Among folk song and dance genres, the *son* is considered to be one of the most characteristically Mexican. Despite its numerous regional differences, the *son* can be defined generally as music associated with dance, with specific literary form and verse contents, and with specific regional instrumental ensembles. It is primarily an instrumental genre but as a rule includes singing. Its most unifying element is an underlying rhythm made up of six-beat measures, variously accented (through *maniqueos* or strumming patterns) and syncopated. The alternating or simultaneous use of 3/4 and 6/8 metrical patterns once more creates a typical Hispanic-American hemiola or *sesquialtera* rhythm. Example 9-8 shows six characteristic rhythmic patterns for *sones* from the Jalisco region. The melodic line also tends to be syncopated and accompanied by simple harmonic progressions. As a predominantly courtship dance, the *son* relies on the *zapateado* (shoe tapping), a conspicuous dance trait which requires the use of a wooden platform (*tarima*) and is closely related to such regional dances as the *huapango*, the *jarabe*, and the *chilena*, to name a few. The most common literary form of the *son* is the *copla*, with repetitions of lines allowing it to extend to five, six, or eight lines. The verse contents are quite varied, with an emphasis on love or lyrical and picaresque subject matters. Certain *son* types are actually defined by their verse contents, and, as such, often identified with a specific tune, as in the case of the *malagueña*, *petenera*, *sandunga*, *indita*, *cuándo*, and *gusto*. The *son*'s most common musical form is strophic, either alternating vocal and instrumental sections, or stanzas and a short refrain. Two or more voices (male, as a rule) sing in alternation or simultaneously in parallel, with frequent falsetto singing in some regional variants.

The regional *conjuntos* in central Mexico include primarily string instruments: a violin, a *jarana*, and a *guitarra quinta* or *huapanguera* for the *son huasteco*; one or two harps, *requinto*, *cuatro*, and *jarana* for the *son jarocho* or *veracruzano*; and the "conjunto de arpa grande" consisting of a large harp whose resonating box is often used percussively (*tamboreo*) and *vihuela*, *jarana*, and two violins for the *son jaliscience* or *abajeño* in Jalisco and Michoacán. *Huapango* is also the name given to the dance accompanied by either *son huasteco* or *son jarocho* ensembles. The well-known "La Bamba" is one of the tunes of the *jarocho* genre. *Sones* also form an integral part of the repertory of the famous *mariachi* ensembles, developed in the state of Jalisco and consisting of male voices, two violins, *vihuela*, *jarana*, and *guitarrón*, to which were added in the 1930s two trumpets, more violins, two guitars, and an occasional female voice. In other areas, the *son* is accompanied by brass bands or typical regional ensembles, such as the marimba ensemble used to accompany the *son oaxaqueño* and the *son istmeño* of Tehuantepec. There, the old tradition of the three-man

EXAMPLE 9-8. Characteristic rhythmic patterns of Mexican *sones*. From Paul Bowles, "On Mexico's Popular Music," *Modern Music*, XVIII, 4 (May–June, 1941), 227.

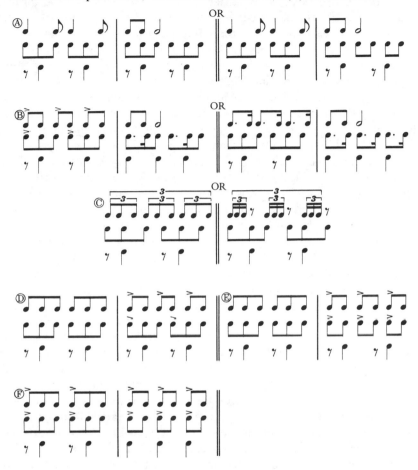

solo marimba has given way to a large orchestra with saxophones, trumpets, and drum sets, in which the marimba is played by one or two men. These types of *sones*, which are strictly instrumental and in which no string instrument is part of the ensemble, represent an exception to the general traits of the genre.

The *jarabe* is one of the oldest and most popular folk dances of Mexico. Indians, rural and urban mestizos, and white people dance to it. In its present form, it consists of a sequence of tunes or *sones*. Such tunes were printed in the early nineteenth century and have remained much alive. Tunes such as "El Palomo," "El Perico," "Los Enanos," and "El

Tapatío" were considered the most representative by the earliest nineteenth-century Mexican nationalist composers. The *jarabe tapatío* is the form of the dance that developed in Guadalajara, became the national dance par excellence, was associated with the Mexican war of independence, and popularized the *charro* (cowboy) and his girlfriend, the *china poblana* (with their appropriate costumes) as the most stereotyped representatives of Mexican popular culture. The name "hat dance," as the *jarabe* is called in the United States, is derived from a choreographic section in which the man puts his sombrero on the ground and his partner dances around the wide brim. The urban *jarabe* has become a conventionalized and abbreviated version of the old dance still performed in many towns and villages.

Similar to the *jarabe* is the *jarana*, the most popular dance of the Yucatán peninsula. The music has the same lively character as that of the *jarabe*, but the dance proper is generally not accompanied by singing. The word *jarana* is said to be derived from the small guitar-like instrument of the same name which probably was once part of the *conjunto*; no string instrument, however, now participates in the accompanying ensemble. Rather it consists of a small band (*banda de pueblo*) with one or two alto saxophones, a tenor saxophone, sometimes a clarinet, a trumpet, a trombone, and drums and rattles of the *güiro* type.

Another important regional folk music style is that of *música norteña* ("northern music") which, like the *mariachi* of Jalisco, has transcended its original regional boundaries. Primarily dance music, the *norteño* repertory developed in the latter part of the nineteenth century from the adaptation of European fashionable dances, such as the mazurka, the schottisch (which became the *chotís*), the polonaise, the varsovienne, and, especially, the polka. Indeed, the polka dominates the *norteño* repertory not only as a dance genre; polka rhythm and symmetrical melodies are also applied to other genres, such as *corrido* and *canción*, in a typical *norteño* performance style. The *conjunto norteño* usually consists of three or four instrumentalists who also sing: an accordion is the melodic instrument (diatonic, button accordion is the norm, although the chromatic piano keyboard type is also used); the *bajo sexto* and the double bass are rhythmic and harmonic instruments. In the urban areas, rhythmic spoons or a piece of hollow wood (called *redova*) played with two wooden sticks are sometimes added to the ensemble. Although the accordion is known as a folk and popular instrument in other regions of Mexico, it has become the main instrument of the *norteño* style and, by extension, of the Mexican-American *conjunto* style. Thus, polkas are frequently played solo on the accordion. Among the songs of the region (*canciones norteñas*) are the *rancheras*, very popular sentimental songs with march-like or waltz-like rhythmic accompaniment in varying tempos. In commercial popular music, the term *ranchero* (from *rancho*, i.e., rural) as in *polka ranchera* or *bolero ranchero*, refers vaguely to a "folk-like" style of singing.

The major secular vocal genres of Mexican mestizo folk music are the *corrido* and the *canción*. Related to the Spanish *romance*, the *corrido* is the main ballad of Mexico, Central America, and some Spanish Caribbean countries. Set in the usual *copla* (four-line stanza) or *décima* form, the *corrido* has many regional designations in Mexico (*romance, historia, trage-dia, bola, mañanitas, versos*), but its general melodic structure consists of one or two symmetrical and isometric phrases, repeated as often as the text demands it (the length varies from 6 to 78 stanzas). It is therefore in a strophic form. Corridos deal with a wide array of subjects, from old and new crime and love stories to historical events and figures (particularly significant is the *corrido* repertory of the Mexican Revolution of 1910), to local current events and sociopolitical protest. The *corrido* singer or *corri-dista* follows certain general formulas in telling the story: calling the audience's attention, statement of the place and date of the event to be narrated and the name of the main character of the story; presentation of the main parts of the story; message; and farewell of the main character and of the *corridista*. A *corrido* is performed by one or two voices, with the accompaniment of a guitar, a violin and a guitar, an accordion, or a harp. With the increased popularity of *mariachis*, *corridos* written by popular composers (José Alfredo Jiménez, for example) are sung by a solo voice with the backup of a true orchestra, all in *mariachi* style.

Although the term *canción* is applied generically to any song, it is more specifically understood as a Mexican mestizo song of lyric expression, outside any dance context (with a few exceptions, such as the polka songs of northern Mexico or the waltz songs of Tehuantepec). This lyric expression is probably an outgrowth of numerous sources of these songs; the range of sources also explains the great diversity of the genre; but many of the characteristics of nineteenth-century Italian opera and musical comedy have exerted profound influence on the *canción*. Thus, the long, expanded melodic phrases prevail over the rhythm. Although the *canción* is not confined within any given meter or rhythm, its general form is a binary structure consisting of the song itself and an instrumental ritornello. Mendoza[14] has classified the *canción* according to the following criteria: the meter of the versification, the musical structure, the geographical features which it describes, the area of the country in which it is sung, the time of day or the circumstances within which it is sung, the character of the tune, the age or occupation of the users, and the rhythm of the accompaniment expressed in terms of European dance forms. Although it is difficult to establish a

---

[14] Vicente Mendoza, *La canción mexicana* (Mexico: Universidad Nacional, 1961).

clear distinction in Mexico between folk and popular music in general, it is especially so in the case of the *canción*, which appears in both rural and urban contexts. Numerous songs (of the *canción romántica mexicana* type) written by such venerated composers of popular music as Agustín Lara, Tata Nacho, and Guty Cárdenas, to name only a few, have won such lasting recognition that they are part of the repertory of the whole mestizo population.

The states of Central America, from Guatemala to Panama, have greatly varied musical traditions. In addition to the same Hispanic foundation of Mexican mestizo folk music, the area has a number of aboriginal Indians with traditional musics and a marked African influence. For example, in spite of the fact that the most popular dance of Guatemala, the *son chapín* or *guatemalteco*, exhibits clear Hispanic traits (6/8 and 3/4 meters with hemiola effects, diatonic melodies, and triadic harmonies), the national instrument of the country is the *marimba*, apparently of African origin. Although there have been numerous attempts in Guatemala to prove the pre-Columbian origin of the Guatemalan *marimba*, there is no definite archaeological evidence to indicate that the original *marimba de tecomates* (i.e., of calabash resonators tuned to a diatonic scale) is of Indian provenance, the popularity of the instrument among Indians since the eighteenth century notwithstanding. The Guatemalan *marimba* was probably introduced in the early colonial period by African slaves. It is remarkably similar to African xylophones, not only in its actual construction but in the particular buzzing sound resulting from a vibrating membrane attached to a circle of wax around an opening at the bottom of the resonators. *Marimba* ensembles (featuring instruments with gourd or wooden resonators) include string instruments of the guitar family, wind instruments (saxophones, clarinets, and trumpets) among mestizos (*ladinos*), and *tun* (the Mayan two-keyed slit drum), *chirimía* (shawm of Spanish origin), and still in traditional dances such as the *baile del venado* (deer dance) the Indian transverse cane flute known as *xul* among Maya Indian musicians. The Maya also have string ensembles with three- and four-string fiddles, guitars and *tiples*, and the diatonic harp (with as many as 32 strings), supported by a snare drum, a bass drum, or a tambourine for various performance occasions, from traditional ritual music to the *ladino* genres.

In Honduras and Nicaragua are found settlements of black Caribs, who are descendants of Arawak and Carib Indian tribes and former African slaves. Despite their Afro-Indian heritage, however, the culture and music are mostly derivative of West Africa, combined with ceremonial dancing of tropical-forest Indian cultural derivation. In Panama, however, a stronger African presence is to be found in musical sound and behavior. Panama's musical traditions reflect clearly its ethnohistory. The Chocós, Cunas, and Guaymíes Indian groups retain many aspects of their traditional music, especially in their festivals, such as the Guaymí *juego de balsería* (game of pole-throwing contest) or the Cuna *inna suid* (hair-cutting ceremony), but these traditions have seen, since the 1940s, a fast rate of change. Mestizo music is represented by various folk song genres and dances, above all the *mejorana* (or *socavón*), but the national dance of Panama, the *tamborito*, preserves a strongly African character. Particularly reflective of the African heritage are the Carnival festivals organized by the *Congos Negros*, who represent associations of black descendants of Panamanian slaves in small towns along the shores of Lake Gatún and on the Atlantic coast near and in the city of Colón. These festivals involve not only singing, hand clapping, and drumming to accompany the dancing in the *tamborito* style, but also the performance of a dance drama (the *Juego de los Congos*) with a sequence of dramatic events enacting the early history of the maroons (escaped slaves) in Panama, combined with some themes from Christian folk plays. To each main scene corresponds the respective *tonada* (tune) of the dance, with two types of *tonadas*: the *corrido*, in 2/4 time, and the *atravessao* or *tambor congo* in 6/8 time.

The *tamborito* displays the most typical form of Afro-Panamanian singing and dancing. Performed by nonembracing mixed couples with much individual choreographic display, the *tamborito* is sung in responsorial fashion by female voices exclusively (the soloist is called *cantadora-alante*, i.e., front singer), accompanied by drums (double-headed *tambora* played with sticks, and the single-headed *pujador*, and *repicador*, of different sizes, played with hands and fingers) and hand clapping. The *tonada* or melody of the *tamborito*, in 2/4 meter, generally consists of two- to four-bar phrases, sung alternately by soloist and chorus, evenly and unevenly distributed between them; in the latter case, the longer phrase is that of the soloist. Complex rhythmic combinations result from the interaction of the drum players and the vocalists.[15]

The *mejorana* is both a song genre (of the ballad type) and a dance. Only instrumental pieces accompany the dance. The vocal genre, exclusively for male voice, is commonly referred to as *socavón* and shows the following traits: a descending tendency of the melodic phrase, progressing by disjunct rather than conjunct motion, and a text based on the *décima* preceded by a quatrain with the typical rhyme scheme ABBA. Although many *mejorana* melodies are cast in the major and minor modes, the Mixolydian mode also occurs frequently. Typically the accompanying instrument is the classical guitar or the native *mejoranera*, a five-string guitar, tuned E, B, A, A, D, or E, C-sharp, A, A, D. A hemiola relationship between the voice and the accompaniment is quite common. The singing style involves a penetrating

---

[15] Fourteen notated examples of *tamborito* are given in *Boletín del Instituto de Investigaciones Folklóricas*, Vol. I, no. 1 (Panamá: Universidad Inter-Americana, 1944).

harsh voice (without vibrato), with frequent alternation of falsetto and normal voice, extending the range to more than two octaves. As a dance genre, the *mejorana* presents traditional Spanish choreography divided into two parts: the *zapateado* (foot figures) and the *paseo* (promenade, as in the square dance). The Panamanian *cumbia* is also known in instrumental and vocal versions. In contradistinction to the Colombian counterpart, it is performed by violin or accordion for the melody, accompanied by the *mejoranera* and the *tambora*.

The Spanish Caribbean

In general terms, two main folk traditions form the basis of the music in such "Latin" Caribbean islands as Cuba, the Dominican Republic, and Puerto Rico: the Hispanic tradition and the African tradition. Among the Cuban peasants (the *guajiros*) of the Eastern province and the interior of the country, there survive such song types as the *décima guajira*, the *guajira*, and the *punto*, showing the same main stylistic peculiarities as most Spanish-related folk music of Latin America. The *décima* represents the improvised song text, frequently in poetic-singing contests. Usually, the first four lines of text propose the main topic, which can be answered or developed in six additional lines. Melodically, the same phrases are used to sing both parts of the text, with the repetition of the first two lines of the first quatrain. The *punto*, as a song and dance, is spread throughout the Caribbean; it is found in Puerto Rico, the Dominican Republic, Venezuela, Colombia, and Panama. The Cuban *punto* is known in two forms: the *punto libre*, or "free" *punto*, in a recitative-like style (hence without a regular or constant pulse), and the *punto fijo*, or "fixed" *punto*, with constant pulse and ostinato rhythm, suitable for dancing. The *guajira*, as a popular song and dance, developed during the early years of the twentieth century, primarily in the urban areas, under the influence of the *son cubano* cultivated by popular composers. Typically, the *guajira* explores systematically the hemiola of the vocal line (in 6/8 time) and the accompaniment (in 3/4 time) and sets its melodies in parallel thirds and sixths.

Afro-Cuban music, in addition to the popular religious music examined in Chapter 10, pervades much folk and popular music in Cuba and is represented by such important dances as the *rumba*, the *conga*, and other well-known forms, such as the *son cubano*, the *danzón*, the *guaracha*, the *habanera*, and the *bolero*. Together with the various drum types associated with cult music, the typical Afro-Cuban instrumental ensemble includes *güiro*, *maracas*, *claves* (two resonant hardwood sticks struck against each other), and bongo drums. The *tres* (small guitar of three courses of double strings) is commonly added to the percussion section. Example 9-9 illustrates the fundamental rhythmic figures of Afro-Cuban music, also found in Afro-

EXAMPLE 9-9. Rhythmic figures of Afro-Cuban music. From Gaspar Agüero y Barreras, "El aporte africano a la música popular cubana," *Estudios afrocubanos*, (1946), p. 77.

Dominican and Puerto Rican folk music. The first figure, called *tresillo* in Cuba, is often notated as a simple triplet (A), but in actual performance appears as in (B) or (C). In other words, by taking the sixteenth note as the pulsating unit, the duple meter is actually subdivided as 3–3–2. The second figure, notated as (D) but performed as (E), is further complicated in the basic *conga* (originally a Carnival dance from Santiago) rhythm by tying together the first two notes of that rhythmic cell (F). The third figure (G) is perhaps the most characteristic formula of Cuban and other Caribbean folk and popular music. It is known as *cinquillo* in Cuba and results probably from a contraction of the rhythm (H), quite African in its symmetry, and very common in the nineteenth-century Cuban *contradanza*. It also forms the basis of much ritual drumming in the Haitian *vodoun*, as well as in the Caribbean dance known as *merengue* in the Dominican Republic and *méringue* in Haiti. It sometimes appears as (I), and it generates the basic rhythm of the Cuban *danzón* (J), which also appears in the *son* and the *bolero*.

The last two patterns in Example 9-9 show the typical figures, in duple and triple meters, associated with the *claves* in almost all Afro-Caribbean dances (hence often referred to as the *clave* rhythmic pattern). The first measure of the duple meter example is the basic *habanera* rhythmic formula (although here similar to the *tresillo* because of the tie into the second beat), which was first found in the early nineteenth-century Cuban *contradanza* and the Spanish *tango andaluz*. The *habanera*, together with the conspicuous syncopation of a sixteenth-eighth-sixteenth, constitutes the rhythmic base of most Latin American dance music, from the Cuban *son*, *mambo*, and *chachachá* to the *merengue*, the Puerto Rican *danza*, certain styles of Jamaican and Trinidadian folk song and dance (such as the *mento* and *calypso*), as well as the popular *cumbia*, the Brazilian *tango*, *maxixe*, and *samba*, and the Argentine *milonga* and *tango*. The most common variants of this formula are shown in Example 9-10.

The Cuban *son*, a genre of song and dance which developed in the province of Oriente at the end of the nineteenth century and became a well-established urban sung dance in the 1920s, combines Hispanic and Afro-Cuban elements, not only in its original instrumentation (*tres*, guitar, *marímbula*, *bongo*, *maracas*, *claves*, and later trumpet) but also in its vocal structure (stanza and refrain alternation in responsorial fashion). The urban *son*, which enjoyed so much popularity among the famous ensembles (*sexteto* and *septeto*) of the 1930s, tended to emphasize syncopated rhythms (*tresillo*, *cinquillo*, and variants) in both accompaniment and vocal melodies.

Among the various Afro-Cuban social dance forms, the *rumba* occupies a particularly significant position, from both a choreographic and musical viewpoint. The term *rumba* has different meanings in Cuban folk and popular music. Originally, the term referred generally to a manner of vivacious and erotic dancing. As a folk music genre, the rumba has three types: the *yambú*, *columbia*, and *guaguancó*, all courtship couple dances that imitate a pursuit. The *guaguancó* is by far the most popular. Its instrumentation includes two conga-type drums, the larger known as *tumbadora* and the smaller as *quinto*, and *palitos* (sticks on wood blocks) or *claves*. The ensemble

EXAMPLE 9-10. Common variants of *habanera* rhythms.

is completed with one or two male solo singers and a mixed chorus. Typically the solo part is sung in the middle of the choral range and is rhythmically and melodically free in contrast to the fixed choral parts. This freedom constitutes an opportunity for improvisation by the soloist or soloists. When two vocalists perform, heterophony often results, although duets in parallel thirds are also common; but the improvisatory possibilities are obviously reduced. The chorus, which sings simple harmonies and octave doublings, frames the soloist vertically by extending higher and lower in pitch and horizontally by repeating the last phrase of the solo line or complementing it. The percussion ensemble follows this same function and structure. The *quinto* player parallels the vocal soloist in the sense that his almost fully improvised part also occupies the middle range of the percussion group. The *quinto* part is musically the most exciting aspect of the *rumba* dances because of this almost complete improvisation. Several pitches are possible on the instrument, but, in general, tonal contrast is established between a low tone and a sequence of high slap tones obtained by slapping the drumhead with a loud, sharp attack. Different tones are also produced through muffling the head, applying pressure to it, or exerting different levels of force in the attack. As opposed to this improvisation, the *tumbadora* and the *palitos* or *claves* perform slightly varied ostinato patterns. As shown in Example 9-11, the resulting performance is made up of the most typically African-like improvised multiple syncopation and multilayered rhythmic activity. The vocal call-and-response practice also stresses the African heritage of this music.

The folk music of Puerto Rico maintains a strong Hispanic and African heritage, the former particularly in the interior of the island, the latter in the coastal areas. Besides the *corrido* in *copla* form inherited from the Spanish *romance*, and the Christmas song known as *aguinaldo* related to the *villancico*, the main dance and song of the Puerto Rican peasants (*jíbaros*) is the *seis*. The Spanish character of the *seis* comes not only from the use of the *décima espinela* in its song text but also from the frequent harmonies based on the "andalucian cadence" (descending conjunct motion of the roots of alternating major and minor triads) and a specific tense vocal style associated with *cante hondo* or *flamenco* music. The typical accompanying ensemble includes a guitar, a *tiple* (small guitar of five courses of single or double strings), a *bordonúa* (large six-string guitar), and the Puerto Rican *cuatro* (a guitar-like instrument of five courses of double strings), to which are added a *güiro* and a *bongo* drum. Among the predominantly Afro-Puerto Rican folk and popular musical genres are the *bomba* and the *plena*. The *bomba* reveals the call-and-response performance pattern of traditional Afro-Caribbean vocal folk music, supported by polyrhythmic drum accompaniment. As a dance and a song type, the *plena*—considered by many to have originated in the southern coastal area, around the city of Ponce—is

EXAMPLE 9-11. *Rumba guaguancó.* "Una Rumba en la Bodega," transcribed by Larry Crook, from the recording *Guaguancó Afro-Cubano* (Grupo Folklorico de Alberto Zayas), Panart LP-2055. From Larry Crook, "A Musical Analysis of the Cuban Rumba," *Latin American Music Review*, Vol. III, no. 1 (1982). Used by permission of the University of Texas Press.

All pitches are transcribed a minor second higher than actual sounding pitch.

la   la rum - ba   o - ye   la ____

un - a rum - ba en la bo - de-e ga ____

al ver - nas a - llá for - mó

etc.

characteristically *criollo* in its combination of Spanish-related melodies with Afro-Caribbean rhythmic structures for the accompaniment, provided by guitar, *cuatro*, wind instruments such as trumpet and clarinet, drums such as the *tambora* and *conga*, and, in more urbanized groups, double bass and accordion. The *plena* has become one of the most significant expressions of Puerto Rican popular culture in its social commentaries—on daily life and sociohistorical events of the island—in frequently derisive, critical, and humorous terms, much like the calypso tradition of Trinidad.

BIBLIOGRAPHICAL AND DISCOGRAPHICAL NOTES

The best and most comprehensive bibliographical discussion of Latin American folk and traditional music is found in Gilbert Chase, *A Guide to the Music of Latin America* (Washington, DC: Pan American Union, 1962). An updated account of the literature appears in the music section (humanities volumes) of the *Handbook of Latin American Studies*, published by the Hispanic Foundation of the Library of Congress. For a general description of Latin American folk and popular music, the entries for the various countries in *The New Grove Dictionary of Music and Musicians* should be consulted. A fairly detailed assessment of "Latin American Ethnomusicology Since About 1945" by Gerard Béhague appears in the *Handbook of Ethnomusicology*, ed. Helen Myers (London: Grove Dictionaries, Macmillan, in press). The state of research in popular music is the subject of Gerard Béhague's chapter "Popular Music," in *Handbook of Latin American Popular Culture*, ed. Harold E. Hinds, Jr., and Charles M. Tatum (Westport, CT: Greenwood Press, 1985). A useful overview of Latin American folk music is provided by Isabel Aretz in her study, *Síntesis de la etnomúsica en América Latina* (Caracas: Monte Avila Editores, 1980).

A very useful study of Aztec and Inca musics and their development is Robert Stevenson, *Music in Aztec and Inca Territory* (Berkeley and Los Angeles: University of California Press, 1968). Mexican folk music is also studied, with numerous musical examples, in Stevenson, *Music in Mexico: A Historical Survey* (New York: Crowell, 1952); in Vicente T. Mendoza, *Panorama de la música tradicional de México* (Mexico: Imprenta Universitaria, 1956); and in Mendoza, *La canción mexicana* (Mexico: Universidad Nacional, 1961). Gertrude P. Kurath and Samuel Martí, *Dances of Anáhuac* (Chicago: Aldine, 1964) discusses the Maya and Aztec traditional dances and music and the extent of their preservation in present-day Mesoamerica. E. Thomas Stanford provides an updated survey of Mexican folk music in the first chapter "La música popular de México," in *La música de México*, ed. Julio Estrada (I. *Historia.* V. *Período contemporáneo* (1958 a 1980) (Mexico: Universidad Nacional Autónoma de México, 1984–86).

Studies of Latin American folk and popular musical instruments abound. John M. Schechter provides a good introduction to native instruments in Meso-america in "Non-Hispanic Instruments in Mexico and Central America: An Annotated Bibliography," *Current Musicology*, XXIV (1977), 80–104. For Central America, see Vida Chenoweth, *The Marimbas of Guatemala* (Lexington: University of Kentucky Press, 1964); Samuel Martí, *Instrumentos musicales precortesianos*, 2nd ed. rev. (Mexico: Instituto Nacional de Antropología y Historia, 1968); Charles L. Boilès, "The Pipe and Tabor in Mesoamerica," in *Yearbook* of the Inter-American Institute for Musical Research (Tulane University) II (1966); and Arturo Chamarro, *Los instrumentos de percusión en México* (Zamora: Colegio de Michoacán, 1984). A very comprehensive single-volume organological study is Karl G. Izikowitz, *Musical and Other Sound Instruments of the South American Indians* (Göteborg: Elanders, 1935; reprint Wakefield, Yorkshire: SR Publishers, 1970). Other useful items are Carlos Vega, *Los instrumentos musicales aborígenes y criollos de Argentina* (Buenos Aires: Ediciones Centurión, 1946); Isabel Aretz, *Instrumentos musicales de Venezuela* (Cumaná: Universidad de Oriente, 1967); Guillermo Abadía M., *Instrumentos de la música folklórica de Colombia (Bogotá: Instituto Colombiano de Cultura, 1981);* Carlos Alberto Coba A., *Instrumentos musicales populares registrados en el Ecuador*, 2 vols. (Otavalo: Instituto Otavaleño de Antropología, 1980, 1984); César Bolaños, Fernando García, Alida Salazar, and Josafat Roel Pineda, *Mapa de los instrumentos musicales de uso popular en el Perú* (Lima: Instituto Nacional de Cultura, Oficina de Música y Danza, 1978); and *Instrumentos musicales etnográficos y folklóricos de la Argentina*, by several authors (Buenos Aires: Instituto Nacional de Musicología "Carlos Vega," 1980). The works that follow also contain sections on instruments.

Most studies of Latin American and Caribbean folk, traditional, and popular musics are in Spanish or Portuguese. Items in English appear in specialized journals, such as *Ethnomusicology* (special Latin American issue, Vol. X, no. 1, January 1966), *Latin American Music Review/Revista de música latino-americana* (published since 1980 by the University of Texas Press), and, on occasion, *The World of Music*, the *Yearbook for Traditional Music*, and nonmusic periodicals (for these, consult the RILM [*Répertoire international de littérature musicale*] abstracts). For the Andean area, Raoul and Marguerite d'Harcourt, *La musique des Incas et ses survivances* (Paris: Paul Geuthner, 1925) is still valuable, leaving aside its obsolete analytic focus. The study *La musique des Aymara sur les hauts plateaux boliviens* (Paris: Société des Américanistes, 1959), by the same authors, is more satisfactory in its analytical conclusions. Max Peter Baumann's work in Bolivia has resulted in some very good studies, among which is his "Music, Dance, and Song of the Chipayas (Bolivia)," *Latin American Music Review*, Vol. II, no. 2 (1981), 171–222. The more recent overview of Peruvian music, *La música en el Perú* (Lima: Patronato Popular y Porvenir Pro Música Clásica, 1985), with chapters on pre-Columbian and contemporary music by César Bolaños and Raúl Romero, respectively, provides a good appreciation of the current knowledge and concerns in Peruvian musical studies. Important collections of folk music for the Peruvian area are *Cancionero andino sur* (Lima: Casa Mozart, 1967) and *Panorama de la música tradicional del Perú* (Lima: Casa Mozart, 1966). Colombian folk music is surveyed in Guillermo Abadía M., *La música folklórica colombiana* (Bogotá: Universidad Nacional de Colombia, 1973); the most detailed study of George List, mentioned in this chapter, *Music and Poetry in a Colombian Village* (Bloomington: Indiana University Press, 1983), deserves careful consultation.

Many music histories of the various South American countries present general accounts of folk and traditional musics. For Chile, consult Samuel Claro Valdés and Jorge Urrutia Blondel, *Historia de la música en Chile* (Santiago: Editorial Orbe, 1973); and Samuel Claro Valdés, *Oyendo a Chile* (Santiago: Editorial Andres Bello, 1979), with an accompanying cassette of recorded examples. For Ecuador, Segundo Luis Moreno, *Historia de la música en el Ecuador* (Quito: Editorial de la Casa de la Cultura Ecuatoriana, 1972), summarizes most of the author's earlier writings. The early Brazilian music history, *História da música brasileira*, 2nd ed. (Rio de Janeiro: F. Briquiet, 1942), by Renato Almeida, remains valuable for some of its treatment of folk and popular music. The same applies to Oneyda Alvarenga, *Música popular brasileira* (Rio de Janeiro: Editora Globo, 1950). A more recent introductory study of Brazilian music, written by various specialists, is *Brasilien. Einführung in Musiktraditionen Brasiliens*, ed. Tiago de Oliveira Pinto (Mainz: Schott, 1986). A good but old survey of Argentine folk music is the study of Isabel Aretz mentioned in the text, which should be supplemented by the various studies of Carlos Vega, especially his *Panorama de la música popular argentina* (Buenos Aires: Editorial Losada, 1944) and *Las danzas populares argentinas* (Buenos Aires: Instituto de Musicología, 1952). For Uruguayan folk music, the works of Lauro Ayestarán remain the best reference, particularly his *La música en el Uruguay* (Montevideo: SODRE, 1953) and *El folklore musical uruguayo* (Montevideo: Arca, 1967). Venezuelan folk and popular music is the subject of Luis Felipe Ramón y Rivera, *La música folklórica de Venezuela* (Caracas: Monte Avila Editores, 1969), *La música afrovenezolana* (Caracas: Monte Avila Editores, 1971), and *La música popular de Venezuela* (Caracas: Ernesto Armitano, 1976).

Cuban folk music is treated in general terms in Alejo Carpentier, *La música en Cuba* (Mexico: Fondo de Cultura Económica, 1946). Particularly important for Cuban folk music are the studies of Argeliers León, especially his *Música folklórica de Cuba* (Havana: Ediciones del Dept. de Música de la Biblioteca Nacional José Martí, 1964) and *Del canto y el tiempo* (Havana: Editorial Letras Cubanas, 1984). A recent study by Olavo Alén R., *La música de las Sociedades de Tumba Francesa en Cuba* (Havana: Casa de las Américas, 1986), sheds new light on the subject. A general account of Dominican folk dance and music is provided by Fradique Lizardo, *Danzas y bailes folklóricos dominicanos* (Santo Domingo: Museo del Hombre Dominicano y Fundación García Arévalo, 1975). A good study of the Dominican *salve* is Martha Ellen Davis, *Voces del Purgatorio. Estudio de la salve dominicana* (Santo Domingo: Museo del Hombre Dominicano, 1981). For Puerto Rican music, besides the study of María Luisa Muñoz, *La música en Puerto Rico* (Sharon, CT: Troutman Press, 1966), and that of Francisco López Cruz, *La música folklórica en Puerto*

Rico (Sharon, CT: Troutman Press, 1967), the general survey by Héctor Campos Parsi, *La música. La gran enciclopedia de Puerto Rico*, Vol. VII (Madrid: Ediciones Madrid, 1976) is recommended.

Recordings of Latin American Indian music and Afro-American music of Latin America are listed in the discographical notes for Chapters 8 and 10, respectively. There are so many recordings of Latin American folk music available on American, European, and Latin American commercial labels that a sample list cannot do justice to the discography. In the United States, the Folkways, Lyrichord, and Nonesuch catalogs contain very useful items. In Europe, many fine recordings appear on labels sponsored by governmental agencies (e.g., the Musée de l'Homme in Paris) or international agencies (e.g., the UNESCO Record series). In Latin America, some of the most representative and authentic recordings have been published by governmental agencies. A series of more than two dozen discs published since 1969 by the Instituto Nacional de Antropología e Historia documents Indian and mestizo traditions of Mexico; the approach has been primarily regional, and nearly all of the volumes consist of ethnographic field recordings. (The recordings are available from Serie de Discos, INAH, Córdoba 45, México 1, D. F., México.) *Documentário sonoro do folclore brasiliero* is an ongoing series of 7-inch, 33 ⅓ rpm discs surveying Brazilian folk traditions (including Afro-Brazilian but not traditional Indian music) issued by the Fundação Nacional de Arte (discs available from FUNARTE, Rua Araújo Porto Alegre, 80, Rio de Janeiro, 20030, RJ Brazil).

TEN

AFRO-AMERICAN FOLK MUSIC IN NORTH AND LATIN AMERICA

by Bruno Nettl and Gerard Béhague

One of the truly important developments in the history of world music was initiated by the forced migration of great numbers of Africans, as slaves, to various parts of the Americas. Coming mostly from West Africa but also from other regions, such as Angola, they brought with them their music and other elements of their cultures, which served to provide a common context for the continuation, at least in part, of the African traditions. The Africans in the New World came into contact with a large variety of European musics, and the nature of the contact was different in North and South America, in the Caribbean, on plantations, and in towns. Their reactions to these European—and sometimes American Indian—musics called into being a whole group of musical subcultures that have had an impact on all strata of twentieth-century music in the West and elsewhere.

Not only are the folk musics of the various black populations and communities in the New World intrinsically interesting and alive, they have also influenced the folk music of the whites to the extent of having played a major role in the development of some typical North and Latin American forms. They are responsible for the development of a great deal of Western popular music; their role in the development of ragtime and jazz cannot be overestimated; their urban outgrowths, such as gospel, rock, and rhythm and blues, are major forces in everyday musical life; and their effect on composers of art music in the United States and Latin America as well as on such Europeans as Antonin Dvořák and Igor Stravinsky has been considerable.

The origin of the styles of black music in the New World has been the subject of much debate. Extreme and opposing views have been advanced: The music is actually African, unchanged by migration; the music is simply a copy of Western form and style; the black American is a superlatively creative individual; he or she is capable of creating nothing but the simplest spontaneous musical utterances. The definition of "black" music has been argued as well: Is all music composed or performed by Afro-Americans black music? Or is it only that part of the repertory of Afro-American musicians that shows a distinctly African-derived character? In fact, it is the former view that corresponds to a great deal of ethnomusicological practice, because scholars, in assessing the musical style of a culture, tend to base their findings on a sample of that culture's complete repertory, whatever its origins.

A more moderate view of the origins of Afro-American styles is now widely accepted. There is no doubt, of course, that the slaves from Africa did bring with them their music. In areas in which they greatly outnumbered their white neighbors and masters, and where they were isolated from whites, they retained this African heritage with relatively little change. It is even conceivable that they now retain some practices that have changed more rapidly in Africa than in the New World. Some of their songs and rhythms can still be found in Africa, but their repertory appears to be largely material actually composed in the Americas, although using styles and patterns very largely derived from Africa. In areas in which Afro-Americans associated more closely with whites, and lived in less self-contained communities, they appear to have taken over a great deal of folk, church, and popular music from whites (while probably also holding on to aspects of the African tradition), gradually absorbing it. Everywhere, in any event, they were influenced by the music of whites (and in some cases by that of the Indians), and accordingly they modified their own traditions to some extent. Thus their musical acculturation could take three forms: they may have learned the music of whites together with white performance practices; they may have learned the performance practices of whites and superimposed these on their own music; or they may have learned the music of whites and superimposed on them African performance practices.

All of these things happened to some degree. The blacks of the United States learned music from their white masters, from missionaries, and from neighbors in the towns. Some songs they sang in styles indistinguishable from those of whites, but on most of them blacks imposed some stylistic traits derived from Africa. They presumably also continued to sing and play African music and to compose new music in the African styles; this appears to have been true more in Brazil and the Caribbean than in the United States, to which slaves were not brought directly from Africa but rather from the Caribbean, where linguistic and social ties were broken down. The African elements that were retained were among those also found, at least to some extent, in European (and therefore American) folk and popular music, a fact that stimulated anthropologists to develop the theory of culture change known as *syncretism*. According to this theory, when two cultures come into contact, elements that are similar or compatible tend to syncretize, or grow into a new hybrid form.[1] Thus, for example, because both African and the Western (European) tradition have harmony, Afro-American music also has it, and its character is derived from both African and European models. In contrast, because North American Indian and European music have little in common, a form of music having features of both did not arise.

What actually are the African features that were carried into the New World? One that comes to mind immediately is the emphasis on rhythm; it appears in many different forms, including the importance of drums and other percussion instruments in the black cultures of the Americas, the use of syncopation and complicated rhythmic figures in North America (and of complex rhythmic ensemble music in Latin America), an emphasis on the beat, and a tendency to adhere very strictly to meter and tempo (the "metronome sense" of West Africa). Another feature is the tendency to use call-and-response patterns, so important in Africa, which is manifested not only in ordinary antiphonal or responsory techniques but also in more complex alternating devices, such as the rotation of the solo part in jazz. The love of instruments and instrumental music is also one of these African features, although only some Afro-American instruments are derived from Africa, others being ordinary Western instruments, such as guitar and harmonica, or adaptations of them, such as the gutbucket. Extremely important

---

[1] See Richard A. Waterman, "African Influence on American Negro Music," in *Acculturation in the Americas*, ed. Sol Tax (Chicago: University of Chicago Press, 1952), p. 212. Syncretism and other responses to musical culture contact are discussed further in Bruno Nettl, "Some Aspects of the History of World Music in the Twentieth Century: Questions, Problems, and Concepts," *Ethnomusicology*, XXII (1978), 123–36, and in Margaret J. Kartomi, "The Processes and Results of Musical Culture Contact: A Discussion of Terminology and Concepts," *Ethnomusicology*, XXV (1981), 227–50.

among African elements is the use of improvisation and a tendency to vary a short theme. Polyphony, although not really typical of West African music or, for that matter, of much black music in the Americas, may perhaps, where it is found, be traceable to African roots. Most important, the manner of singing, the way in which the voice is used and the typical vocal timbre in the black musics, appears to be closely related to Africa.

These are the features of music that appear to have been brought from Africa. They are techniques of making music, and the actual musical sounds that Afro-Americans produce when using such techniques may not, in fact, seem very much like African music. It is frequently difficult to decide whether a given feature of a piece of black music results from the African heritage or not. As has been pointed out, African musical techniques have maintained themselves in a hostile cultural environment largely because their counterparts in Western folk and popular music are somewhat similar. But it is interesting to find that, on the whole, those features of music that were most strongly developed in Africa have to some extent also been retained in Afro-American music, and, conversely, those elements which were not developed to any great degree of complexity or distinctiveness (such as scale) seem to have given way to traits bearing the European trademark.

Students of the relationship between African and Afro-American cultures have often remarked on the extent to which African characteristics have remained in the Afro-American musical repertories, in contrast to the lower degree of retention in most other aspects of culture. At times this fact has been ascribed to a presumably special native musical talent of blacks, and it has even been supposed that certain elements of music are part of the black's biological heredity. But it has never been possible to demonstrate a connection between musical talent and race or to prove the biological inheritance of specific aspects of musical behavior. The explanation is probably much closer at hand. Music plays an important role in African life, especially in ritual; as such, it is of major cultural value. It is not surprising that Africans cherished their musical heritage when they were brought to the New World. (Similarly, we find that European immigrant groups also tended to lay greater stress on their musical traditions in the strange environment of America than they did in the old country.) Furthermore, music was in various ways more complex and more highly developed in Africa than in the Western folk cultures with which the blacks came into contact in the Americas.

It is possible to rank the various Afro-American communities by the degree to which their musical styles adhere to African models. Among the musics that are reasonably well known, those of Haiti, the Guianas, and northeastern Brazil (particularly the state of Bahia) are closest to the African. Jamaica, Trinidad, and Cuba are next, followed by the southern

United States and, finally, the northern United States. Generally speaking, religious music tends to be closer to African styles than does secular. In general, also, Africanisms are more readily found in rural than in urban situations, for the culture of the cities is more conducive to Westernization and modernization. (This is particularly true of the United States.) But there appear to be exceptions. In the city of Salvador, Brazil, West African religious cults remain an important force, and are accompanied by music that sounds characteristically African.

The kind of ranking produced here is complicated by the fact that each Afro-American community has a variety of styles. The island of Jamaica provides a characteristic microcosm of this variety. Inhabited almost entirely by blacks, it contains a number of distinct musics related in various ways to Africa. In the rural areas there are remnants of cult music with African-sounding melodies and drum patterns; there are also the songs of revival cults, based on Protestant fundamentalism, with songs that are European in character but sung with African modes of performance. In the port of Kingston, dock workers sing work songs in a style closely related to the music of Haiti and Cuba. The popular music of Kingston, however, is distinctively Jamaican, having developed three types of style, the Ska, the Rock-steady, and Reggae, all based essentially on North American models but with prominent African and Latin American elements. And Jamaica participated along with Trinidad, in the development of a distinctive song type, the *calypso*. Thus, although we may rank Jamaica at a particular point in the scale denoting degrees of Africanism or African retention in music, we must realize that this ranking is not based on a homogeneous musical culture. The same sort of statement could be made about each Afro-American community.

AFRO-AMERICAN INSTRUMENTS

A great many instruments that are at least partly of African origin are used by the Afro-American communities of Latin America. For example, in Haiti certain drums are made of hollow logs. Normally they have single heads and are cylindrical in shape. Their height varies from six feet to eighteen inches. Among the idiophones, the *ogán*, a kind of iron bell struck with an external clapper, is being replaced by other metal objects which are called by the same name. Gourd rattles and double-headed drums are also used, and so are shallow, single-headed open drums similar to a tambourine. Various kinds of sticks are used to beat the drums, each cult having its own type of drumsticks and combination of drums. The mosquito drum, a type of musical bow, of which one end is attached to the ground while from the other extends a string attached to a piece of skin covering a hole in the ground, is used as an accompaniment to singing. In this instrument, the hole in the ground functions as a resonance chamber, much as the calabash or the player's mouth adds resonance to the sound of musical bows in southern and central Africa.

Stamping tubes, hollow tubes struck on the ground or on a board, provide another kind of rhythmic accompaniment. A rather large and deep-sounding version of the African *sansa* or *mbira* (called *marimba* in Haiti and *marimbula* in Puerto Rico) is also found in the Caribbean. Horns and trumpets made of bamboo, each capable of playing only one pitch, are used, as are cows' horns, conch-shell trumpets, and horns improvised from various objects, such as phonograph loudspeaker horns. The *claves*, short sticks made of hardwood that are struck together by hand, are important in the Caribbean. The xylophone, common in Africa, is not as widespread in the Afro-American cultures but does seem to have become one of the important instruments of Central America. In Guatemala, the marimba (xylophone with gourd resonators) has become a national instrument. A form of musical bow with gourd resonator, called *berimbau*, is used in Brazil and played in an essentially Central and South African manner. Throughout the area under discussion, the black community has brought instruments directly from Africa, has adapted Western materials and technology to the needs of African instruments, and has exerted an African cultural influence by its interest in instruments and instrumental music and its creation of many musical types, also by the prestige and ritual significance that it has placed on the instruments themselves and on the instrumentalists.

The steel drum, an instrument invented in Trinidad during or after World War II, is a fascinating example of the results of the acculturation of African practices in modern Western civilization. Steel oil containers, abandoned and available, their tops hammered into shapes producing the desired pitches, were combined into groups of three or four different sizes and accompanied rhythmically by idiophones—rattles, *claves*, or bells. Later, the bottom sections of the containers were cut off, and the steel drums were placed on special stands. Each drum is capable of playing simple melodic material. The result is music of a strongly rhythmic character, with polyphony of an ostinato nature, and with each drum (or "pan," as they are called by the players) having a particular musical function, as in a jazz band. Aside from African-derived and invented instruments, Western instruments such as the guitar and the banjo (which may itself have been developed under African influences) are widely used in the black communities of Latin America and the Caribbean.

In the black folk music of the United States, instruments play a larger role than in the Anglo-American tradition, although interest in instru-

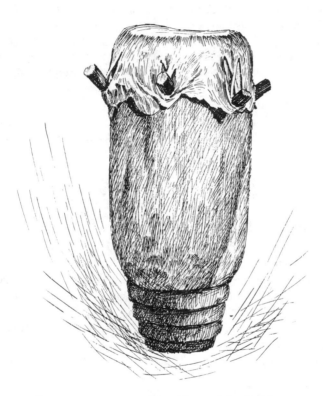

Drum type common in West Africa and the Caribbean

ments appears to have increased considerably in white communities in the course of the twentieth century. Many of the Afro-American instruments in the United States are European-derived (harmonica, fiddle, brass instruments). Others are either actually derived from African models or fashioned so as to produce sounds similar to those produced by African instruments. In the former category are several that are hardly found today but are reported to have been present in the United States in the nineteenth century and earlier: the *sansa* or *mbira*, hollowed log drums, and gourd rattles. In the latter category we find the gutbucket or washtub, related to the musical bow and to the Haitian mosquito drum; washboards used as scrapers and placed on baskets for resonance; and frying pans, cowbells, bottles, and wood or bone clappers to replace the bells and rattles of the West African percussion ensembles. These instruments are not themselves descendants of African forms, but they seem to have been invented or improvised to fulfill the functions once performed by African instruments.

AFRO-AMERICAN MUSIC IN LATIN AMERICA

In the Latin American context, the definition of "black" music becomes extremely complex. First of all, the general acceptance of what constitutes, culturally and ethnically, an Afro-American is not as unequivocal as in North America. There are several examples in Central and South America of black groups whose African cultural identity is difficult to assess, such as the Caribs of Honduras and Nicaragua who are black representatives of an Indian culture. Conversely, important nonblack segments of certain communities have perfectly definable African-related cultural traits, such as, for example, some East Indian groups of Trinidad, or the Cayapa Indians of Western Ecuador. In many areas of Latin America, acculturation of African peoples has been considerable and has affected other ethnic groups or the wide range of mixed groups. In such cases we are confronted with ethnically diverse groups with a remarkably homogeneous "black" culture. Race alone cannot, then, be considered a valid criterion for identifying Afro-American musical styles in Latin America. Although we'are stressing Africanisms in our discussion here, it should always be borne in mind that Afro-American music cuts across ethnic lines.

Black music in Latin America functions in both sacred and secular contexts, but generally it is in the sacred context that African musical elements are most strongly preserved. Various cults involving deities (called *orishás*, *vodouns*, saints, etc.) that have been transferred from the West African homeland but whose character has often changed in the process are found

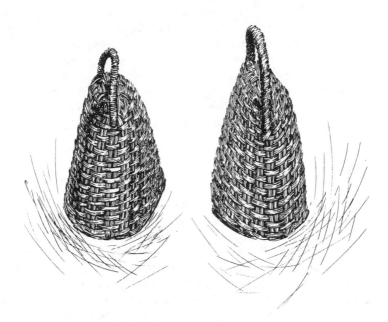

Basket rattles, as found in Haiti or West Africa

in Cuba, Haiti, Jamaica, Trinidad, and Brazil. Among the Afro-American communities of Latin America a cult implies the recognition of African deities and a belief system essentially African. Syncretism, however, has taken place almost everywhere, in varying degrees. Most cults show features of Christian belief systems, although not necessarily a recognition of a Christian god or saint. Often, as a result of sociohistorical accommodation, a Catholic saint has been assimilated into the personality of an African deity, but the equivalence of saints and deities is by no means uniform throughout the continent. West African religions as developed in the Americas are monotheistic, animistic in nature, and involve a pantheon of major and lesser deities, each of which is worshipped with characteristic ceremonies, songs, and drum rhythms. The most obvious African features prevailing in such ceremonies include the ritual use of blood (animal sacrifices), initiatory rites, ritual dancing with a highly symbolic choreography, personification of the *orishás* through spirit possession, and offering of food to the gods. The most outstanding Christian or reinterpreted Christian elements include the use of the Bible, Catholic prayers, cross and crucifixes, candle burning, and lithographs of saints. Misconceptions about Afro-American belief systems, epitomized by the term *black magic*, arise from the fact that most cult leaders practice some aspect of folk medicine.

The most important Afro-Cuban cults include the *Lucumi* (derived from the Yoruba of Nigeria), the *Kimbisa* or *Mayombé* (from the Congo area), and the *Abakuá* (combining beliefs and practices of the other cults; its members are referred to as *ñáñigos*). In Brazil, the cult groups are called the *candomblé* in Bahia, *xangô* (shango) in Pernambuco, and *macumba* in the central and southern states. The Bahian groups include the *Ketu* (or *Nago*) and *Jesha* (Yoruba), the *Gêgê* (Dahomey), the *Congo-Angola*, and the *Caboclos* (derived from some Amerindian beliefs combined with those from the other cults). Most important among the Haitian cult groups are the *Vodoun* or *Rada* cult (*Arada-Nago* family) and the *Pétro* group (*Congo-Guinée* family). According to Courlander,[2] other lesser family groups include the *Ibo-Kanga*, the *Congo*, and the *Juba-Martinique*, each with a distinct set of dances and accompanying songs. In Jamaica and Trinidad the groups include respectively the *Kumina* and the *Shango* cults, in addition to Afro-Christian groups under Protestant denominations' influence, such as the Pukkumina, Revival and Revival Zion of Jamaica, and the Spiritual Baptists (or Shouters) of Trinidad. Revivalist cult music in these areas is quite similar to much black Protestant music of the southern United States. It is basically a mixture of various types of traditional Protestant hymnody,

---

[2] Harold Courlander, *The Drum and the Hoe* (Berkeley: University of California Press, 1960).

with an important body of gospel hymns of the type composed by Ira Sankey and disseminated throughout the area by various evangelical crusaders during the nineteenth century. (In both Jamaica and Trinidad the word "Sankey" has become a generic term for "hymn.") A basic difference of revival cult music from that of the other cults is the constant presence of harmonized choruses, much like congregational hymn singing in southern United States black churches, and the nature of the accompanying rhythmic patterns, substantially less African than in the Cuban, Haitian, or Brazilian cults. The type of call-and-response practice in Jamaican revivalist music could be considered a retention of an African feature, although it is not unlike that of the gospel music in the United States today.

Protestant-related cults excepted, the most obvious stylistic trait common to the musics of cult groups in Latin America is the predominant use of call-and-response patterns. The leader or solo singer may be either a woman or a man, but the chorus is usually composed of women. The chorus sings in monophonic fashion, but occasionally individual singers deviate from the main melodic line. Among the most acculturated groups (*Abakuá* in Cuba, *Caboclo* and *Umbanda* in Brazil), heterophony is not uncommon. Sometimes soloist and chorus overlap. Tempo varies considerably from one cult group to another and, within the same cult, in accordance with a particular song cycle. Gradual acceleration in many songs or in drum music is fairly frequent, depending on their particular ritual function. Scales are most commonly pentatonic without semitones, although diatonic scales are found in many songs. The ranges of the melodies are not uniform; for example, the *Gêgê* cult of Bahia has songs with wide range (most with more than an octave), whereas those of the *Jesha* cult in the same area average less than an octave. The melodic contours are generally descending, but pendulum-like movements are also characteristic, as in the series of songs to the deity *Exú* in the Bahian *Ketu* cult. Melodic intervals are often quite large. Whenever there is leader-chorus alternation, the melodic phrases tend to be short, but with solo songs or duets the melodic line becomes longer and more complex. The form, within the framework of the solo-chorus alternation, is frequently based on the repetition of a single phrase, with some variations through ornamentation. The soloist is likely to present a theme with variations as the basis of his or her tune. Leader and chorus often use the same tune, but may use related tunes or completely unrelated materials. Occasionally the chorus uses material from the last portion of the soloist's line. The large majority of songs follow the strophic form. Examples 10-1 and 10-2 illustrate some of the characteristics of the Afro-Bahian cult songs. In Example 10-2, the *rumpí* and *lê* figures, taken together, form the following pattern:

EXAMPLE 10-1. Brazilian Gêgê cult song (text omitted), from Alan P. Merriam, "Songs of the Gêgê and Jesha Cults," *Jahrbuch für musikalische Volks- und Völkerkunde,* I, ed. Fritz Bose (Berlin: Walter de Gruyter, 1963), 122.

EXAMPLE 10-2. Brazilian Ketu cult song (Field collection of Gerard Béhague). Transcribed by Robert E. Witmer and Gerard Béhague. Text omitted.

The singing styles of most Afro-American cults are essentially like the relaxed, open manner of singing common in Africa. Female voices present a characteristically hard, metallic quality, with a preference for the upper range of the voice. Falsetto is often used by both soloist and chorus.

The song repertories of Afro-American religions have not been fully codified, but we know that a multitude of songs attributed to a given deity form the bulk of the repertories. Cycles of songs are performed in a ritual order, according to a well-established tradition. Song texts appear in various languages, from Yoruba (Nago), Fon, and various Congo dialects, to Spanish and Portuguese, Haitian *créole*, or a combination of these. Typically, song texts are simple praise or imprecation directed to the gods; sometimes they refer to specific events in the lives of the deities or to their remarkable feats, following West African mythology as reinterpreted in the New World through the influence of popular Christianism.

Although the large majority of song repertories are traditional, evidence has been gathered that points to stylistic changes and to the elaboration of a more recent repertory. According to the testimony of cult leaders in Salvador, Bahia, many songs attributed to specific deities have disappeared from the repertory, and new songs are being incorporated. These are not, in general, songs composed by the priest or priestess of a cult house; they are spontaneously created when an initiating member, in a state of possession, sings his or her song to his or her *orixá*. Such songs are apparently remembered afterward. Especially among the *Congo-Angola* and the *Caboclo* cults, these "new" songs frequently include elements from folk music or urban musical culture (such as Carnival street music) foreign to the tradition but familiar to the songmakers.

The single most important ritual and musical element in Afro-American cults is the drumming. Drums are considered sacred instruments. They undergo ritual baptism by means of animal sacrifices and food offering. In the case of the Cuban *Abakuá*, some drums have an exclusively symbolic function and are never played. Complex ritual involving drums is essential because they alone are thought to have the power to communicate with the deities. In most cult groups, drums are played in a battery of three, in conjunction with an iron gong or a rattle. They vary in size and shape among the various cults, but the trio always comes in three different sizes. The largest drum (called *rum* in the *Ketu* of Bahia, *iyá* among the *Lucumis* of Cuba, *maman* in the *Vodoun* cult, *mama* or *bemba* in the *Shango* of Trinidad) is played by the master drummer. The medium size drum (known as *rumpí*, *itótele*, *seconde*, and *congo*, in the same order) and the smallest one (respectively *lê*, *okónkolo*, *bébé*, *oumalay*) usually repeat a single steady rhythm. In contrast, the largest and lowest drum varies its beats, producing some of the complex and intensely exciting rhythms typical of the Afro-American styles. The gong (variously called *agogô* or *gan* in Brazil and *ogán* or *ekón* in Cuba) or the rattle generally sets the fundamental beat; the drums join in a few seconds later. As Herskovits has pointed out, the melody of the song is but the accompaniment to the rhythm of the drums. This emphasis on rhythm is an obvious African heritage. Each cult, dance, ceremony, or deity has its characteristic rhythms, on the basis of which the master drummer improvises. Drum music per se, that is, separate from an accompanimental function, also exists in large quantity. Its major function is to call the gods and to bring on possessions, also to provide materials for the many ritual dances. Cross rhythms and polyrhythms form the major substance of the music. Examples 10-3 and 10-4 show several rhythmic patterns, with their respective names, of the Bahian *Ketu* cult, and the Afro-Cuban *Lucumi*. The *rum* part of the *avaninha* pattern often presents a subtle duple-triple ambivalence. For example, it sometimes sounds like ♪ ⅞ ♪ ⅞ ♪ ⅞ ♪ ♪ ⅞ ⅞. Likewise, in the *toque de Iansã*, the 4/4 gong pattern often approaches a triple feeling, as for example ♪ ⅞ ♪ ⅞ ♪ ⅞ ⅞ ♪ ⅞ ♪ ♪ ⅞ ⅞. In the same pattern, the *rum* also expresses a duple feeling, like the gong: 𝄴 ♪ ♪♪ ♪ ⅞ ♪ ♪ ⅞.

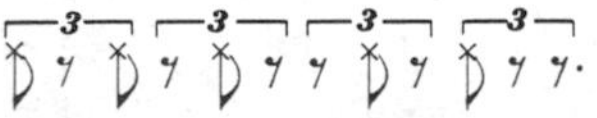

In general, the meters of this cult music are most commonly duple but often also triple, and the hemiola rhythm—African par excellence—finds its way into much of the drum music repertory. Although there is no definite evidence of the retention in Latin America today of the African talking drum techniques, it is believed that the various ritual drum patterns (attributed to each deity) were, originally, rhythmic renditions of the melodic shape of certain phrases of the Yoruba language (which is a tone language). Such renditions would have been learned, memorized, and transmitted by use of onomatopoeias.

Within the social structure of the Afro-American cults, women have a particularly important position. In the Afro-Bahian cults, although many leaders are men, the great majority are women; so are most of the initiates. The leaders, referred to in Bahia as "Pai" or "Mãe-do-santo," in Cuba as "Padrino" or "Madrina," represent the maximum spiritual and temporal authority of the cult house, and determine the degree of orthodoxy in it. They are, for the most part, leading singers themselves, responsible for transmitting the knowledge of their vast repertory and for the supervision of instruction in music and dancing in the house. Drummers have a very exalted position. They are musicians par excellence. According to Herskovits, the master drummer "moves about the scene, confident, respected. . . . Relaxed, the drum between his legs, he allows the complex rhythm to flow from his sure, agile fingers. It is he who brings on possession through his manipulation of these rhythmic intricacies, yet he himself never becomes possessed."[3] Drummers go through a series of tests before they are allowed to perform in ritual ceremonies. Their acceptance into the cult is publicly signified by means of a "confirmation" ceremony. A drummer may become

---

[3] Melville J. Herskovits, "Drums and Drummers in Afro-Brazilian Cult Life," *Musical Quarterly*, XXX (1944), 477–80.

EXAMPLE 10-3. Abstract of some basic patterns in Afro-Bahian drumming.

"Avaninha"

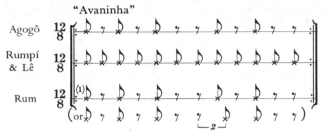

(1) The duple triple ambivalence is subtle,

e. g.,

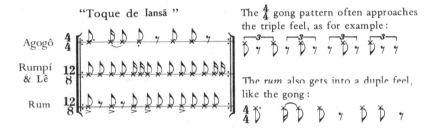

sometimes sounds like:

"Toque de lansã"

The $\frac{4}{4}$ gong pattern often approaches the triple feel, as for example:

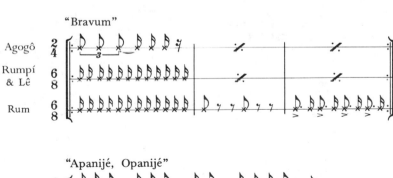

The *rum* also gets into a duple feel, like the gong:

"Bravum"

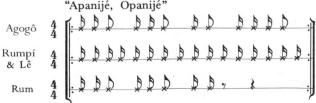

"Apanijé, Opanijé"

EXAMPLE 10-4. Lucumi Bata drum pattern to the deity Obba. From Fernando Ortiz, *La africanía de la música folklórica de Cuba* (Havana: Ediciones Cardenas y Cia., 1950), pp. 417–18.

a master drummer only after many years of experience, and only under certain circumstances, for it is considered a very special privilege.

There also exist, in Latin American black culture, instances of what might be termed "secular rituals" in which, once more, music appears as a cultural focus. The *currulao*, or marimba dance, of southwestern Colombia and northwestern Ecuador is such a ritual, that is, a socializing occasion at which highly symbolic behavior takes place. According to Whitten, the *currulao* gives us an excellent example of the function of music not only in social integration but also in the "development of personal networks." One of the important conclusions of Whitten's study is that "the currulao provides an expressive context which permits household and marital structure to be realigned when necessity demands it. . . ."[4] The music itself of this marimba dance preserves many African patterns. It requires an ensemble of six to seven male musicians, two of whom play the marimba and the others drums. The marimba may have from twenty to twenty-eight hardwood keys (each with bamboo resonators), and it functions both melodically and harmonically. The player called *bordonero* is in charge of the melody on the lower half of the instrument; the *tiplero*, on the upper half, of the counterpoint and harmony. The tuning of the marimba is by no means uniform. Solo-chorus alternation predominates in the *currulao*. Many female singers, called *respondedoras*, participate in the chorus. The leading male musician is the *glosador*; his function is to lead the singing, to give the shouts, and to indicate to the women what part of the repertory should be sung at a given time. Accompanimental drumming is produced by two *bombos* (large double-headed drums), two *cununos* (single-headed cone-shaped drums played with the hands), and rattles (maracas and *guasás*, the latter being bamboo tubes filled with seeds and into which hardwood nails are driven).

The relationship of the religious material to social dance and song is, in Latin American black culture, always a close one, and one for which explanations vary from area to area. Some of the Haitian and Afro-Bahian ceremonial material has lost its religious significance and has become part of the social side of musical life. This is also true of the *candombe*,[5] an Afro-Uruguayan ritual dance performed at the time of the Mardi Gras carnival

---

[4] Norman E. Whitten, Jr., "Personal Networks and Musical Contexts in the Pacific Lowlands of Colombia and Ecuador," in *Afro-American Anthropology, Contemporary Perspectives*, ed. Norman E. Whitten, Jr. and John Szwed (New York: The Free Press, 1970), p. 214. See also, by the same author, "Ritual Enactment of Sex Roles in the Pacific Lowlands of Ecuador-Colombia," in *Afro-Hispanic Culture* (Cambridge, MA: Shenkman Press, 1972), and *Black Frontiersmen, A South American Case* (Cambridge, MA: Shenkman Press, 1974).

[5] Paulo de Carvalho Neto, "The Candombe," *Ethnomusicology*, VIII (1963), 164–74 See also Nestor Ortiz Oderigo, *Calunga, Croquis del Candombe* (Buenos Aires: Editorial Universitaria de Buenos Aires, 1969), pp. 29–41.

in Montevideo. Here are found certain stock characters—the *gramillero* (an agile young dancer representing a tottering old man), an old black woman, a broom maker, a drummer, and a trophy bearer. These characters dance in the parade; but it is likely that they represent figures from the earlier time of slavery and the period after emancipation, when African cults and tribal rivalries dominated the life of the urban black community.

Among the Afro-Bahians, a particular secular form of singing and dancing, although not entirely dissociated from the sacred context, is the sort of athletic game known as *Capoeira Angola*. In spite of its name, this game seems to have been invented in Brazil by former slaves, and must have been, in its original form, a simple offensive and defensive type of fight.[6] Today it is reduced to a simulated fight, with the preservation of stylized steps (strokes). Only the legs and feet are involved in this dance-like game. The *capoeira* makes use of a small instrumental ensemble, including the *berimbau* (musical bow, also called *urucungo*), the tambourine (called *pandeiro*), a cone-shaped drum (*atabaque*), and a little basket rattle (*caxixi*) of the type illustrated in this chapter. Sometimes, though infrequently nowadays, a *ganzá* or *reco-reco* (*güiro*-type of rattle) and an *agogô* (iron gong) may participate in the ensemble. Specific rhythmic patterns (each with a special name, such as *São Bento Grande*, *Benguela*, and *Angola*) accompany the dancing and the singing. *Capoeira* songs are among the oldest in Brazil; very often they originate in repertories of the music of other folk dances and from songs such as the children's round songs or *samba de roda* described in the previous chapter. One of the most significant characteristics of the *capoeira* song is its dialogue form, between the *capoeira* singer and some abstract, imagined character. Fernando Ortiz[7] has observed the same characteristic, under its multiple aspects, not only in Cuba but in various other Afro-American areas of Latin America. Strikingly similar genres still exist in distant areas of the continent. For example, the well-known stick-fight game of Trinidad associated with the *kalinda* and accompanied by drum music has its equivalent in Bahia: the *maculelê*.

Although the ceremonial music (sacred and secular) of the black communities of Latin America and the Caribbean is its most prominent—and stylistically most African—musical expression, we must not forget that other kinds of music are also produced. There are work songs, social dance songs, narrative songs of various sorts, and love songs. The *calypso*, which presumably originated in Trinidad and spread rapidly throughout the Caribbean (but there are also satirical songs in Africa), is a unique kind of satirical

[6] Cf. Waldeloir Rego, *Capoeira Angola, Ensaio Sócio-Etnográfico* (Salvador, Bahia: Editora Itapuã, 1969), pp. 30–46.

[7] Fernando Ortiz, *Los bailes y el teatro de los negros en el folklore de Cuba* (Havana: Ediciones Cárdenas, 1951), pp. 6–36.

song that grew out of the racial tensions present in the island; musically, it is a combination of African, North American black, and Spanish popular styles. Jamaican blacks sing spirituals and sea shanties whose words are of English and North American origin but also preserve the call-and-response pattern of the African tradition (which may have been reinforced by the existence of similar forms in the English sea shanties). Likewise, Afro-Cuban, Afro-Brazilian, Afro-Colombian, and Afro-Venezuelan urban popular musical species exhibit various patterns that can be related to several stylistic origins. Some of these are mentioned in Chapter 9.

AFRO-AMERICAN FOLK MUSIC IN THE UNITED STATES

The musical development of North American black communities has proceeded rather differently from that of other Afro-American groups. Rather than living in relatively closed communities in which African social structures could still function, the blacks were brought to the United States from the West Indies, where elements of African culture had already begun to change and to disappear, and, once on the continent, they tended to live in close contact with their white masters. Although the survival of the West African religious cults was to some extent assured in Latin America because of their similarity to some aspects of Roman Catholicism, the impact of the Protestant denominations in the United States was of such a nature as to annihilate many, if not most, of the West African religious practices. Nevertheless, much of the value structure of the African heritage was retained, and although most of the black folk music in the United States does not sound like African music in the way that the cult music of Haiti and Bahia does, it does contain some African stylistic features. More important, African musical values often played a role in the independent developments that took place in Afro-American music. For example, call-and-response patterns, in pure form, are not found too frequently in black folk song in the United States. But the original importance of this kind of practice—essentially alternation, dividing up a tune between leader and chorus, and the encouragement of improvisatory variations—seems to have led to other practices involving alternation and improvisation, for instance, the sophisticated dividing up of a performance among different soloists in jazz and the principle of improvisatory variation that is the essence of jazz. Similarly, the importance of rhythm in West African music became part of the American black tradition, even though the rhythmic structure of North American black folk songs is very distant from that of Africa. When it comes to singing style, of course, black Americans share the qualities of other Afro-American groups and exhibit a really close tie to West Africa.

There are reports of the American South by nineteenth-century observers which mention the existence of musical practices, such as African-derived cults and cult music, similar to those that can be observed in twentieth-century Brazil and the Caribbean. The songs of the southern slaves were numerous and were associated with a large number of uses. There were work songs, many of them rhythmic to accompany the hard labor performed by groups but some, such as the field blues, slow and languid. The work songs with driving rhythms were related to similar songs used in Africa to accompany rowing and other group activities, but they also derived in part from British work songs, such as the sea shanties. Dance and play songs, related to the play-party songs of whites, were used when time for recreation was available. A few narrative songs, similar to the Anglo-American broadside ballads, or derived from the African practice of singing while telling stories about animals (like the stories of Uncle Remus, with heroes like Br'er Rabbit or Anansi, the spider), are still used and were probably once much more numerous. Short field and street cries or hollers, consisting of a single, repeated, and varied musical line, are also an important ingredient of the black folk tradition. Most important, perhaps, is the *spiritual*, the religious musical expression of the slaves, which exists in many different forms and styles, from the slow, lyrical, and devotional spirituals sung at services, to the quick, driving, and ecstatic "shout spirituals" of the revival meetings.

The spiritual, in its basic content, is closely associated with the "white spirituals" sung in the South, particularly in the Appalachians. Many of the black spirituals use words and tunes also found in the white spirituals but feature more percussion accompaniment, the use of antiphonal techniques, and improvised variation. (Parenthetically, we should point out that the question of the origin and development of the black spiritual's style has not been answered in a satisfactory way, for the white spirituals are also frequently sung in a very vigorous and rhythmically un-hymn-like way, whether through black influence or not, we don't know.)

George Pullen Jackson (1874–1953)[8] found, in tunes he took largely from nineteenth-century published collections, a great number of parallels between black and white spirituals. However, his notation gives us no information about the style or styles of singing used. Nevertheless, it is obvious that some tunes were used as both white and black spirituals, like the one shown in Example 10-5: It is the famous "Swing Low, Sweet Chariot," which is similar in melodic content to a white American hymn tune entitled "Gaines."

---

[8] George Pullen Jackson, *White and Negro Spirituals* (New York: J. J. Augustin, 1943); also his *White Spirituals in the Southern Uplands* (New York: J. J. Augustin, 1933).

EXAMPLE 10-5. Black spiritual, "Swing Low, Sweet Chariot," and analogous white spiritual, from George Pullen Jackson, *White and Negro Spirituals* (New York: J. J. Augustin, 1943), pp. 182–83.

Swing low, sweet char - i - ot, Com-ing for to car-ry me home, Swing low, sweet char - i - ot, Com-ing for to car-ry me home.   I look'd o - ver Jor-dan and what did I see— Com-ing for to car-ry me home, A band— of an - gels com-ing af - ter me,— Com-ing for to car-ry me home.

O— for a thous - and tongues to sing My— great Re-deem - er's praise, The glo-ries of my God and King,— The— tri umphs of— his grace, The tri umphs of— his— grace.

Many songs of black Americans have simply been taken over from the heritage of the whites, and others, although composed by blacks, are patterned after the music of the Anglo-American community. The black tradition in the United States has always been influenced by whites, and much of the basic material in it is essentially of European origin; it is primarily in the style of performance that we can detect definitely African roots.

Yet some types of black music are not patterned after forms used in white music. A case in point is the blues, a term actually referring to a number of different types of forms. The so-called "field blues" are simply short calls and wails, frequently with indefinite pitch, repeated several times, which perhaps originated as communication by field hands in the cotton fields; sometimes they are sung alternately by two persons. This type of song gradually developed into the "rural blues," accompanied most frequently by guitar, and, eventually, to the "urban blues" style, which is based on a specific harmonic pattern and has a definite though flexible musical and textual form.

The Afro-American community in the United States has produced a great number of prominent musicians who have become widely known outside the folk culture and have gone on to become nationally famous. Leadbelly, whose real name was Huddie Ledbetter, was a Texas convict discovered in 1933 by the pioneer folk song collector, John Lomax. Leadbelly sang many songs, but perhaps his main contribution was a number of blues songs. The form of these was also adopted by the early jazz bands that played blues. It consists of three parts, the first two similar both musically and textually, with a third contrasting. This form can be observed in such well-known pieces as "St. Louis Blues" and also in some of Leadbelly's songs, such as "Shorty George" and "Fort Worth and Dallas Blues." Many songs in the rural blues category have different forms, some of them based essentially on one musical phrase. For example, "Now Your Man Done Gone" (Example 10-6), collected in Alabama, is essentially a descending set of variations on a single phrase. Typically, Afro-American folk songs tend to be based on a smaller number of different melodic phrases than

EXAMPLE 10-6. Afro-American folk song, "Now Your Man Done Gone," collected in Alabama, from Harold Courlander, *Negro Folk Music, U.S.A.* (New York: Columbia University Press, 1963), p. 108.

are most of the songs of American whites—another possible survival of African music.

A frequently mentioned characteristic of Afro-American music is the use of so-called blue notes, or the slight lowering of notes—in particular the third and seventh—using the major scale as a pattern. This phenomenon cannot with certainty be traced to Africa. But if indeed it is African in origin, it must have been selected from a considerable number of differences that exist between African and Western scales. Its survival must have a special reason, such as compatibility with Western musical patterns. Possibly it originated among urban Afro-American musicians and moved from them into the folk music repertory.

Another group of black songs in North America that is rather distinct from its counterpart in white culture consists of counting-out rhymes and other children's game songs and rhymes. These, again, are performed in a style perhaps derived from Africa, with strict adherence to metric patterns, some rhythmic complexity such as syncopation, and the undeviating tempo typical also of much West African music. These rhymes, among the most popular of which are "I asked my mother for fifty cents" and "Head-shoulder baby," are sometimes sung, sometimes spoken. Call-and-response techniques are very common. The melodic materials are part of a worldwide pattern of children's songs with few tones, intervals of the minor third and major second, and repetitive structure. These children's songs are found not only in the South, but also in the black neighborhoods of the Northern cities, and they are frequently disseminated from black to white children.

In the work songs of Afro-Americans, African patterns also appear. Work songs that are actually sung to accompany rhythmic labor are not common in the white American tradition, with the exception of sea shanties. But they are widespread in West and Central Africa, and their existence may have contributed to their prominence in the Afro-American folk tradition, as may the fact that rhythmic labor was very much a part of the slaves' way of life. The style of these songs is a mixture of Anglo-American and African elements. Some of the songs, such as "Pick a Bale of Cotton," actually deal with the work. Others, such as Leadbelly's "Elnora," are simply a group of words, euphonious but hardly related to the job, which supply a pleasant rhythmic accompaniment to work.

The use of the voice by Afro-American folk singers is often traceable to African singing styles. The relaxed, open way of singing, sometimes varied by the use of purposely raucous and harsh tones, is rather similar to African singing and certainly quite different from the rather tense and generally more restrained manner of singing that is traditional among southern whites. Very likely, the difference is due to the persistence of African musical ideals in the Afro-American community, and possibly also to the difference between the culture patterns of the Anglo-Americans and the

Afro-Americans, which in turn is due both to the latter's African heritage and to the lifestyle developed from slavery and gradual, though partial, emancipation.

BIBLIOGRAPHICAL AND DISCOGRAPHICAL NOTES

Many publications dealing with Afro-American folk music in the United States are available. Among the older ones, the following are most useful: Harold Courlander, *Negro Folk Music, U.S.A.* (New York: Columbia University Press, 1963); John and Alan Lomax, *Negro Folk Songs as Sung by Leadbelly* (New York: Macmillan Press, 1936); and, for its study of the relationship between black and white spirituals, George Pullen Jackson, *White and Negro Spirituals* (New York: J. J. Augustin, 1943). More recent studies include Dena J. Epstein, *Sinful Tunes and Spirituals: Black Folk Music to the Civil War* (Urbana: University of Illinois Press, 1977), and "The Folk Banjo: A Documentary History," *Ethnomusicology*, XIX (1975) (U.S. Black Music Issue), 347–71; and the survey by Eileen Southern, *The Music of Black Americans: A History*, 2nd ed. (New York: Norton, 1983). Art and Margo Rosenbaum, *Folk Visions and Voices: Traditional Music and Song in North Georgia* (Athens: University of Georgia Press, 1983), is an intriguing collection of songs and tunes gathered from black and white informants. The relationship between published tune-books and oral tradition hymnody in the rural South (both black and white) is explored by Brett Sutton in "Shape-Note Tune Books and Primitive Hymns," *Ethnomusicology*, XXVI (1982), 11–26 (and illustrated on *Primitive Baptist Hymns of the Blue Ridge*, American Folklore Recordings 39088).

Informative studies of the blues include Charles Keil, *Urban Blues* (Chicago: University of Chicago Press, 1966); Jeff Todd Titon, *Early Downhome Blues: A Musical and Cultural Analysis* (Urbana: University of Illinois Press, 1977); William Ferris, Jr., *Blues from the Delta* (Garden City, NY: Anchor Press/ Doubleday, 1978; reprint New York: Da Capo Press, 1984); and Robert Palmer, *Deep Blues* (New York: Viking, 1981). David Evans, *Big Road Blues: Tradition and Creativity in the Folk Blues* (Berkeley and Los Angeles: University of California Press, 1982), is a collection and comparative study. Among the many publications on jazz are Gunther Schuller, *Early Jazz* (New York: Oxford University Press, 1968); Frank Tirro, *Jazz: A History* (New York: Norton, 1977); and James Lincoln Collier, *The Making of Jazz: A Comprehensive History* (New York: Dell, 1979). *Journal of Jazz Studies* is the basic scholarly journal of the field. A standard bibliography is Donald Kennington and Danny L. Read, *The Literature of Jazz: A Critical Guide*, 2nd ed. (Chicago: American Library Association, 1980).

Two publications by Richard A. Waterman provide theoretical background for the study of black music in the New World: " 'Hot' Rhythm in Negro Music," *Journal of the American Musicological Society*, I (1948), 24–37, and

"African Influence on American Negro Music," in *Acculturation in the Americas*, ed. Sol Tax (Chicago: University of Chicago Press, 1952). Black music of Africa and the New World is also the subject of Olly Wilson, "The Significance of the Relationship between Afro-American and West-African Music," *Black Perspective in Music*, II (1974), 3–22; Ashenafi Kebede, *Roots of Black Music: The Vocal, Instrumental and Dance Heritage of Africa and Black America* (Englewood Cliffs, NJ: Prentice-Hall, 1982); and John Storm Roberts, *Black Music of Two Worlds*, rev. ed. (New York: Morrow Press, 1974), a book complemented by a set of Folkways recordings under the same title (see further on in this list).

The bibliographical notes for Chapter 9 list several studies of Latin American music that include discussion of Afro-American traditions. Alan P. Merriam, "Songs of the Ketu Cult of Bahia, Brazil," *African Music*, I (1956), 53–82; Melville J. Herskovits, "Drums and Drummers in Afro-Brazilian Cult Life," *Musical Quarterly*, XXX (1944), 447–92; and Luis Felipe Ramón y Rivera, "Rhythmic and Melodic Elements in Negro Music of Venezuela," *J-IFMC*, XIV (1962), 56–60 are also important reading. Black music in the Caribbean is discussed, with musical transcriptions, in Harold Courlander, *The Drum and the Hoe* (Berkeley: University of California Press, 1960), a study of Haitian voodoo culture. Also recommended are Peter Seeger, "The Steel Drum: A New Folk Instrument," *Journal of American Folklore*, LXXI (1958), 52–57, and Jocelyne Guilbault, "Fitness and Flexibility: Funeral Wakes in St. Lucia, West Indes," *Ethnomusicology*, XXXI (1987), 273–99. Important studies of Afro-Cuban music have been carried out by Fernando Ortiz. In addition to the work mentioned in the text, see his *Los instrumentos de la música afrocubana*, 5 vols. (Havana: Ministério de Educación, 1952–55). For Jamaican music, see the introductory study by Olive Lewin, "Jamaican Folk Music," *Caribbean Quarterly*, XIV (1969), 49–59. A systematic study of cults in Jamaica is George E. Simpson, "Jamaican Revivalist Cults," *Social and Economic Studies*, V, i–ix (1956), 321–42.

Useful bibliographies include Dominique-René de Lerma, *Bibliography of Black Music*, 4 vols. (Westport, CT: Greenwood Press, 1981–84); John F. Szwed, Roger D. Abrahams, and others, *Afro-American Folk Culture: An Annotated Bibliography of Materials from North, Central, and South America and the West Indies*, 2 vols. (Philadelphia: Institute for the Study of Human Issues, 1978); Jo Ann Skowronski, *Black Music in America: A Bibliography* (Metuchen, NJ: Scarecrow Press, 1981); and Irene V. Jackson, *Afro-American Religious Music: A Bibliography and a Catalogue of Gospel Music* (Westport, CT: Greenwood Press, 1979).

Important recordings of black music in Latin America are *Music of Haiti*, collected by Harold Courlander, Folkways 4403, 4407, 4432 (3 discs); *Spiritual Baptist Music of Trinidad*, recordings and commentary by Stephen D. Glazier, Folkways FE 4234, which updates George Eaton Simpson's earlier recording, *Cult Music of Trinidad* (Folkways FE 4478); several discs on the Areito (Egrem) label under the title *Antologia de la música afrocubana* (available from Ediciones Vitrales, P. O. Box 701394, Trains Meadows, NY 11370); *Cult Music of Cuba*, Folkways 4410; *Jamaican Cult Music*, Folkways FE 4461; *From the Grass Roots of Jamaica*, Dynamic (Kingston, Jamaica) 3305; *Music from Saramanka: A Dynamic Afro-American Tradition*, recorded and annotated by Richard and Sally Price, Folkways FE 4225; *Afro-Bahian Religious Songs of Brazil*, Library of Congress AAFS 61–65; and *Afro-Brazilian Religious Songs: Cantigas de Candomblé*, recorded by Gerard Béhague, Lyrichord LLST 7315. Several volumes of Afro-Brazilian music are included in the series *Documentário sonoro do folclore brasiliero* (on 7-inch, 33 ⅓ rpm discs), produced by the Fundação Nacional de Arte (FUNARTE, Rua Araújo Porto Alegre, 80, Rio de Janeiro, 20030, RJ Brazil). Samples of music from the West Indies, South America, the United States, Africa, and the Middle East are available on *Black Music of Two Worlds*, compiled by J. S. Roberts, Folkways FE 4602 (3 discs).

As an introduction to North American black music, we recommend two large sets of records, *Music from the South*, recorded by Frederic Ramsey, Folkways FA 2650–59 (10 discs), and *Southern Folk Heritage Series*, edited by Alan Lomax, Atlantic 1346–52 (7 discs, including white and black music). Among excellent recent field recordings of black music are *Georgia Sea Island Songs*, New World Records NW 278, with notes by Alan Lomax; and *Sorrow Come Pass Me Around: A Survey of Rural Black Religious Music*, Advent 2805, and *Afro-American Folk Music from Tate and Panola Counties, Mississippi*, Library of Congress AFS L67, both recorded and with commentary by David Evans; *Drop on Down in Florida*, produced by Dwight DeVane and Brenda McCallum, Florida Folklife LP 102–103; and *Powerhouse for God: Sacred Speech, Chant, and Song in an Appalachian Baptist Church*, American Folklore Recordings 39089, recorded by Jeff Todd Titon and Ken George and with extensive commentary by Titon. *Children of the Heav'nly King: Religious Expression in the Central Blue Ridge*, ed. Charles K. Wolfe, Library of Congress AFC L69–70, presents music of black and white congregations. In the area of folk blues we cite *Leadbelly's Last Sessions*, Folkways 2941–42 (4 discs); *The Rural Blues*, ed. Samuel B. Charters, RFB Records RF 202 (2 discs); and *South Mississippi Blues*, recorded and with notes by David Evans, Rounder 2009. The best overall introduction to jazz is *The Smithsonian Collection of Classic Jazz*, SI R2100. The Smithsonian and Folkways Records have produced many notable jazz reissues.

ELEVEN

FOLK MUSIC IN MODERN
NORTH AMERICA

The culture of modern North America is essentially a European one; its most prominent ingredients have come from Great Britian and, to a somewhat smaller extent, other Western European countries. But there have been other major influences as well, for example, from Hispanic culture and from the cultures of eastern and southern Europe. And among the most important distinguishing features is the influence of two non-European cultures: the African, which has had an enormous impact, and the American Indian, whose thrust has been less noticeable but is nevertheless pervasive. At certain levels of activity and thought, North American culture is a rather homogeneous blend of these and many other ingredients. At other levels, however, it is a conglomeration of enclaves—Scotch-Irish in the Appalachians, Mexican American in Arizona, French Canadian in the province of Quebec and in northern New England, Polish American in Chicago and Detroit, Afro-American in areas of large cities and in parts of the rural South, with small pockets of separation, such as the Indian tribes on reservations and various communities of religious groups (the Amish in the Midwest or the Doukhobors in the western United States and Canada). Each of these enclaves has kept a distinctive way of life; thus, in certain respects, there is enormous variety in the panorama of North American culture. In some ways, then, this continent is in the vanguard of what appears to be a gradually developing universal culture; in other respects, it functions as a museum, preserving in isolated and archaic forms the otherwise rapidly changing cultures of other lands.

The profile of folk music in modern North America is similar. The musical traditions of peoples from everywhere have been brought here, sometimes maintained for generations, sometimes rapidly forgotten; sometimes developed into new, more distinctly American phenomena, sometimes preserved in old forms; sometimes combined with the music of other groups from elsewhere, and with different styles, but sometimes held in isolation. We find that the enclaves of European, African, and American Indian cultures have retained some of their old musical traditions, but we also find that new styles, resulting from combinations, have come about. We are forced to conclude that the homogeneity of modern American life, and particularly the prominence of radio, television, and the recording industry, has also homogenized musical life to the extent that the old tripartite view of music (art, popular, and folk) has lost much of its meaning. It would appear that nearly all elements of the population share in a musical culture dominated by what we have for some time called popular music, based on rock, with elements of jazz, blues, country, folk, and even to some extent art music— a musical culture with a certain amount of stylistic unity based on aesthetic as well as technological criteria.

Our task here is to describe the role of the surviving traditional folk music in this complex situation; to a smaller extent, it is to point out those elements in the homogeneous culture that are derived from folk music.

ETHNIC MINORITIES IN RURAL AMERICA

We have mentioned the existence of isolated groups which retain their traditional culture essentially outside the framework of modern American civilization. Among them are the English-descended New England farmers and the Scotch-Irish of the Appalachians. We have already (in Chapter 4) examined their retention of older British songs and singing styles. Although their place in American history and the character of their culture is different, the American Indians occupy something of a similar role. In both cases, distinctiveness of musical culture helps to provide a feeling of cultural and, to some extent, racial identity. The most dramatic examples of such conservatism in both lifestyle and music are found in some of the religion-based enclaves.

In many cultures, religious and ceremonial life tends to reveal the most conservative elements, and the most archaic aspects of a tradition are usually to be found in its religious manifestations. Thus, perhaps the oldest European folk music preserved in the Americas is that which is associated with religion. The Spanish liturgical dramas are one example; another is the tradition of German spiritual folk song which is found especially in Pennsylvania and also among the Amish of the midwestern United States.

The Amish are a religious community related to the Mennonites. Of Swiss and German origin, they began leaving Germany in the seventeenth century, some migrating first to Russia and then, in the early nineteenth century, to the United States, others coming directly to America. Their austere manner of living and their conservative traditions have kept them essentially out of contact with other German Americans. Devoting themselves exclusively to farming, they use music only for worship. Their hymns are of two types, an older one that is possibly a survival of a medieval hymn-singing tradition, and a newer one evidently part of the German-American spiritual tradition of Pennsylvania.

To most listeners, the older hymns of the Amish scarcely sound like products of Western musical culture. They are monophonic and sung without accompaniment, without perceptible meter, with syllables drawn out over many tones, and with slowly executed ornaments. Only when one becomes acquainted with the style does one see in it any resemblance to the hymn tunes of the German reformed churches. The resemblance is apparent if one connects the first notes of the textual syllables to each other, even when these notes are short and seemingly insignificant. Since this style of singing is not found in Europe today, how did it come about? Possibly the Amish, after arriving in Russia or the United States, began to slow down the hymns they had sung in Germany, to add ornaments, and to draw out the metric structure until it was not to be recognized. Or, possibly their way of singing was once widely used in the German-speaking rural areas of Europe, and has simply been retained by the Amish in America although undergoing complete change in Europe under the impact of the all-pervading musical influence of the cities and courts. Whatever the case, the Amish hymns are an example of the marginal survival that characterizes some of the musical culture of the Americas.[1]

The newer hymns of the Amish correspond to the spiritual tradition of the Pennsylvania German culture. This culture represents an interesting

[1] Bruno Nettl, "The Hymns of the Amish: An Example of Marginal Survival," *Journal of American Folklore*, LXX (1957), 327–28. This style of congregational singing is examined in Nicholas Temperley, "The Old Way of Singing: Its Origins and Development," *Journal of the American Musicological Society*, XXXIV (1981), 511–44.

mixture of German—particularly south German—and British elements, including a special dialect of German that includes certain elements of American English phonology. The songs of the Pennsylvania Germans draw on both the German and the Anglo-American traditions. The so-called Pennsylvania spirituals, folk hymns with German words, are really products of the spiritual revival of the early 1800s, which involved Methodists and Baptists in the English-speaking community, and the influence of black music and of black spirituals, all converging on the Pennsylvania German community. Thus the tunes are of various origins. Some are those of secular German folk songs; a few are derived from early German hymns; some come from the white spiritual tradition ("The Battle Hymn of the Republic" appears with several sets of words). The Pennsylvania German spiritual is not, of course, a purely folkloric type of music in the strictest sense of the word. Hymn books were printed and professional hymn writers contributed to them. But much of the musical material was and is identical to that which lives in the authentic folk culture, and most of the tunes, in contrast to the words, were actually passed on by oral tradition, performed at camp meetings without the use of books, and lived by means of variation and communal recreation.

Just as the German folk culture lives on in the small towns of eastern Pennsylvania, other Western European traditions can be found thriving in other rural areas of North America. Northern Michigan and Minnesota are repositories of Scandinavian and Finnish folklore. In the southern Midwest and Louisiana there are people who still sing, or at any rate can occasionally remember for a collector, the folk songs of France. Of course the eastern part of Canada, especially the province of Quebec, is rich in the folklore of French Canadians. Much as the United States yields a repertory of English songs at least as large as that of England, the French-Canadians sing essentially all of the older French folk songs; Marius Barbeau, veteran collector of songs in this tradition, recorded that for song upon song more variants have been found in America than in France. One group of individuals who in particular carried the French tradition was the *voyageurs*, French Canadians who paddled canoes through the Great Lakes in the fur trade, and who sang for amusement and in order to provide rhythmic accompaniment to paddling. On the whole, the French-Canadian folk song heritage does not seem to differ appreciably from that of France, and in its wealth it parallels the Anglo-American folk song tradition. The penetration of French melodies to other repertories can be seen in some of the tunes of the Haitian cults, whose musical style is generally Caribbean and closely related to African music but among whose songs are tunes and fragments of melodies highly reminiscent of French music. A similar situation obtains among the Cajuns of southern Louisiana, descendants of the Acadians whose deportation from Canada to Bayou Teche, Louisiana, in 1755 was chronicled by Henry

Wadsworth Longfellow in "Evangeline." The Cajuns continue to speak French and to sing French songs, but their music has also absorbed elements of Anglo-American and Afro-American styles, particularly in the repertories of their string bands.

THE ROLE OF FOLK MUSIC IN URBAN AMERICAN CULTURE

The early settlers in America who came from the British Isles, Scandinavia, France, and Spain developed a largely rural culture, and their folk music is preserved mainly in small towns, in villages, and on farms. On the whole, the peoples who came to North America from Italy, the Balkan peninsula, and Eastern Europe arrived later, when cities had already developed into centers of industry; they emigrated at the end of the nineteenth century and the beginning of the twentieth to work in these cities. Thus their folk music, to the extent that it is preserved, is found in an urban milieu. These same cities also draw upon the rural population, and thus many of the Western European immigrants also found their way into them as did non-Europeans—for example, blacks, Mexican Americans, Chinese, Japanese, and even some American Indians. The rapidly expanding North American city—different from the typical European city, which took centuries to reach its present size—tended to become a complex of sections, neighborhoods, villages almost, which served as focal points for various ethnic groups. These tended to try to maintain in some respects the culture and tradition of their countries and places of origin, as a way of preserving identity and of easing the dislocations of Americanization, Westernization, and modernization. They could obviously not retain their rural work habits, economic systems, transportation, and so on, but they could attempt to retain their folklore, art, and music.

At the same time, the North American cities, in the twentieth century, have been wellsprings of technical innovation and social change. It is difficult to imagine that music could have escaped the impact of developments resulting from the turmoil caused by the throwing together of many disparate cultural groups, and of the constant pressure to change the approach to all of life's problems. Thus the folk music of the American city also reflects the most important social attitudes that developed, and we find song associated with various movements of social and political forces, particularly with movements whose function is to protest.

Preservation and response to the pressures of modernization are both evident in the music of Eastern European groups in those cities, particularly in the Midwest, which grew primarily as industrial centers. By no means have the folk repertories of all groups been collected and studied, but a generous sampling is available. For example, large collections of Hungarian and Slovak songs have been made in Cleveland;[2] Yiddish and Puerto Rican folk music has been studied in New York, and the songs of Poles, Syrians, and many other groups have been recorded in Detroit. In some cases, old songs can be found relatively undisturbed, and the American city acts as the agent of marginal survival. At other times, the European traditions are changed because of the pressures of urban American culture. There seems to be a tendency to favor dance and instrumental music over other types of traditional music; perhaps this is due to the fact that young Americans of foreign descent have less interest in the words of the songs, which they may not even understand, than in the tunes. Organized teaching of folk songs, even from song books, by members of the ethnic group who are noted for their knowledge may be one way of preserving the material. Indeed, group singing is more prominent than in the European parent traditions. Singing clubs and dance groups are formed in order to keep the tradition alive, for music and dance play an important part in keeping an ethnic group in a city from losing its identity.

Furthermore, the musical style of Eastern European folk songs sung in the American cities may change, for those songs which come closest to being acceptable in terms of the American popular tune tradition are those which are preserved by the ethnic groups. The younger individuals in these communities, who by the middle of the twentieth century were no longer able to speak the languages of their grandparents, have been stimulated by the appearance in concerts of professional dance and instrumental groups from Europe. The original functions of Eastern European folk songs on the whole have disappeared in the American city, and the music serves mainly as entertainment, as an expression of sentimental feeling, and as accompaniment to dancing. Occasionally, new songs in Polish, Hungarian, Slovak, or other languages are created, though in such cases it is usually only the words, dealing with American life, that are new. On the whole, the European ethnic groups in the United States perform the music of the old country, sometimes preserving tunes already forgotten in Europe, but more frequently singing the old tunes in less ornamented, shorter, and frequently impoverished style, and often tending to change modal tunes to major or minor, heterometric structure to isometric, and unaccompanied tunes to songs with chordal accompaniment or singing in parallel thirds. Example 11-1 illustrates a Polish folk song (possibly unchanged in transit) collected in Detroit.

---

[2] Stephen Erdely, "Folksinging of the American Hungarians in Cleveland," *Ethnomusicology*, VIII (1964), 14–27. Further collections and studies of the music of ethnic groups are cited in the bibliographical notes for this chapter.

EXAMPLE 11-1. Polish folk song, "Czterty mile za Warszawa" ("It was four miles out of Warsaw"), collected in Detroit. Reprinted from *Merrily We Sing, 105 Polish Folksongs* by Harriet M. Pawlowska by permission of the Wayne State University Press. Copyright 1961.

One genre of Eastern European dance music has flourished in North America. The *polka* is well known among Americans of Polish, Czech, or German extraction and also by many of other backgrounds. This genre thrives on the edge of popular culture, in dance clubs, on a few smaller radio stations (largely but not exclusively in the upper Midwest), and on minor record labels and homemade tapes. Fans may keep in touch with one another and learn of opportunities to dance or buy recordings through a semimonthly newspaper, *The Polka News* (St. Charles, Michigan). The issue for April 8, 1987 gives the membership count of the Polka Clubs United as 14,317. Thus, although the mass media can (and often do) overwhelm folk music, they can also accommodate and even further the lives of some genres.

The Anglo-American and black communities in the cities also have a folk music tradition, largely because many members of these two groups are recent immigrants from the countryside. The older, traditional sort of Anglo-American folk song, when known to urban individuals or families, tends to live essentially in the memories of singers or in the intimate family circle rather than functioning in more broadly social situations. In the music of urban Afro-Americans, on the other hand, folk music has served as an inspiration for the creation of various popular styles and musical forms, like jazz, blues, and gospel song.

Throughout Western history, music has been used as a symbol of political actions and positions. Songs of political and social protest are known even from the late Middle Ages; nations and political parties developed solemn anthems for inspiration and rousing songs to stimulate rallying to a cause. It is not surprising that folk music, the music identified with the common person, and more specifically with the poor, minorities, and the disestablished, has provided the natural stylistic symbol, even in the mainstream of society, for social criticism and for protesting intolerable conditions, whereas music associated with the established order has been more likely to hew closely to a stylistic line derived from art music. Folk songs voicing protest have been composed in many corners of the world; it appears that thoughts that would not be acceptable in speech are frequently permitted in song.

Of great interest in this connection is the body of songs revolving about, and in some cases integrally a part of, the labor movement. These are songs of relatively recent origin, their poets and composers are normally known, and they are usually learned first from song books and taught by trained organizers. Stylistically they are part of the broadside ballad tradition, and they use either original tunes composed in the broadside idiom or tunes from other folk songs, hymns, or popular music. One of the best known is the ballad of "Joe Hill," a martyred leader of the IWW, whose ghost returns to exhort laborers to organize. Some of these songs have passed into oral tradition and are also sung outside the labor movement. Many of them have words protesting the bad treatment of factory workers, miners, migrant farmers, or minority groups. Others sing the praises of labor organizations. Usually, tunes of older folk songs, hymns, music hall ditties, and minstrel songs are used. Often the words parody songs already in the folk tradition. For example, a song sung during a New York State milk strike in 1939 is a parody of "Pretty Polly," a version of the British ballad of the "Cruel Ship's Carpenter":

> Mister farmer, mister farmer, come go along with me (twice)
> Come hitch up with the milk trust and we'll keep the system free.
> So they followed the milk trust stooges and what did they find? (twice)
> Nothing in their pockets and a knife from behind.[3]

The use of folk songs as protest has deep roots in Afro-American culture and is an essential ingredient of the texts of entire genres such as blues and spirituals. It was not adopted as rapidly by the white mainstream of American society. But beginning in the 1930s, the idea of protesting through folk song began to spread to segments of the white population. One of the characteristics of this movement was the development, especially

---

[3] John Greenway, *American Folksongs of Protest* (Philadelphia: University of Pennsylvania Press, 1953), p. 215.

in the 1950s and 1960s, of star folk singers who performed songs with important elements of Anglo-American folk song styles (e.g., characteristic melodic devices and contours, text patterns with the basic structure of folk poems, and accompaniment by folk instruments, such as the guitar, dulcimer, and banjo). But although traditional folk songs were occasionally used, it was more typical of these singers to perform original songs only reminiscent of the rural tradition. Many of these songs—and indeed, the most famous—were songs of protest. The Vietnam War in particular produced a large number of such protest songs; many of the performances of singers Bob Dylan, Joan Baez, and others fall in this category. Although some performers, including Dylan and Baez, were very close to the traditional folk styles, others, such as Simon and Garfunkel, adopted styles intermediate between folk music and the mainstream of urban popular music; still others (such as the Byrds) exhibited a style essentially in the realm of popular music but influenced by folk song.

Precursors of the "folk" movement in popular music—Pete Seeger, Burl Ives, and others—tended to adhere relatively closely to the folk tradition. The urban folk singing movement in the middle of the twentieth century followed a course of gradual (though partial) assimilation into the mainstream of popular music, and became known and accepted by a larger portion of the population. Toward the end of the century, folk music has lost much of its share in the popular music marketplace. Some performers have maintained their careers by entering established pop music genres, particularly country music. Of those performers remaining in the folk movement, some, such as Doc Watson, have kept small but enthusiastic audiences by playing "old-timey" music, using traditional tunes (though now virtuosically performed), and others continue to write new songs emphasizing current social concerns. The American folk movement has sparked and strongly influenced similar movements in Europe, resulting in some curious mixtures of styles. For instance, intended preservers of German folk songs in the Plattdeutsch dialect, such as Hannes Wader and Knut Kiesewetter, perform and record these songs with the accompaniment of American folk instruments—steel string guitars, fiddles (played in American styles), and banjos.[4]

Those who believe in authenticity as a major criterion may decide that the phenomena we have described are not really folk music. But the roles of folk music in contemporary popular culture are worthy of detailed study. These kinds of folk music differ from the "authentic" folk traditions mainly in the following ways: the songs are learned not from friends and family but from books, recordings (field recordings and professional perfor-

---

[4] *Hannes Wader*, Philips 6305 218 (1974); *Liederbuch Knut Kiesewetter*, Polydor 2630 107 (1978).

mances), and trained musicians; many of the songs are composed especially for urban consumption (but this may have been true of many older folk songs as well); the performer consciously tries to develop certain idiosyncracies and to repeat them in an identical way each time; and the style of singing—in some instances polyphonic, sometimes with virtuoso accompaniment on banjo, guitar, piano, and so on—may be completely different from the style in which the same songs are sung elsewhere. Also, an urban folk singer may draw on several traditions and many languages.

As was pointed out in Chapter 1, it may be possible for a song to be a folk song and not a folk song at the same time. And thus we may insist that folk songs sung by musicians in the popular music tradition, by professionals who make use primarily of the mass media, in styles which may have little to do with any rural folk tradition, are no longer really folk songs. It may be simply a semantic problem. But perhaps a good solution to this definitional dilemma is to regard the music that consists of actual folk songs, and of songs composed in a style derived from folk music by urban song writers and performed by professional entertainers, as the true folk music of urban culture.

This kind of music exhibits important parallels with the broadside ballad traditions of the eighteenth and nineteenth centuries. Both make use of a variety of musical sources; both depend on the current interest of their subject matter for rapid dissemination; both deal with content close to the interests of many segments and classes of society; and both depend on rural and perhaps ancient singing traditions for important elements of their performance practice. Thus there is at least some justice in calling this urban material folk music, and in considering it the logical extension, in a rapidly urbanizing and modernizing society, of the rural folk music tradition.

Although this chapter focusses on modern North America, we should perhaps point out that folk music has been used as a way of representing political and social views, and also as a method of music education, in Europe and elsewhere as well. In the Soviet Union, songs praising the communist way of life and Joseph Stalin were introduced and passed into oral tradition in city and countryside early in the twentieth century. In Nazi Germany, the singing of German folk songs was obligatory in patriotic organizations. In Hungary, folk music has become the mainstay of elementary music education. Even in Vietnam, a folk singing movement using traditional tunes with new words treating matters of war and liberation, and with American-style guitar acccompaniment became widespread, largely due to the efforts of the famous singer Pham Dui. Thus the kind of urban folk singing that is current in the United States has precedents and analogues in many parts of the world.

THE RURAL ANGLO-AMERICAN TRADITION

In the United States, the development of an urban folk music culture is partly a result of the maintenance of a strong folk music tradition in the rural Anglo-American community. We have pointed out the importance of this tradition to the survival of British folk music, and we have noted that British material is often better preserved in the New World than in the Old. But the British tradition has also undergone changes in America, influenced by the peculiar course of American history and the development of American culture.

The music of Anglo-American folk songs is partly composed of British and Irish tunes that are not easily distinguished, individually, from their forms as they are found in the British Isles. Some come from popular song and from broadside ballad tunes. The differences between American and British song are greater in the words than in the music, for the words are much more frequently of American origin (often they are parodies of British songs), embodying specific events of American history or reflecting particular features of American culture—the frontier, the religious revival of the 1880s, the love of humor and exaggeration, the presence of various ethnic minorities, and the particular occupations (cowboys, miners, Indian fighters, etc.) in which Americans engaged while building a new country.

Taken as a whole, the style of American folk music in English has more melodies in major, fewer pentatonic tunes, more songs in duple meter, and less use of accompaniment (but more use of the drone principle in instrumental accompaniment) than the style of Britain. Like the British tradition, but unlike the Afro-American styles and some other groups in the United States, it is essentially one of solo singing. Melodies that are obviously of nineteenth-century origin, with a definite implied harmony, are common. The words of the English songs in America have also been changed, and Americans have made a special selection of material from the British repertory. Thus there are more humorous folk songs in the American repertory than in the British. Tall tales and other exaggerations are typical. Folk heroes, such as the black superman John Henry, the bad man Jesse James, and the Slavic steel worker Joe Magarac, abound. Broadside ballads telling of the murders and railroad wrecks of a locality are particularly popular, and songs telling of shipwrecks are a specialty of the populations of Newfoundland, Labrador, and New England. Besides preserving British broadsides, Americans have composed a body of broadsides of their own, especially during the nineteenth and early twentieth centuries. These are more apt to deal with violence and romantic love and less with the supernatural and with battles than are their British counterparts.

Regional differences do, of course, appear in folk singing of the United States. According to Alan Lomax,[5] northern folk singers produce a rather relaxed, open-voiced tone, whereas southern ones are tenser and "pinched-voiced," and those of the West are a blend of the two. Lomax has attributed these differences to deep-seated cultural differences involving the relationship between the sexes, the hardships of frontier life, and the presence of the black minority in the South.

The fact that dancing was prohibited or at least frowned upon by many religious leaders of early America tended to drive dance music from the British Isles into the background, but produced a distinctly American type of song, the *play-party song*, which accompanies marching and dance-like movements similar to those of some children's group games. Dancing has, however, played a part in the British-American folk culture, as may be seen from the prominence of the square dance, which is derived from the eighteenth- and nineteenth-century quadrilles of European high society. A distinctive American feature is the presence of a caller, who speaks or sings verses instructing the dancers in the routine required in the execution of the dance.

There is also in the American tradition a large body of instrumental music that is used for dancing, some of which was at one time also used for marching. As a matter of fact, the earliest jazz bands in New Orleans were brass bands that played marching music for funerals and other processions. At the same time, in the white North, fiddle and fife players played ornamented versions of song tunes as well as tunes of popular and art music origin. The main instruments of the American folk tradition are the guitar, the banjo, the mandolin, the dulcimer, the violin (fiddle), and the harmonica. The dulcimer appears in various forms, some of them similar to those of the Swedish dulcimer described in Chapter 4. As in Europe, the American string instruments are frequently used for music in which the drone principle somehow appears.

Just as many of the instrumental tunes came from the vocal repertory, many tunes originally played were eventually sung. Again, this is a tendency found also in some European cultures. Example 11-2 is a fiddle tune with words; its large range suggests that it may have originated as an instrumental piece which only later began to be used vocally.

In recent years, however, North American fiddling has increasingly taken on a life of its own, independent of previous connections with folk song and even with dancing. Like many folk arts, fiddling was declining in importance during the first half of the twentieth century. However, in the 1950s and following, an organized revival attracted new players of various

[5] Alan Lomax, *The Folksongs of North America in the English Language* (New York: Doubleday, 1960), p. 1.

EXAMPLE 11-2. Fiddle tune and song, "Prettiest Little Gal in the County, O," collected in Florida, from Alton C. Morris, *Folksongs of Florida* (Gainesville: University of Florida Press, 1950), p. 226.

Pret-tiest lit-tle gal in the coun-ty, O, Dressed in silk and cal-i-co; And

if she mar-ries let her go, Plen-ty more in the coun-ty, O,

Pret-tiest lit-tle gal in the coun-ty, O; Mam-my and dad-dy both say so;

And if she mar ries let her go, Plen-ty more in the coun-ty, O.

social backgrounds, while retaining strong rural roots (something that had *not* happened in the folk song revival). Contemporary fiddling is an extremely vigorous contest and concert art. The nature of performance has been radically transformed. Earlier, dance-related styles might feature a great deal of variation, but this was generally unobtrusive, so that the music would not fail to give solid support to the dancing, and so that a performance could end gracefully at any eight-measure interval. In the contest setting (which is not new, but newly central), performances have become virtuosic, featuring elaborate, carefully shaped variation. Rhythmic and melodic vocabularies have been enriched through borrowings from jazz, and a new array of styles has emerged. Fiddlers and fans, spread throughout rural and to a lesser extent urban populations, are linked by a network of low-distribution records and tapes and by numerous fiddlers' organizations. At the same time, fiddle tunes form part of the repertory of bluegrass, a tradition-oriented subgenre of country music. Fiddle tunes give bluegrass performers, nearly all of whom are virtuosos on one or more acoustic string instruments (guitar, mandolin, banjo, dobro, fiddle), chances to display their abilities in jazzy breaks. The fact that these tunes are quite frequently performed is also due, to some extent, to their cost-saving exemption from copyright.

Finally, the Afro-American impact on the white American folk song tradition has been enormous. It can be felt in the occasional "hot rhythm" of singing and accompaniment, in the development of the so-called hillbilly style, in the tendency to stick to one meter (although many white singers sing instead in the parlando-rubato style), in the use of rhythmic handclapping by white folk performers and audiences, and, of course, in the many black songs that have become part of the white repertory.

If the singing of Joan Baez, Pete Seeger, Bob Dylan, and Simon and Garfunkel is the consequence of the impact of urbanization on folk music, then the result of modernization and the use of the mass media in rural American must be the large body of country music. Beginning with music growing directly out of the traditional folk songs of the Appalachians, taking with it musical elements of the broadside ballad and a large repertory of folk hymnody that goes back to colonial times, and constantly interacting with the developments in urban culture, this highly distinctive musical style remains exceedingly prominent in contemporary American culture despite the shrinking of rural America and the all-pervading influence of television, to which it has readily adapted. And although country music has traveled far from traditional folk song in its style, its origins nevertheless remain obvious. The relationship to the old Appalachian folk music is evident in the structure of the melodies, the instruments used for accompaniment, the physical stance of the singers, and particularly the singing style, that least changeable aspect of musical performance.

CONCLUSION

The American folk music scene is a fitting one for closing a survey of folk and traditional music in the Western continents, for it shows us many of the things that are typical and interesting in folk music everywhere—the preservation of archaic forms, the creation of new styles under the impact of acculturation, special developments due to particular trends in cultural values, and the growth of a special kind of folk music culture in the modern city and, through the pervasiveness of the media, elsewhere.

One of the things that our consideration of folk music in the Americas and, indeed, of folk and traditional music everywhere, has shown is the condition of flux in which the material is constantly found. Change, brought about through intercultural contact and through the creative elements within each society, has evidently been present in even the simplest cultures, and it has increased in rapidity as the world's traditions are thrown into contact and conflict with each other as a result of the accelerating Westernization of the entire planet. Will it be possible for traditional musics to survive and to retain some measure of the distinctiveness that has characterized them in the past? If we consider folk music or traditional music solely as the product of the rural, unlettered classes or of backward peoples, we are bound to find that the traditions in which we are interested are receding and will eventually disappear. On the other hand, if we can retain an interest in the musical cultures of nations and peoples rather than only that of a musically professional elite, and if we are willing to broaden our definitions of folk and traditional music to include such things as popular music, jazz, and urban folk song, we may be in a position to investigate the kinds of music that are rapidly replacing, in their social functions, the folk and traditional musics of the past and present.

Although we must perhaps concede the eventual disappearance of traditional musics in the narrower sense of the concept, we should not assume that this demise is imminent. For many decades, some collectors have pursued their material with the attitude of a last-minute rescue operation, proclaiming the doom of authentic folklore. And indeed, because traditional music is always changing, something of it must always be disappearing. Nevertheless, each year brings new discoveries of unknown styles, unexplored musical cultures, unexpected instruments, and new distributions of musical types, always requiring changes in theory and reorientation of scholarly thought. As long as this is the state of traditional music, one can hardly claim that it is a dying art.

BIBLIOGRAPHICAL AND DISCOGRAPHICAL NOTES

General works on North American folk and traditional musics have been cited in the bibliographical notes for Chapter 8. To these we add D. K. Wilgus, *Anglo-American Folksong Scholarship Since 1898* (New Brunswick, NJ: Rutgers University Press, 1959), a survey of developments in collecting and studying American folk song; Malcolm G. Laws, *Native American Balladry* (Philadelphia: American Folklore Society, 1950), a bibliographic survey of ballads originating in America; and Samuel L. Forcucci, *A Folk Song History of America: America through Its Songs* (Englewood Cliffs, NJ: Prentice-Hall, 1984). The role of folk music as entertainment and education is discussed in Sven Eric Molin, "Leadbelly, Burl Ives, and Sam Hinton," *Journal of American Folklore*, LXXI (1958), 58–78; and Charles Seeger, "Folk Music in the Schools of a Highly Industrialized Society," *J-IFMC*, V (1953), 40–44. Eric von Schmidt and Jim Rooney, *Baby Let Me Follow You Down: The Illustrated Story of the Cambridge Folk Years* (Garden City, NY: Doubleday/Anchor, 1979), and Jerome L. Rodnitzky, *Minstrels of the Dawn: The Folk-Protest Singer as a Cultural Hero* (Chicago: Nelson-Hall, 1976), deal with aspects of the American folk music revival of the 1960s. *Folk Music and Modern Sound*, ed. William Ferris and Mary L. Hart (Jackson: University Press of Mississippi, 1982), is a collection of essays concerning folk music in urban settings and in the media. Philip V. Bohlman, *The Study of Folk Music in the Modern World* (Bloomington: Indiana University Press, 1988), examines contemporary folk musics and scholarship.

Ethnic music in North America is discussed in Stephen Erdely, "Ethnic Music in the United States: An Overview," *Y-IFMC*, XI (1979), 114–37; Charles Seeger, "The Cultivation of Various European Traditions in the Americas," in *International Musicological Society, Report of the Eighth Congress* (Kassel: Bärenreiter, 1961), pp. 364–75; and Nicholas Tawa, *A Sound of Strangers: Musical Culture, Acculturation, and the Post-Civil War Ethnic American* (Metuchen, NJ: Scarecrow Press, 1982). Vol. III, no. 1, of the UCLA *Selected Reports in Ethnomusicology* (1978), ed. James Porter, is devoted to studies of the musics of European immigrants. The article "European-American Music," by Philip V. Bohlman and others in *The New Grove Dictionary of American Music*, II, 64–86, surveys these traditions, and includes a large bibliography. *Ethnic Recordings in America: A Neglected Heritage*, with a foreword by Alan Jabbour (Washington: American Folklife Center, Library of Congress, 1982), is a valuable compendium of essays, interviews, and resource materials. Studies of individual ethnic groups and communities include Bruno Nettl, "The Hymns of the Amish: An Example of Marginal Survival," *Journal of American Folklore*, LXX (1957), 323–28; Stephen Erdely, "Folksinging of the American Hungarians in Cleveland," *Ethnomusicology*, VIII (1964), 14–27, and "Traditional and Individual Traits in the Songs of Three Hungarian-Americans," UCLA *Selected Reports in Ethnomusicology*, Vol. III, no. 1 (1978), 98–151; Jacob A. Evanson, "Folk Songs of an Industrial City" (Slovak songs in Pittsburgh), in *Pennsylvania Songs and Legends*, ed. George Korson (Philadelphia: University of Pennsylvania Press, 1949); Mark Forry, "*Becár* Music in the Serbian Community of Los Angeles: Evolution and Transformation," UCLA *Selected Reports in Ethnomusicology*, Vol. III, no. 1 (1978), 175–209; James P. Leary, "Old Time Music in Northern Wisconsin," *American Music*, II (1984), 71–87; and a historical study by Mark Slobin, *Tenement Songs: The Popular Music of the Jewish Immigrants* (Urbana: University of Illinois Press, 1982), accompanied by a one-hour cassette of early recordings (1880–1920). Among collections of songs and tunes are Rochelle and Robert L. Wright, *Danish Emigrant Ballads and Songs* (Carbondale: Southern Illinois University Press, 1983); Harriet Pawlowska, *Merrily We Sing, 105 Polish Folk Songs* (Detroit: Wayne State University Press, 1961); Kenneth Peacock, *A Garland of Rue: Lithuanian Folksongs of Love and Betrothal* (Ottawa: National Museum of Man, 1971), collected in southern Ontario and accompanied by four 7-inch flexidiscs. Sources pertaining to the music of Afro-Americans are listed in Chapter 10.

Several fine works on Hispanic-American music have been published. *The Texas-Mexican Conjunto: History of a Working-Class Music* (Austin: University of Texas Press, 1985) is one of several studies by Manuel Peña of a popular style of music developed by Texas Mexicans during and after World War II; a companion disc edited by Peña is available. Américo Paredes, *With A Pistol in His Hand* (Austin: University of Texas Press, 1958; reprint Austin: University of Texas Press, 1981), deals with the Texas-Mexican ballad, "El Corrido de Gregorio Cortez." Two good collections of Hispanic-American folk music are Américo Paredes, *A Texas-Mexican "Cancionero:" Folksongs of the Lower Border* (Urbana: University of Illinois Press, 1976), and John Donald Robb,

Hispanic Folk Music of New Mexico and the Southwest: A Self-Portrait (Norman: University of Oklahoma Press, 1980). William A. Owens, *Tell Me a Story, Sing Me a Song: A Texas Chronicle* (Austin: University of Texas Press, 1983), with a one-hour cassette of field recordings made by Owen in the 1930s and 1940s (sold separately), documents white, Mexican, and black traditions in the state. French folk songs of North America are collected in Irène Thérèse Whitfield, *Louisiana French Folk Songs*, 3rd ed. (Eunice, LA: Hebert Publications, 1981), and in Marius Barbeau, *Le rossignol y chante*, rev. ed. (Ottawa: National Museum of Man, 1979).

Two classic collections of British song in North America are Cecil J. Sharp, *English Folk Songs from the Southern Appalachians*, 2 vols. (London: Oxford University Press, 1952), and Alan Lomax, *The Folk Songs of North America in the English Language* (New York: Doubleday, 1961). Ira Ford, *Traditional Music in America* (New York: Dutton, 1940; reprint Hatboro, PA: Folklore Associates, 1965), is a collection of instrumental pieces and songs. Regional collections include Maud Karpeles, *Folk Songs from Newfoundland* (London: Faber and Faber, 1971); Helen Creighton, *Folksongs from Southern New Brunswick* (Ottawa: National Museum of Man, 1971), with four 7-inch flexidiscs; David S. McIntosh, *Folk Songs and Singing Games of the Illinois Ozarks* (Carbondale: Southern Illinois University Press, 1974); Vance Randolph, *Ozark Folksongs*, ed. and abridged by Norm Cohen (Urbana: University of Illinois Press, 1982); and Norman Cazden, Herbert Haufrecht, and Norman Studer, *Folk Songs of the Catskills* (Albany: State University of New York Press, 1982), with a companion volume containing notes and source references. Bill C. Malone's *Southern Music, American Music* (Lexington: University Press of Kentucky, 1979) is a fine regional history. The relationship between oral and written traditions is explored in Brett Sutton, "Shape-Note Tune Books and Primitive Hymns," *Ethnomusicology*, XXVI (1982), 11–26, adapted from his notes to *Primitive Baptist Hymns of the Blue Ridge*, American Folklore Recordings 39088. Good topical studies include Archie Green, *Only a Miner: Studies in Recorded Coal-Mining Songs* (Urbana: University of Illinois Press, 1972); Edward D. Ives, *Joe Scott, the Woodsman-Songmaker* (Urbana: University of Illinois Press, 1978), for which a one-hour cassette is also available; a collection compiled by Edith Fowke, *Lumbering Songs from the Northern Woods*, with tunes translated by Norman Cazden (Austin: University of Texas Press, 1970); Norm Cohen, *Long Steel Rail: The Railroad in American Folksong* (Urbana: University of Illinois Press, 1981); and Jim Bob Tinsley, *He Was Singin' This Song: A Collection of Forty-Eight Traditional Songs of the American Cowboy* (Orlando: University Press of Florida, 1981). The oral folklore of one family is presented in Leonard Roberts, *Sang Branch Settlers: Folk Songs and Tales of a Kentucky Mountain Family*, with music transcribed by C. Bull Agey (Austin: University of Texas Press, 1974).

American instrumental folk music is examined in Samuel P. Bayard, *Dance to the Fiddle, March to the Fife: Instrumental Folk Tunes in Pennsylvania* (University Park: Pennsylvania State University Press, 1982); Earl V. Spielman, "The Fiddling Traditions of Cape Breton and Texas: A Study in Parallels and Contrasts, *Yearbook* of the Inter-American Institute for Musical Research, VIII (1972), 39–48; Linda C. Burman-Hall, "American Traditional Fiddling: Performance Contexts and Techniques," in *Performance Practice: Ethnomusicological Perspectives*, ed. Gerard Béhague (Westport, CT: Greenwood Press, 1984), pp. 149–221; and Chris Goertzen, "American Fiddle Tunes and the Historic-Geographic Method," *Ethnomusicology*, XXIX (1985), 448–73, and "The Transformation of American Contest Fiddling," *Journal of Musicology*, VI (1988), 107–29. Neil V. Rosenberg, *Bluegrass: A History* (Urbana: University of Illinois Press, 1985), is an excellent survey. A country music pioneer is the subject of Gene Wiggins, *Fiddlin' Georgia Crazy: Fiddlin' John Carson, His Real World, and the World of His Songs* (Urbana: University of Illinois Press, 1987).

Among guides to the enormous literature of European-American folk music on disc are Larry Sandberg and Dick Weston, *Folk Music Source-Book* (New York: Knopf, 1976), which lists commercial recordings and recordings documenting the folk revival; Dean Tudor, *Popular Music: An Annotated Guide to Recordings* (Littleton, CO: Libraries Unlimited, 1983), which covers all American music except art music; the annual "Selected List of Recordings" issued since 1983 by the American Folklife Center, Library of Congress; and the lists of recordings appearing in each issue of *Ethnomusicology*.

For the United States, the series *Folk Music of the United States* issued by the Library of Congress is excellent. Especially to be mentioned among these recordings are *Folk Music from Wisconsin*, AAFS L55; *Songs of the Michigan Lumberjacks*, AAFS L56; *Anglo-American Songs and Ballads*, AAFS L12, 14; *Songs and Ballads of the Anthracite Miners*, AAFS L16; and *Sacred Harp Singing*, AAFS L11. Lectures on collecting by John Lomax appear on *The Ballad Hunter*, AAFS L49–53 (5 discs). Two U.S. bicentennial efforts have contributed more recently to the repertory of North American folk music available on records. A series entitled *Folk Music of America*, ed. Richard K. Spottswood and issued by the Library of Congress (LBC 1–15), draws on commercial recordings, field recordings, and other recorded materials to document the musical traditions of a wide spectrum of Americans; and New World Records' *Recorded Anthology of American Music* includes approximately three dozen volumes of folk and popular musics and jazz.

Music in a New World: America's Ethnic Traditions consists of twenty-six open-reel tapes or cassettes (one-half hour each) of recordings made by Karl Signell, each tape devoted to the music of a different ethnic group. This series, which is particularly well suited to classroom use, is available from NFBC, 1314 14th St. NW, Washington, DC 20005. Other recordings presenting European-American musics include *Traditional Norwegian-American Melodies from Wisconsin*, 2 vols., produced by Phil Martin, Folklore Village Farm FVF-201 and FVF-202 (available from Wisconsin Folklife Center, Folklore Village Farm, Route 3, Dodgeville, WI 53533); *From Sweden to America: Emigrant and Immigrant Songs*, Caprice CAP 2011 (2 discs), with notes by Marta Ramsten and others; *Memories of Snoose Boulevard* and *Return to*

Snoose Boulevard, Olle SP-223 and SP-224, products of the Scandinavian and American folk music revivals consisting of performances by the professional Swedish singer, Anne-Charlotte Harvey (discs available from Olle i Skratthult Project, P.O. Box 14171, University Station, Minneapolis, MN 55414); *James Morrison—Tom Enis*, TOPIC 127390, recordings made in New York in the 1920s by two well-known players of Irish music (a fiddler and a piper); *Italian Folk Music Collected in New York and New Jersey*, 2 vols., recorded and edited by Anna L. Chairetakis, Folkways FES 34041–42; and *Lithuanian Folk Songs in the United States*, Folkways FE 4009, with notes by Jonas Balys. Also to be recommended is the series of discs *Texas-Mexican Border Music*, ed. Chris Strachwitz and available on Folklyric Records; and *Caliente = Hot: Puerto Rican and Cuban Musical Expression in New York*, New World Records NW 244, with notes by Robert Friedman and Roberta Singer.

Among good recordings of American fiddling are *American Fiddle Tunes*, collected and with notes by Alan Jabbour, Library of Congress AFS L62; *Texas Fiddle Favorites*, County 707; *The Riendeau Family: Old-Time Fiddling from Old New England*, County 725; and *Fishers Hornpipe and Other Celtic-Traditional Tunes*, Folkways FS 3520. *The Hammons Family: A Study of a West Virginia Family's Traditions*, Library of Congress AFS L65–66, recorded and edited by Carl Fleischhauer and Alan Jabbour, presents one family's instrumental music and oral folklore. Logging ballads and songs are recorded on *Ted Ashlaw: Adirondack Woods Singer*, Philo 1022.

Fine Canadian collections are *Maritime Folk Songs from the Collection of Helen Creighton*, Folkways FE 4307; *Folk Music from Nova Scotia*, Folkways FM 4006, also edited by Creighton; and *Songs of French Canada*, Folkways FE 4482. *Danses pour veillées canadiennes*, Philo FL 2006, highlights the accordion playing of Philippe Bruneau; a French-Canadian fiddler is featured on *Henri Landry*, Philo FL 2002.

INDEX